AF564756

Social Implications of Schooling

Knowledge, Pedagogy and Consciousness

Social Implications of Schooling
Knowledge, Pedagogy and Consciousness

Avijit Pathak

Social Implications of Schooling: Knowledge, Pedagogy and Consciousness
Avijit Pathak

First Published, 2002
Republished by Aakar Books 2013
Reprinted, 2017
Reprinted 2021

ISBN 978-93-5002-208-5 (Hb)

Published by
AAKAR BOOKS
28 E Pocket IV, Mayur Vihar Phase I
Delhi 110 091, India
www.aakarbooks.com

Printed at
Sapra Brothers, Noida.

To my daughter Ananya and all those who have been experiencing an alternative form of schooling

Contents

Preface to the New Edition

The clock time moves—from 2002 to 2012. Is there any reason to bring out the new edition of a book that I wrote in 2002? I do not know. Things change, new experiments evolve, and new ideas grow. Yet, the old book with a new preface... It is Mr. Saxena—the enthusiastic leader of Aakar Books—who insists, who inspires; and I obey.

I continue to exist in the realm of formal education. I continue to reflect on teaching, curriculum and pedagogy. I love to read children's books; I look at their eyes; I feel them; I enter the world of Illich, Tolstoy, Tagore, Krishnamurthy; I sense the burden of schooling—the oppression implicit in a learning machine; I strive for alternatives. And it was this same feeling that guided me when I wrote this book. Hence I wish to believe that, despite the flow of time, the book has not lost its relevance.

True, I am aware of many changes. Look at Chapter 2. The NCERT books that I analysed have been replaced. New experiments, new authors, new texts, new sensibilities. Yet, I have retained the Chapter because it sensitises the reader, makes her reflect on ideology and curriculum; and the insights the reader gains might help her to look at the texts that exist today. Or, for that matter, look at Chapter 4. Has *Mirambika* as an alternative school changed? I am not very certain. Yes, I continue to visit the school. Not for a 'field study'. As a matter of fact, I cherish my nostalgia; I love its ambience, its openness; I love to see its children, the rhythm of their bodies, the spontaneity of their minds. And I guess that as an alternative school it continues to experience the tensions, anxieties and ambiguities that I narrated. I have retained this Chapter.

As far as the other chapters are concerned, my fundamental philosophy has not altered. Possibly I could have added a couple of more references, footnotes, case studies; but I have not done so. Why should I burden the reader with more quotes, more technicalities when, for me, the essential philosophy remains the same? Let the book retain its original flavour.

We all realise that our children are growing up in an environment not very conducive to the cultivation of a positive spirit. Corruption is all-prevading; television spectacles devalue all great ideals; the political realm refuses to arouse hope; the cult of consumption promotes greed and aggression; poverty, violence and insurgency disturb the rhythmic flow of existence. What is the role of education? Should our children grow up with despair and cynicism? Or should we search light amidst darkness, innate human possibilities when it is so easy to be depressed? There is indeed a challenge confronting all or us: parents, adults, teachers. We need to rethink education—its vision, its priorities, its pedagogic practices. Does this book act as a catalyst? Let my readers decide.

I keep writing. My wife's invisible presence, my daughter's questions, a tree, its shade, my students, my young gurus, green tea, music, reflections on poetry, music and life—I have not yet lost my romance with utopias. My book is just a humble offering nothing more. Nothing less.

November 24, 2012

Avijit Pathak
Jawaharlal Nehru University
New Delhi

Preface

Education is something on which, I feel, I am destined to reflect. As a teacher, there is no way I can ignore what is happening in the domain of education. In the process of self-reflection, I am required to cope with many pertinent questions: What am I teaching? Is there a hidden meaning in the texts that I ask my students to study? Or, how do I relate to my students? Is teaching an exercise of power, or is it an art of relatedness? As a parent, I too am growing up with my child, and rediscovering the meaning of schooling. I begin to enquire into the social implications of schooling: its socialising functions, its disciplinary devices, and its pedagogic methods. As a student of sociology, I am invited to the domain of education. I am expected to know how education is a process of communication through which schools pass on to the children their social heritage, knowledge and skills, and prepare them for adult roles. And finally, the *ideal* of education fascinates me. Education—I have been told by many saints, prophets and revolutionaries—elevates us, brings us closer to all that is noble and beautiful. Education is a process of inner transformation! But then, with my sociological imagination, I can see the widening gap between the ideal and the real. As a result, I begin to ask: what has gone wrong with the prevalent form of education?

Is it possible to intervene, to bring about radical changes and implement the *ideal* of education?

Yet, one could ask: Is there any reason at all to write a book on school education? One may also argue that there is not enough reason to over-emphasise the role of school education, because there are many other influences in life which can neutralise the effect of schooling. For example, schools can teach the child all good things: morality, tolerance, secularism, human dignity and so on. Yet, despite going through school education, one may end up becoming communal, violent and intolerant. In other words, as it is debated, schools do not, and cannot dictate the way one chooses to lead one's life.

There are limits to what schools can do, because school knowledge is often delegitimised. It is also possible to cite its many *unintended* consequences. For instance, one of the main objectives of colonial education was to create docile subjects loyal to the British Empire. But then, we know that the same education also created many rebels who fought against colonialism, and gave new meaning to the struggle for freedom. In other words, there need not necessarily be any symmetry between the intended educational objective and what really emerges out of that. It is also possible to argue that school education need not necessarily be taken very seriously, because one may evolve a purely strategic/instrumental orientation to it: consume all that the school is teaching for the purpose of passing the examination or getting the degree, and then, forget everything! The 'ideal' of education is one thing, but life itself is quite another story!

I can understand the significance of these arguments. I do agree that life is too complex to be comprehended on the strength of one's formal education alone. Yet, I would insist that the meaning of school education is worth examining; for good or bad, it does have an impact on one's life. In modern/complex societies one spends a significant part of one's formative years at school. In a way, the school is the first institution where one learns to interact with the world outside of his/her home and family. Moreover, as knowledge becomes more and more complex, formal school education acquires greater importance in its production and transmission. No wonder, what schools can do to one's life in terms of how one perceives and relates to the world is something that has aroused the imagination of many great minds. From John Dewey to Ivan Illich, from Leo Tolstoy to Mahatma Gandhi, from Rabindranath Tagore to Jiddu Krishnamurthy—we have seen how the thinkers/activists/visionaries spoke of and intervened in the domain of school education. We realise that it is important to understand and participate in the debate on the implications of schooling. This book is also an effort—albeit a modest/humble one, with its own limitations—to contribute to this critical/reflexive exercise.

Education has a broader meaning, as it is a life-long process of learning that takes place everywhere. Hence, it is not uncommon to find people who, in spite of not having had proper school education, are full of knowledge and wisdom. Likewise, degrees/diplomas may not necessarily provide one with what is generally expected of a 'cultured/educated' being: the spirit of love and tolerance, honesty and courage. However, in this book I have concentrated primarily on formal/institutionalised school education. This is not to devalue the importance of the other agencies of learning—say, the family, the community, the workplace or the media. The reason for concentrating on school education is to limit the range of the study and to develop a sharp focus. Moreover, it is also important to realise that in modern/complex societies, school education has acquired much greater importance than ever before. It is, however, true that in India millions of children have not yet been able to get school education. The *absence* of schooling in their lives is a reality to reckon with. But the focus of this project is not on this absence. Instead, I am eager to explore the meaning of schooling; of what it means to those 'lucky' ones who get school education.

There is much that can be studied about school education —its diverse forms and practices, caste/class/gender issues relating to knowledge and curriculum, the economics of education and, above all, the 'dropout' phenomenon: how the children belonging to the poor and the marginalised sections of society fail to survive in the system. It is obvious that a single book cannot cover all these issues. Here, our effort is to study and initiate a discussion on what can be termed as the social meaning of schooling: how it is related to the larger society; the social functions it serves; the way its functions alter in the process of social transformation; the social construction of school knowledge and its politico-ideological implications; and, above all, how schooling can also be perceived as a language of protest to promote emancipatory education for a just society. In other words, this book deals with the macro issues/debates relating to the significance of school education in India. It is an enquiry into the sociology of education, the politics of curriculum, and the pedagogic implications of the dominant as well as alternate forms of teaching and learning.

To begin with, the Introduction gives us an insight into how social scientists—mainly, sociologists and educationists —have studied the phenomenon called schooling, that is, the reason for its existence, the purpose it serves, the difference it makes in one's life, and its relationship with the larger society. The idea is that life at school is a worthwhile experience to study. No wonder, social scientists have been debating on its implications: whether it socialises and restores order; whether it legitimises and perpetuates inequality; whether it empowers, subjugates or controls; whether it has the power to transform and radicalise the society. This theoretical insight, I would like to point out, helps us make sense of the issues we are dealing with: schooling and society, ideology and curriculum, pedagogy and politics.

Chapter 1 is a study of how, in the Indian context, we have been debating on the objectives of education. As the society undergoes changes from time to time, so do the social expectations from education. The chapter seeks to capture and narrate the sociology of this living debate: how, for instance, colonialism undermined the ideals of ancient education; how a group of dissenters questioned the hegemony of colonial education; how the post-colonial Indian state visualised its educational agenda; or how, in our own times, because of the prevailing contradictions in the process of nation-making, divergent and conflicting educational perspectives have emerged. This broad sketch, I assume, would help us understand the socio-historical context in which schooling and its agenda have to be located.

In Chapter 2, I have examined the sociology of school knowledge: why certain ideas acquire more legitimacy than others, or why what is being taught at school needs to be seen as a *perspective,* rather than something that is 'pure', 'objective' and 'value neutral'. To substantiate my arguments, I have concentrated on the *NCERT* and *Eklavya* texts, and examined why the understanding and knowledge of India differs in these two projects. With this familiarity with the politics of knowledge, I have reflected on the challenges confronting the educationists: how the complexity of India —its diversity and civilisational unity, its contradictions and promises—can be or ought to be presented to the young learners.

Following this reflection on the contents of school knowledge, I have tried to examine some of the deep-rooted effects of schooling in terms of one's engagement with the world. This explains the rationale of Chapter 3—a chapter in which, as I see it, the discontent with the dominant/ mainstream pattern of school education has been revealed. The idea is that the prevalent practices—the hierarchy of knowledge, the ritual of examinations, the anti-dialogic form of teaching/learning—tend to distort the worldview of children.

In fact, with this discontentment begins a new quest: the search for alternatives. Chapter 4 is an in-depth study of an alternative school—*Mirambika* which is situated in the Sri Aurobindo Ashram of New Delhi and is based on the philosophy of 'free progress education'. It is important to state why we have chosen *Mirambika* as a site for alternative education. It is not my contention to argue that Mirambika is the only alternative. In fact, in a vast and complex country like ours, it is not impossible to find other equally important alternative projects catering to the divergent sections of society. For instance, as I have stated in this book, *Eklavya* is a striking example of this alternative venture: the way it experiments with textbook writing and brings knowledge closer to the social reality as experienced by the marginalised sections of society. Hence, to speak of Mirambika is not to negate or undermine the importance of other alternatives.

Perhaps, as Max Weber would have argued, the selection of a problem for investigation is related to the researcher's 'value-relevance'. I, therefore, cannot deny the 'subjectivity' involved in choosing Mirambika as an alternative project. It is possible that its philosophic roots and its culture of learning fascinate me. But then, I would also like to state that, despite this 'subjective' orientation, I have tried to study Mirambika from all possible angles. I have tried to examine its possibilities and achievements, its crises, contradictions and failures. There is yet another reason for choosing Mirambika. It is a school that derives its inspiration from the educational philosophy of Sri Aurobindo—a visionary, a revolutionary, a saint, and a mystic. It is, therefore, interesting to examine whether his educational ideals are merely Utopian, or whether they can be translated into reality. Moreover, as Mirambika is located in a metropolitan social milieu, it becomes necessary to observe how it copes with the metropolitan aspirations and deals with the typical middle class desires for material gains and success in life. In other words, a study of Mirambika enables us to explore the dynamics of spirituality and modernity, harmonic aspirations and the competitive social milieu, Utopian ideals and realistic concerns.

And finally, in Chapter 5, I have outlined the salient features of an emancipatory educational project and reflected on the questions many of us have been trying to find answers to: What kind of a society do we need to implement a radical educational project? And what are the tasks—both immediate and long-term—that you and I can initiate so that schooling can be an experience of joy, fulfilment, creativity and emancipation for the children of the new age?

A book of this kind, which is theoretical as well as empirical, academic as well as interventionist, has also got its limitations. I, therefore, ought to tell the reader what she/he should not expect from it. For example, this book is not about, say, the state of rural education in India: how poverty, hunger, hostile social situations and terribly poor infrastructural facilities destroy and distort the process of learning. Likewise, this book is not on 'gender issues' in school education. Nor is it about alternate politico-educational projects (say, the *Shiksha Karmi* and *Lok Jumbish* projects in Rajasthan or the *Neel Bagh* School in Andhra Pradesh) trying to make a difference in the life-practices of the poor and the oppressed. Perhaps those who are trying to find answers to 'socially/politically relevant practical questions' may not find much meaning in this book, because this book, as I would state without feeling apologetic, is about deeper sociological/philosophical questions rooted in the practice of schooling, knowledge, pedagogy and curriculum. One may sense a certain 'theoretical idealism' in a work of this kind. But then, this theoretical or socio-philosophical sensitivity and reflexivity that the book seeks to evoke, I would stress, is needed for any meaningful intervention in the arena of education.

I can imagine my potential readers. True, I would like the book to be read by the scholars and students of the sociology of education. But then, I have not written it just for the purpose of preserving it in the university libraries. This is not just another 'academic' book, written exclusively for a core group of specialists. I would like my book to be read by school teachers, textbook writers, educational activists and, above all, by the parents of school-going children—the parents who want to make sense of what happens in schools, or who want to understand the meaning of the texts that their children study. In other words, the reader of my book can be anyone who is given to asking the following questions:

a. What do schools do to one's life?
b. What are the social functions of school education?
c. Is it possible to think of an alternative system of learning for creating a new society?

The purpose of this book is in line with its form, the mode of presentation and writing. In this context I wish to make three points. First, I have tried my best to reduce the use of 'technical idioms'. My goal is to communicate and write in a manner that retains its simplicity without losing its depth. Second, I am not particularly fond of 'academic neutrality'. In fact, I have written this book with a purpose: to make my readers aware of the shortcomings of the prevalent pattern of school education and understand the desirability of alternative pedagogic experiments. For me, writing this book is also a therapeutic process: it releases my tensions and anxieties; it heals and shows me a way. Third, there is no trace of positivism in my study. Because in this study, I have experienced the unity of what the positivists regard as opposites: reason and passion, thinking and feeling, critical distance and emotional involvement. As a result, my study transcends the disciplinary boundaries time and again. I have drawn inspiration from insights into sociology, philosophy, and even mysticism. The sources I have used are diverse and many. I have studied books and articles; interviewed educationists, school teachers, children and parents. I have read school texts and other material. I have participated in classroom activities. And, above all, I have, *felt* the tension of the anxiety-ridden parents; the agony of the tender minds burdened with examinations, homework and the heavy load of learning material. I have felt the missionary zeal of those who have been trying to establish an alternative form of teaching and learning. To sum up, this book is a combined effort of thought and feeling; an active participation of the brain and the heart.

I have been teaching a course on the sociology of education. Teaching, I have felt, is a process of learning. I am indeed grateful to my students whose questions, interventions and comments have helped me develop my arguments. With deep gratitude, I remember my three students—Disha Nawani, Amman Madan and Bikram Mishra. Their research interest in education has always been a source of inspiration. In fact, the culture of learning that continues to prevail in the Jawaharlal Nehru University has given me the strength to undertake a project of this kind. Urmila did the editing job with extreme care. I am grateful to her.

Time and again, I have read out the manuscript to my wife. Her art of listening and suggestions have helped me move ahead with the project. In fact, I am grateful to everyone in my family, particularly my mother and elder brother who helped me cultivate my faculties of learning. I also recall my late mother-in-law, with whom I used to share my ideas. I am grateful to my friends and well-wishers. They have given me the strength. I have realised that without love, there is no faith; and without faith, there is no creativity. In a way, they are my teachers. If this book makes sense, the credit must go to all of them.

April 2002

Avijit Pathak
Jawaharlal Nehru University
New Delhi

Introduction

Life at School

Need for a Critical Enquiry

It would be difficult for anyone to overlook the crucial role played by schools in shaping our lives, especially in the context of modern/complex societies. Formal schooling, it is thought, gives one the necessary information, the required skills, and the much needed specialised knowledge. It is a measure of one's level of education; a deciding factor in the selection or rejection of people for professional roles. It trains the mind to adapt to a modern, technologically advanced civilisation. No wonder, there is an ever increasing emphasis on universal/compulsory schooling. As a result, one also gets to witness the parents' anxiety with respect to their children's school education. Without good schooling, it is argued, life cannot unfold its full potential!

It is, therefore, important to understand the phenomenon called schooling. To begin with, it is possible to look at schooling from a positive angle. School, as a formal educational institution, is viewed as a necessity in the modern society; a society that can no longer rest on the *particularistic* values of family and kinship. It can also be argued that schools, with their organised structure and disciplinary devices, legitimate knowledge and certified texts, examinations and hierarchies, systematise one's mind and evolve a 'scientific' way of looking at things. In other words, schooling (or its widespread networks) is seen as an index of societal progress. It is believed that the school is an agent of social change; it leads to modernity. Moreover, it makes social mobility possible.

But then, there are dissenters who are not happy with the way schools function. They are of the opinion that as schools tend to monopolise the domain of education, alternative possibilities or orientations to knowledge get undermined. The schooled mind, as a result, tends to become closed and conservative. It begins to conform. It is also argued that schools perpetuate inequality and reproduce the values of an unequal social order. They make one believe in competition, social divisions, and in one's success at the cost of someone else's failure. Moreover, schools, it is believed, tend to become oppressive. The spontaneity/naturalness of the child is killed, and a regimented mind is produced. This critique has also led many to innovate and experiment with new schools that are emancipatory, and are more sensitive to the child's needs and natural growth.

A rigorous study of education, therefore, demands a critical enquiry into the meaning of schooling—its functions and dysfunctions, promises and contradictions, possibilities and ambiguities.

I
School as a Necessity of Modern Existence

Why is it that schools play such an important role in a modern/complex society? We know that in order to be certified as 'educated', all of us have to attend schools, study the appropriate texts, and pass innumerable tests at different stages of our 'cognitive development'. In other words, what is called education seems to be impossible to acquire without schooling. It is, therefore, important to understand the reasons that make schooling a 'necessity'.

What characterises a human society is its ability to renew itself, because 'life', wrote John Dewey, 'is a self-renewing process' (Dewey 1966: 2). And this self-renewal, it ought to be realised, is not just the renewal of mere physical existence. It is, as Dewey argued, the renewal of the entire experience of the group—its 'beliefs, ideals, hopes, happiness, miseries and practices' (Ibid: 2). 'And education', he wrote, 'in its broadest sense, is the means of this social continuity of life' (Ibid: 2). In other words, education is a process of transmission/communication of the group heritage. It is this educative process that allows a society to continue and renew itself. Needless to add, education means that the adults who retain the knowledge and customs of the group transmit and communicate their 'habits of doing, thinking, and feeling' (Ibid: 3) to the younger generation.

Education as a means of the renewal of group heritage is common to all societies. But there is a qualitative difference between the 'under-developed social groups' and modern, complex societies. In the case of the former, as Dewey would say, there is no need of formal schooling. Children learn their customs and acquire their emotional set- and-stock of ideas by sharing in what the adults are doing. But then, as Dewey observed, things began to change as civilisations advanced and became more complex, because with the tremendous advancement in knowledge, resources and skills, children could no longer learn about the richness of their social heritage by merely observing the adults, one of the main reasons being that 'in an advanced culture, much which has to be learned is stored in symbols and it is far from translation into familiar acts and objects' (Dewey 1966: 8).

Take, for example, the advancement in literature, philosophy, or natural/mathematical sciences. It is impossible to learn all these 'abstract symbols' merely from the familiar setting of family and kinship. What is important, therefore, is a formal educational institution with its planned curricula and professionals who are capable of communicating these complex knowledge systems to the child. That perhaps explains the necessity of the school as a formal educational institution. To quote Dewey:

> Much of what adults do is so remote in space and in meaning

> that playful imitation is less and less adequate to reproduce its spirit. Ability to share effectively in adult activities thus depends upon a prior training given with this end in view. Intentional agencies—schools—and explicit material—studies—are devised. The task of teaching certain things is delegated to a special group of persons (1966: 8).

One thing is becoming clear. Given the complexity of our society, the importance of school as a formal educational institution cannot be overlooked. What further adds to this complexity is that a modern society, for its existence, rests on abstract/universalistic values. This is what distinguishes it from a simple society that depends on particularistic values of family and kinship. In other words, human beings, in order to participate in a modern/complex society, must go beyond family/kinship ties, relate to a vast/impersonal social order and learn abstract/universalistic values. Schools, it is felt, are designed to serve this purpose, because here, surrounded by professional teachers and children from divergent families, one learns the abstract/universalistic values. It is, therefore, said that the school is a place that takes the child away from the protective context of family-kinship ties and places him/her in the ocean of the larger society. It is in this context that cultural anthropologists distinguish informal socialisation from, say, formal education.

Yehudi A. Cohen, for example, has drawn a sharp distinction between socialisation and education. For Cohen, socialisation means 'the activities that are devoted to the inculcation and elicitation of basic motivational and cognitive patterns through an ongoing and spontaneous interaction with parents, siblings, kinsmen, and other members of the community' (Cohen 1971: 22). In contrast to socialisation, 'education is the inculcation of standardised and stereotyped knowledge, skills, values and attitudes by means of standardised and stereotyped procedures' (Ibid: 22). The reason why Cohen makes this distinction has to be understood. What he calls 'socialisation' is the characteristic of a society in which 'kinship is the primary principle in the organisation of economic, political and other social relations' (Ibid: 25). And socialisation means an over emphasis on the 'particularistic values of kinship'.

What he calls 'education' is 'the predominant mode of shaping the mind in social systems in which non-kinship and universalistic considerations are of primary significance in the organisation of economic, political and other social relations' (Cohen 1971: 36). The point that Cohen makes is that the need for 'education' arises more in a society that has become modern and complex in the sense that it has gone beyond the kinship networks and has adopted universalistic values.

It is at this juncture that Cohen speaks of the relevance of schools. 'The development of schools—the institutionalised predominance of education over socialisation in the shaping of men's minds—is a characteristic feature of state societies' (Cohen 1971: 39). Cohen reminds us of two major characteristics of a state society. First, it seeks to subvert local—especially kin—sources of solidarity, loyalty and authority. Second, in order to legitimise its authority, it seeks to establish an ideology of uniformity among its people. In other words, a state society requires the predominance of universalistic values—a set of standardised, uniform symbols and aspirations so that the state can exist as the ultimate authority. And schools, according to Cohen, serve this very purpose, because schools are designed to promote uniformity, standardised aspirations and universalistic values. There are many ways of doing this. For example, one can speak of 'uniform dress for school children (or even for their teachers), standardised sacred books and the paraphernalia of fetishes, flags, pictures of culture heroes or rulers that students face throughout the school day' (Ibid: 40). Or, one can speak of a universalistic curriculum like 'learning the multiplication tables,' remembering 'the dates of wars and treaties' or memorising 'the names of rivers, mountains, cities or ports' (Ibid: 43). What is interesting is that 'such learning is wholly independent of family background, ethnic or religious affiliation, regional membership or any other nexus that is a natural breeding ground for particularistic orientations' (Ibid: 43). Moreover, children are taught by a variety and succession of teachers. This reduces the possibility of any tendency to identify with any particular teacher. Finally, 'the allocation of standardised rewards and punishments for standardised performance' is yet another characteristic of school education. The fact, as Cohen intends to establish, is that there is a fair degree of resemblance between school education and state society, because the goals are uniformity, standardisation and promotion of universalistic values and discouragement of particularistic differences. In a way, while establishing the need of school education in a state society, Cohen makes a critical point: 'schools were not established originally to foster the life of the mind or the spirit of free enquiry' (Ibid: 41). As a matter of fact, Cohen's primary thesis is that schools were designed to promote loyalty—'the establishment of conformity to the aims and imperatives of a state system.'

In fact, there is no dearth of critical reflection with respect to the meaning of schooling in our life. Imagine, for instance, the positive dream centred around mass schooling: it leads to democratisation of society, it distributes knowledge, skills, information, and creates a conscious/articulate public for a democratic society. But then, there is also a counter-argument that refutes this dream. It claims that in our society, schools exist for an altogether different reason. Schools exist not to create a democratic society or a civic ideal, but for 'certifying, sorting and selecting personnel' (Green 1971: 133.). True, there need not be a close relationship between the skills required for a particular job and a high school diploma. But what is significant is that the school diploma certifies 'a certain measure of dependability, acquiescence, and plasticity of personality' (Ibid: 134)—the qualities needed for participating in the economy. The point is that schools are necessary, particularly in a complex/technologically advanced society, for certifying and selecting people for their contributory roles in the economy.[1]

It is at this juncture that we can make the following observations regarding the necessity of schooling in a contemporary society.

- In a complex society, schools—as formal institutions with planned curricula and professional teachers—exist to transmit and communicate our rich social heritage: its knowledge systems, beliefs, practices, skills and technologies.
- Schools enable the child to go beyond the particularistic values of family/kinship ties and adopt universalistic values without which a modern/ complex society cannot function. In other words, schools are necessary for bringing about social transformation.
- Schools serve the requirements of a state society by promoting uniformity and loyalty to the state.
- Schools, by certifying and selecting people for future adult roles, justify their existence.

II
Schools, Morality and Social Order

It is, therefore, obvious that there are many ways of looking at the existence of schools. We will, however, begin with a positive orientation to schooling—how, for example, it disciplines the mind, reduces egotism, instils a sense of morality, and stabilises the social order. In other words, it is believed that schools ought to play an important role in the development of a healthy society where there is a general consensus regarding the moral authority of the collective. It is at this juncture that Emile Durkheim's contributions to the sociology of education acquire relevance. Durkheim, a master sociologist, we know, put great emphasis on the power of the collective over the individual. For him, society cannot be reduced into its parts; it is independent of individuals. And, as he thought, one of the major functions of schools is to make the child realise and internalise this moral power of the society. Before we go any further, it is important to see how Durkheim understood education.

To begin with, it has to be realised that for Durkheim, education has a distinctive societal meaning. What we call education cannot be seen without locating it in the context of a given society; its specific needs and requirements. 'It is idle to think', wrote Durkheim (1956: 65), 'that we can rear our children as we wish'. In fact, he wrote, 'each society considered at a given stage of development has a system of education which exercises an irresistible influence on individuals' (Ibid: 65). In other words, there is no abstract/universal content of education; it varies from society to society. This societal education—a specific way of acting, doing, thinking and believing—is difficult to escape.

Education, Durkheim thought, would mean interaction: adults exercising an influence on the youth and making them learn the needs/requirements of the society, its traditions, and heritage. Durkheim also reminded us of the diversity of occupations in advanced civilisations. Each occupation needs a specific aptitude and specialised knowledge. As a result, argued Durkheim, education in advanced civilisations cannot be the same for everyone; it would vary from person to person depending on one's occupation. But then, there is something more than this 'specialised education'. For Durkheim, the proponent of collective conscience, no society can survive without a 'common base—a certain number of ideas, sentiments and practices which education must inculcate in all children indiscriminately, to whatever social category they belong' (Durkheim 1956: 69). Education should, therefore, serve two functions: (a) it should prepare the child for a specific occupation, and (b) it should enable the child to internalise the core values of the society.

To quote Durkheim:

> Education is the influence exercised by adult generations on those who are not yet ready for social life. Its object is to arouse

> and develop in the child a certain number of physical, intellectual and moral states which are demanded of him by both the political society as a whole and the special milieu for which he is specifically destined. (Durkheim 1956: 71).

The deeper meaning of education, as he thought, could be understood only if we look at its social function. Essentially, education creates a new being; an egotistic individual gets transformed into a social being. Without education, man's social existence is impossible. After all, it should not be forgotten that 'there was nothing in our congenital nature that predisposed us necessarily to become servants of divinities, symbolic emblems of society, to render them worship, to deprive ourselves in order to do them honour' (Durkheim 1956: 72). It is education that enables one to become a civilised being and to internalise the language of the society.

> To the egoistic and a social being that has just been born, it must, as rapidly as possible, add another, capable of leading a moral social life. Such is the work of education and you can readily see its great importance. ...It creates in man a new being. (Ibid: 72).

True, education is not spontaneous. It has to be forced. But this does not mean that it has to be oppressive, because the new being that education creates 'represents what is best in us'. The beginning of education means that the child learns to exercise 'strong self-control' in order to contain his 'natural egoism' and subordinate himself to 'higher ends'. One learns self-control because of two factors: (a) physical necessity, and (b) moral grounds. But the child, stressed Durkheim, cannot understand the importance of physical necessity, because he is not yet directly faced with the harsh realities of life. As a result, for the child, self-control is possible only through learning. And herein lies the necessity of schools. For Durkheim, a major function of school education is that it evokes a sense of morality in the child. The child learns self-control and eventually becomes a disciplined/social being.

While reflecting on the social function of schools, he spoke on morality, discipline and punishment, the role of the teacher, and the meaning of the school curriculum.

Schools instil a sense of morality into children. But what is morality? Durkheim made two relevant points. First, the function of morality is 'to determine conduct, to fix it, to eliminate the individual arbitariness' (Durkheim 1961: 27). This means regularity. 'Morality', wrote Durkheim, 'presupposes a certain capacity for behaving similarly under like circumstances, and consequently it implies a certain ability to develop habits, a certain need for regularity' (Ibid: 27). Second, morality implies 'the idea of authority'. The nature of this authority has to be understood. Let us take an example. When we fall sick, we accept the doctor's authority, follow his orders. There is obviously a utilitarian meaning involved in it: we want to recover. But moral authority is qualitatively different. There is no such utilitarian reason. One must obey a moral command out of respect for it and for this reason only. In a way, according to Durkheim, 'morality is a system of commandments' (Ibid: 31). What is important is that it is the spirit of discipline that reconciles these twin aspects of morality. Discipline regularises conduct, and discipline does not come about without authority. 'The fundamental element of morality,' Durkheim concluded, 'is the spirit of discipline' (Ibid: 31). At schools, he argued, children learn how to discipline themselves and emerge as moral agents of society.

Yet, a question remains unanswered: Why should schools occupy such an important place? Can't children learn lessons on morality in their homes, with their families? Well, in the family, one learns altruistic values—how to feel, and live for others. But then, according to Durkheim, the familial education alone is not sufficient for generating a sense of morality and discipline that the larger political society demands. Because the family is full of emotion and sentiment; there is no abstract notion of duty, no impersonality. Things, however, begin to change at school. Teachers and students who form a part of the school are not family members. There is something cold and impersonal about the obligations imposed by the school. In a way, the schoolroom society resembles the society of adults, and to enter it is to enter the bigger world. It serves as an 'intermediary' between the affective morality of the family and the more rigorous morality of civil life. With schooling, Durkheim would argue, begins serious life. In other words, to live as a disciplined citizen in the larger political society, one has to adopt a moral/ responsible attitude even towards those who are not one's immediate family relatives. And schools teach this abstract notion of moral responsibility and civil duty, that is, how to relate to and participate in the larger society. In a way, with schooling begins a child's journey towards the bigger world.

> The bonds uniting the citizens of a given country have nothing to do with relationships or personal inclinations. There is, therefore, a great distance between the moral state in which the child finds himself as he leaves the family and the one towards which he must strive. This road cannot be travelled in a single stage. Intermediaries are necessary. The school environment is the most desirable. It is a more extensive association than the family or the little societies of friends. It results neither from blood relationships nor from free choice, but from a fortuitous and inevitable meeting among subjects brought together on the basis of similar age and social conditions. In that respect, it resembles a political society. (Durkheim 1961: 230-31).

Besides, the school conveys a message to the child: he must come to his class regularly and at a specified time; he must not disrupt things in the class; he must learn his lessons and do his homework, etc. Discipline is important, because 'a well-disciplined class has an air of health and good humour.' (Durkheim 1961: 152). Discipline also involves punishment. Durkheim wrote a great deal about the necessity and meaning of punishment at school. For him, the moral authority of the society is sacred. And if this authority is violated, it begins to lose its sacred character. 'A sacred thing profaned remains no longer sacred if nothing new develops to restore its original nature.' (Ibid: 165).

In fact, the moral harm caused by misbehaviour has to be understood. It shatters the child's faith in the authority of the school law. Hence, the law must assert itself and make the child believe that its refutation or violation cannot be tolerated. 'Punishment', wrote Durkheim, 'is nothing but this meaningful demonstration.' (Durkheim 1961: 166). In other words, the main purpose of punishment is that it restores the child's faith in the moral authority of the school law.

It is, therefore, obvious that, for Durkheim, the aim of punishment is not to cause terror and restore superficial order in the classroom. It is not to cause physical pain or suffering to the child. His voice against corporal punishment was clear and categorical: corporal punishment defies what moral education is all about—belief in the dignity of man. Because 'in beating, in brutality of all kinds, there is something we find repugnant, something that revolts our conscience—in a word, something immoral' (Ibid: 183). Punishment exists only to make the child see the sacredness of moral authority.

The importance that Durkheim attached to school education—its importance in the social and moral development of the child, and discipline and punishment—means that he was deeply concerned about the role of the teacher. The teacher, for him, is entrusted with a major responsibility. To the child, he represents the bigger world; the world that extends beyond the child's milieu of intimate family/ kinship relations. It is for the teacher to make the child respect the moral authority of the larger collective. It is the teacher's task to discipline and punish the child. The teacher should, therefore, be a man of character. To begin with, he must have a strong will, because 'the child cannot have confidence in anyone whom he sees hesitating, shifting, going back on his decisions' (Durkheim 1956: 88). Second, it is also important to realise that 'just as the priest is the interpreter of his god, the teacher is the interpreter of the great moral ideas of his time and of his country' (Ibid: 89).

The child has a tendency to equate the rule with the persona of the teacher. This is not desirable. Because a rule ceases to be a rule if it is not impersonal. The teacher should, therefore, make the child realise that the rule transcends him; that he is merely the instrument of a great moral reality which surpasses him.

Durkheim was equally concerned about whether or not the school curriculum was suitable for his celebrated ideal of moral education. An example would suffice: Durkheim did not attach much importance to art and aesthetics as a part of the curriculum, because he saw a certain contradiction between art/aesthetics and moral education. True, he admitted that there was an ideal in art—one's ability to get outside of oneself, to overcome the immediate/mundane interests of life. And this 'devotion to some transcendent objective,' he felt, leads to morality. Yet, what should not be forgotten is that art, after all, is about dreams and images; 'natural laws do not exist for the artist' (Durkheim 1961: 271). And that is why there is a fundamental contradiction between art and morality.

> ... the world of morality is precisely the world of the real. Morality demands that we love the group of which we are a part, the men who compose this group, the land they live on—all concrete and real things which we must see as they are, even though we are trying to perfect them as much as possible. Morals are in the domain of action... (Durkheim 1961: 271).

Art, however, takes us to an imaginary world and, therefore, should be considered as a 'play', of not much relevance to moral education. Durkheim attached great importance to history, whereas aesthetic education, he felt, was merely 'secondary and incidental'. History, according to him, enables the child 'to live in close intimacy with the collective consciousness' (Durkheim 1961: 278); and to feel that he is a part of the society.

All that we have learned from Durkheim suggests that his is a *functionalist* view—an attempt to see the school as an institution contributing to the development of social cohesiveness; a moral order. This positive/comfortable relationship between the school and the society has further been elaborated by another well known sociologist—Talcott Parsons—who too saw school education serving a positive function: causing appropriate socialisation and selecting people for future adult roles.

While reflecting on the 'school class as a social system,' Talcott Parsons made some interesting observations regarding the role of school education in American society. For him, schools socialise children and also prepare them for adult roles in different walks of life. To begin with, the school class as the 'focal socialising agency' has to be understood. Like Durkheim, Parsons too believed that school is the starting point of the child's journey to the bigger world; it weans the child away from the 'primary emotional attachment to his family' and familiarises him with the 'societal norms and values that are a step higher than those that he can learn in his family alone' (Parsons 1968: 210). True, there are similarities between the family and the elementary school. For instance, like a parent, the teacher too is an adult, 'characterised by the generalised superiority.' Second, like the mother, the teacher is usually a woman.

But then, according to Parsons, there are fundamental differences between these two institutions. The teacher, unlike the mother, is not ascriptively related to the child; hers is essentially an 'occupational' role. Moreover, unlike the mother, the teacher's responsibility towards the child is much more 'universalistic'. She is not supposed to be emotional and biased towards the child; in fact, 'she is not entitled to suppress the distinction between high and low achievers' (Parsons 1968: 208).

Besides, according to Parsons, the socialising function of the school class can be realised most effectively as the 'development in individuals of the commandments and capacities which are essential prerequisites of their future role-performance' (Parsons 1968: 200). In other words, the school trains the child, makes him knowledgeable, and equips him with the necessary skills for a vocational role in the future. But what is really significant is that it is at school that the child learns the basic values of a competitive/ achievement-oriented society: 'It is fair to give different rewards for different levels of achievement, so long as there has been fair access to opportunity, and it is only fair that these rewards lead on to higher order opportunities for the successful' (Ibid: 210). In a way, this is like learning 'the fundamental American value of equality of opportunity' (Ibid: 210). And this is important, because the child, in order to adjust to a competitive society, must learn the value of achievement: the desirability of differential rewards on the basis of one's level of achievement.

Parsons further states that when children join the elementary school in an American society, they experience what can be termed as 'initial equalisation', the reason being that the elementary school is normally a neighbourhood school and as a result, there is a fair degree of similarity among children in terms of their family/economic backgrounds. Moreover, children are given a 'common set of tasks', and the teacher is engaged in a 'relatively systematic process of evaluation of the pupils' performances'. In other words, children realise that the school situation is like a 'race' and that everyone has an equal opportunity. It is, therefore, desirable to differentiate and hierarchise people on the basis of their achievements. Even the losers, despite the initial difficulty, begin to accept this logic.

This, according to Parsons, is a great socialising function. And this leads to another major function that the school serves: selecting people for manpower allocation. At schools, children are evaluated on the basis of their level of achievement. For example, those who do well at the secondary school, would join colleges for higher learning; and those who cannot do well would join the labour force. Moreover, those with relatively high 'cognitive' abilities would do better in technical occupations, for example, 'operatives, mechanics, or clerical workers'. And those with relatively high 'moral' achievement would be inclined towards more 'socially' or 'humanly' oriented roles like 'salesmen and agents of various sorts' (Parsons 1968: 214).

Essentially, according to Parsons, schools are doing a very important job. They enable the child to become an integral part of the system. They also create a mindset that makes it easier for the child to take on a specific adult role later in life. Hence, from Emile Durkheim to Talcott Parsons, there is a positive story on schools—the story about their integrative functions.[2] Schools, we are told, help the child adapt to a new society whose primary ethos is universalistic rather than particularistic. They generate a sense of morality and create the mindset needed to accept the reality of a competitive society based on the principle of achievement. Schools, in other words, contribute to the stability of a consensual/cohesive social order!

III
Towards a Critique of School Practices

It is obvious that not everyone agrees with this functionalist approach. There are many reasons why a critique of school practices has developed. Take, for instance, the most powerful functionalist argument: 'schools contribute to social cohesiveness'. Here, the question arises: whose society are the functionalists talking about? Modern society is not, after all, homogeneous. Nor is it egalitarian. What characterises it is its divisiveness, inequality and asymmetrical power relations. As a result, it is quite possible that school education may promote the interests of the dominant sections of society. As the argument goes: in the name of retaining social order and cohesiveness, school education reproduces the existing inequality.

There is another functionalist argument: schools socialise and discipline the child, thereby strengthening the moral foundation of the society. But there are dissenters who would argue that schools are essentially oppressive institutions. As 'disciplinary institutions', schools destroy the child's spontaneity, hamper his inner growth, and create a passive/ submissive attitude to authority. Similarly, it can be argued that schools create a conservative/conformist mind. The schooled mind accepts the given order of things without questioning; without an urge to overcome it or to think of better alternatives. As we go deeper and elaborate on these points, we would try to present a critique of school practices, primarily from three angles.

Reproduction of the Existing Order and its Inequality

As we have already said, what characterises the contemporary society, particularly the class-divided capitalist society, is its inequality and asymmetrical power relations. It is, therefore, argued that education cannot remain neutral; it is inseparable from class interests. In other words, schools, instead of bringing about social transformation and creating an egalitarian society, tend to do just the opposite. It is in this context that a significant work by S. Bowles and H. Gintis (1976) deserves attention. There are three important points that Bowles and Gintis make in order to establish their thesis of reproduction. First, they argue that schools promote the 'technocratic-meritocratic' ideology: a belief that economic success essentially depends on the possession of the appropriate skills or education. This, they argue, is an 'ideological facade', because in reality, economic success or access to a job is linked to the individual's class, sex, age, race etc., rather than on talent, ability or qualifications. In other words, the 'technocratic-meritocratic' ideology creates a false belief, prevents one from seeing the real reason behind economic inequality, and legitimises it by arguing that success or failure depends upon one's level of education. Second, Bowles and Gintis assert that schools prepare young people for their place in the world of class dominated and alienated work by creating capacities, qualifications, ideas and beliefs which are appropriate to a capitalist economy. Because 'the reproduction of the social relations of production depends on the reproduction of consciousness' (Bowles and Gintis 1976: 127). No wonder, 'schools reward docility, passivity and obedience... [and] penalise creativity and spontaneity' (Ibid: 42). As a matter of fact, schools tend to kill the creative ability of an individual. It is believed that there is 'a close correspondence between the social relationships which govern personal interaction in the work place and the social relationships of the educational system.' (Ibid: 12). For example, students, like workers, have little power. Workers do not have any control over the content of their jobs; likewise, students do not have any control over the curriculum. Again, education, like work, is seen as a means to an end rather than an end in itself, because neither are intrinsically satisfying but are undertaken for the sake of external rewards (qualifications and wages) and to avoid unpleasant consequences (educational failure, and unemployment). Moreover, there is a correlation between the narrow range of work opportunities and specialisation/ compartmentalisation of knowledge.

In a way, Bowles and Gintis speak a different language —different from that of, say, Talcott Parsons, who too, as we know, wrote about American education. For Parsons, as we have discussed, school education, through socialisation and selection, contributes to social consensus and restoration of the social order. However, Bowles and Gintis question the social system that Parsons took for granted. By questioning the social system they critiqued the role of the schools.

This *Marxist* approach—an attempt to debunk the 'neutrality' of schools and see education as an articulation of the dominant class ideology—can be seen in the writings of Ralph Miliband and Louis Althusser. For Miliband, schools reproduce and legitimise the existing capitalist society; its inequality and class divisions. 'Educational institutions at all levels', wrote Miliband, 'generally fulfil an important conservative role and act, with greater or lesser effectiveness, as legitimising agencies in and for their societies' (Miliband 1972: 239).

Public schools, according to Miliband, have done this job quite openly. But what is significant is that the schools for the masses seek 'to instil... a submissive acceptance of the social order' (Miliband 1972: 240). This 'class-confirming' role of schools can be seen in many ways. For example, schools teach working-class children that their failure is due to some deficiency in themselves. Moreover, they teach 'middle-class values' and impose on working-class children 'an alien culture, values, and even language' (Ibid: 242).

Likewise, Louis Althusser saw education as a part of the 'state apparatus'. For Althusser, this state apparatus has two components—the repressive state apparatus (police, army, legal system, government and administration) and the ideological state apparatus (religion, education, politics, communication, literature, etc.). No ruling class, according to Althusser, can rule by means of force or repressive apparatus alone. Herein lies the relevance of the ideological state apparatus for establishing the hegemony of the ruling class. And education, as an ideological apparatus, has a central place in contemporary capitalist societies. For example, it spells out the 'rules of good behaviour' for the child's later economic role. For future wage-earners/labourers, it fosters the feelings of 'modesty, resignation and submissiveness'; for future capitalists and managers, education instils a sense of 'cynicism, contempt, arrogance, self-importance, even smooth talk and cunning' (quoted in Blackledge and Hunt 1985: 161). What is significant is that this whole 'class-maintaining' process is concealed from public view. Instead, the school is projected as a 'neutral' place, free from all ideological influences!

Essentially, what we are witnessing here is an argument that establishes the school as an institution serving the interests of the ruling/dominant class in the capitalist society. Another proponent of this argument is Pierre Bourdieu. For Bourdieu—a leading French sociologist—there is a fair degree of likeness between the culture of the educational institution and that of the dominant classes. It is no wonder, as Bourdieu points out, that the children of the dominant classes tend to perform better at schools and universities, whereas working class children fail. This explains why education seeks to reproduce the prevalent class inequality.

To begin with, Bourdieu points out that different cultures exist in a class-based society. But not all cultures are given equal importance at the educational institution. It is essentially the culture of the dominant classes that is given primary importance. Or, to use Bourdieu's words, the educational system has its own 'cultural arbitraries' which are variants of the cultural arbitraries of the dominant classes. As a result, it becomes easier for the children of the dominant classes to adjust to the educational system or to excel. Besides, as the school, in the name of teaching/learning, attempts to impose the cultural arbitraries of the dominant classes on the children who come from other cultures, a 'symbolic violence' is perpetuated. In other words, the school is instrumental in making the children of the working class feel that their culture is inferior and that it is the culture of the dominant classes that is worth learning!

According to Bourdieu, it is through spontaneous interaction with their family, kinsmen, and other members of their community that children get to learn about their culture: values, norms, ways of thinking and perceiving. It is in this context, he says, that the children of the dominant classes acquire their 'cultural capital'. Being cultured, in terms of high culture, is a measure of cultural capital. For example, cultural capital can be equated with the 'linguistic and social competencies and such qualities as style, manners, know-how as well as aspirations and perceptions of the objective chances of success' (Bourdieu and Passeron 1977: 167). Its manifestation can be seen in acquired interests such as listening to classical music, visiting art galleries, reading non-professional books, etc. It is this cultural capital that enables the children of the dominant classes to excel at the educational institutions. Because the educational institutions, far from being neutral, are biased towards the cultural capital of the dominant classes. The examples that Bourdieu gives to establish his point are interesting. For instance, in France, as he reminds us, there are two forms of language: bourgeois parlance and common parlance. A major characteristic of bourgeois parlance is that it verbalises feelings and judgements. But common parlance is devoid of 'fine words'. Now, Bourdieu says, university French is closer to bourgeois parlance. The literate tradition in education assumes that all experiences can be turned into a literary exercise where style and forms of expression are important. Not surprisingly, in the domain of higher education in France, the upper classes and Parisians dominate. The conclusion that Bourdieu draws is essentially critical in nature: what goes on in the name of education is not expected to create an egalitarian society. Instead, its primary objective is to reproduce the existing class hierarchies and inequalities.

The point emerging from this discussion is that what the schools teach need not be seen as something neutral. Instead, it is important to problematise it and relate school knowledge to the larger socio-economic reality. In Michael Apple—a leading American sociologist of education—we see a very sharp articulation of this perspective. The question that bothers Apple is, 'why certain social and cultural meanings and not others are distributed through schools' (Apple 1979: 27).

What is being regarded as 'legitimate' school knowledge, Apple argues, has to be seen as a 'value governed selection from a much larger universe of possible knowledge' (Apple 1979: 45). And the meaning of this selection—selected by 'specific social groups and classes in specific institutions, at specific historical moments' (Ibid: 45)—cannot be comprehended unless we understand the dominant socio-economic ideologies. For example, in American schools, technical knowledge acquires 'high status'. The reason is that technical knowledge does serve the interests of the corporate economy.

> A corporate economy requires the production of high levels of technical knowledge to keep the economic apparatus running effectively and to become more sophisticated in the maximisation of opportunities for economic production. Within certain limits, what is actually required is not the widespread distribution of this high status knowledge to the populace in general. What is needed more is to maximise its production. As long as the knowledge form is continually and efficiently produced, the school itself, at least in this major aspect of its function, is efficient. (Apple 1979: 36-37).

This close relationship 'between economic structure and high status knowledge' explains why, for instance, 'substantial funding was given to mathematics and science curriculum development while less was given to the arts and humanities' (Apple 1979: 37). Indeed, it is argued that technical knowledge is 'macro-economically beneficial in terms of long run benefits to the most powerful classes in society' (Ibid: 38), because its 'economic utility' cannot be questioned. Moreover, it is 'discrete' in nature with an identifiable content and a stable structure. With such knowledge, Apple points out, it becomes easier to stratify and hierarchise individuals.

In other words, for Apple, the American school with its emphasis on 'high status technical knowledge' is engaged in retaining the *status quo* and reproducing the dominant class hegemony. This invariably implies that schools seek to create a technical/conformist mindset; criticality is denied, and institutions or commonsense rules are projected as something 'pre-given, neutral and unchanging because they all continue to exist by consensus' (Apple 1979: 83). Essentially, a negative meaning is attached to conflict. It is thought that conflict is 'inherently and fundamentally bad'. The avoidance of conflict is clearly visible in the way science is taught in elementary/ secondary schools. Apple argues that what schools teach is a 'consensus theory of science' or a 'positivistic ideal of science'. In other words, science is projected as 'bodies of knowledge organised around certain fundamental regularities'; science, it is thought, is always 'subject to empirical verification with no outside influences, either personal or political' (Ibid: 89). As a result, children are not told that the scientific community too consists of individuals and groups of scholars, and, science 'has had a significant history of both intellectual and interpersonal struggle' (Ibid: 88). For example, competition over priority and recognition in new discoveries is a characteristic feature of all established sciences.

Even in social studies, one sees the same orientation: the primacy of consensus and avoidance of conflict. For example, children are taught that all elements of a society are 'linked to each other in a functional relationship, each contributing to the ongoing maintenance of society' (Apple 1979: 93). But Apple asserts that this taboo on conflict is not desirable, because there is not just 'law or rule breaking dimension of conflict'. Conflict leads to new awareness; it is the beginning of a new journey towards social transformation. Furthermore, it is through conflict, as Apple argues, that the oppressed sections of society define their distinctive identity and strive for liberation.

Schools systematically distort the functions of social conflict in collectivities, and, as a result, contribute significantly to the 'ideological underpinnings that serve to fundamentally orient individuals towards an unequal society' (Apple 1979: 102). Apple concludes:

> When a society 'requires' at both an economic and cultural level, the maximisation (not distribution) of the production of technical knowledge, then the science that is taught will be divorced from the concrete human practices that sustain it. When a society 'requires' at an economic level, the 'production' of agents who have internalised norms which stress engaging in often personally meaningless work, acceptance of our basic political and economic institutions as stable and always beneficient... then we would expect that the formal and informal curricula, the cultural capital, in schools will become aspects of hegemony. (Apple 1979: 102).

There is yet another important point that Apple makes. Schools tell the child that there is a fundamental distinction between work and play. Apple's study of a kindergarten leads him to believe that children are trained to see the incompatibility between work and play. For example, children learn that 'work activities are more important than play activities' (Apple 1979: 55). Not solely that, children are also trained to believe that 'work includes any and all teacher-directed activities'. Work is 'compulsory'; work means what one is told to do. But only 'free time activities' are called play. What is equally important is that work-activities have to be done. It is this compulsion that enables children to appreciate the values of diligence, perseverance and obedience.

The point that Apple makes is that little children are made to see that there cannot be any reconciliation between work and play. Work cannot be an experience of freedom and choice. In other words, it is like preparing oneself for a world that is fragmented, alienated and devoid of creativity. As Apple says, 'unquestioning acceptance of authority and of the vicissitudes of life in institutional settings are among a kindergarten's first lessons' (Apple 1979: 57).

As we reflect on all that we have discussed so far regarding the theory of reproduction, we realise that its power lies in its criticality. It raises critical questions relating to the functioning of schools in class-divided capitalist societies; it sees the ideological character of knowledge; it reveals the hidden curriculum and establishes its relationship with the politico-economic interests of the dominant classes. In other words, it tells us that society is not a cohesive whole, and the question of education cannot be comprehended without locating it in the context of power: how education is being controlled, defined and modulated by the privileged sections of society.

Yet, there are problems. The theory of reproduction, despite its potency, tends to be deterministic. It reduces education into a mere instrument of the economy. As a result, it tends to undermine everything about the traditional curriculum. But then, it is possible to argue that not everything about the traditional curriculum, or for that matter, the 'bourgeois knowledge', is necessarily bad. Science, for example, can be intellectually and cognitively desirable, and even beneficial for the working class and the socialist revolution.[3] Again, this theory refuses to see the possibility of even the minimal autonomy of schools. It also denies the agency of the participants: students and teachers. It treats them as passive receivers of class ideologies, norms and values. But the point we wish to state is that human agency is never dead. For example, it is always possible to find innovative teachers who, despite all odds, may relate meaningfully to the children of the lower classes and generate alternative ideals for them. It is also possible to see *resistance:* how the working class children, far from blindly accepting the dominant class values, refuse to grant legitimacy to school knowledge. Henry Giroux articulates this point rather sharply:

> One of the most important assumptions of resistance theory is that working-class students are not merely the by-product of capital, compliantly submitting to the dictates of authoritarian teachers and scholars that prepare them for a life of deadening labour. Rather, schools represent contested terrains marked not only by structural and ideological contradictions, but also by collectively informed student resistance. (Quoted in Blackledge and Hunt 1985: 181).

In other words, it is possible to speak of a 'counter culture' that emerges out of a protest against what schools tend to symbolise.[4]

School as a Disciplinary Institution

It is also possible to see the school as a disciplinary institution. Well, discipline, for Durkheim, is inherently positive. It brings out what is best in man, reduces egotism and nurtures the moral foundations of society. But then, there is yet another meaning of discipline: the school as a disciplinary institution based on 'surveillance' creating 'docile' bodies! In other words, the school is seen as a place where power is exercised over the child for 'normalcy'. Here, unlike what Durkheim thought, discipline acquires a negative meaning; it is for creating 'meticulously subordinated cogs of a machine'; it is to produce 'automatic docility'; beneath it lies a 'military dream of society.'[5]

To comprehend the meaning of the school as a disciplinary institution, Michel Foucault's insights are of great help. It was in *Discipline* and *Punish* that Foucault elaborated how the modern era witnessed a shift from a medieval penal theory to the institutionalisation of imprisonment. Physical pain was no longer a necessary element in punishment. What emerged was the 'new techniques of discipline' that act in depth on the heart, the mind, the will—in fact, 'a whole set of assessing, diagnostic, prognostic, normative judgements'. No wonder, as Foucault demonstrated, in the eighteenth century, a whole army of technicians gradually took over from the executioner: the wardens, doctors, chaplains, psychiatrists, psychologists, educationalists.

What is significant is, as Foucault said, that these techniques of discipline were not limited to the prison. In fact, there was an astonishing coincidence between the new prison and other contemporary institutions: hospital, factory, school and the barracks. It was, therefore, not surprising, as Foucault pointed out, that Jeremy Bentham's famous 'panopticon'—a circular building enclosing a central inspection tower—was recommended in all these institutions. As a matter of fact, modern societies, as the argument goes, are maintained not so much by the army, police and a centralised state apparatus, but essentially by these 'carceral' institutions armed with techniques of discipline and surveillance.

It is in this context that Foucault viewed the school as yet another illustration of a disciplinary institution. And for discipline, what is important is the distribution of individuals in space—something that the school learned from the monastery. This distribution of space was needed for constant supervision and observation of each pupil. As a result, the old system of teaching, whereby the pupils of all ages and ability were placed under the authority of one master was replaced by the class system which made the supervision of each individual possible. Simultaneously, it also facilitated the assigning of similar work for all. As Foucault put it, the educational space functioned like a learning machine that supervised, hierarchised, rewarded and punished.

Discipline also called for the control of activity, and the chief instrument for doing this was the time-table. The time-table, as its monastic origin suggests, was designed for a precise division of one's days for measured/regulated activities. Foucault gave an illuminating example of the use of the time-table in the early nineteenth century in the French 'mutual improvement schools':

> 8.45 entrance of the monitor, 8.52 the monitor's summons, 8.56 entrance of the children and prayer, 9.00 the children go to their benches, 9.04 first slate, 9.08 end of dictation, 9.12 second slate, etc. (Quoted in Sarup 1982: 16).

The time-table meant the measurement of time. It was needed for the 'proper' use of time. Time, to put it otherwise, became 'disciplinary time'. As a result, the school, like other institutions, became subject 'to a whole micro-penalty of time (latelessness, absences, interruption of tasks), of activity (inattention, negligence, lack of zeal), of behaviour (impoliteness, disobedience), of speech (idle chatter, insolence), of the body ('incorrect' attitudes, 'irregular' gestures, lack of cleanliness), of sexuality (impurity, indecency)' (Quoted in Sheridan 1980: 154).

As a matter of fact, discipline meant hierarchical observation, normalising judgement, and their combination in examination. It required a new kind of architecture that would make it possible for those on the inside to be kept under constant observation. As we have already said, for Foucault, Bentham's 'panopticon' became the ideal model of such architecture; it could be seen in the prison, in the school, in the factory. Moreover, this constant observation and supervision was needed for 'normality'. A centralised/ coercive normality was introduced. The medical profession dictated the norm of normal health; the industrial system was designed to produce standardised products, and the school—with its disciplinary tools—must create the normal child! To quote Foucault:

> The judges of normality are everywhere. We are in the society of the teacher-judge, the doctor-judge, the educator-judge, the 'social-worker' judge; it is on them that the universal reign of the normative is based; and each individual, wherever he may find himself, subjects to it his body, his gestures, his behaviour, his aptitudes, his achievements. The carceral network, in its compact or disseminated forms, with its systems of insertion, distribution, surveillance, observation, has been the greatest support, in modern society, of the normalising power. (Quoted in Sheridan 1980: 162).

This 'normalising gaze' made it possible to classify, compare, reward and punish. In other words, it meant the necessity of the examination as a disciplinary device. The examination, according to Foucault, is the 'ceremony of power'; it 'establishes over individuals a visibility through which one differentiates them and judges them' (quoted in Sheridan 1980: 154). The examination, as a disciplinary tool, was an integral part of the school. It was needed to compare, hierarchise, grade and rank the pupils, and eventually to restore the required 'normality'. Examination reduced each individual to a 'case': an object for knowledge as well as a site for the exercise of power. It was necessary not only to identify 'normal' individuals. It was also necessary to identify those who had to be trained or corrected, classified, normalised, or excluded.

The significance of Foucault's work cannot be underestimated. It enables us to see what is often overlooked by those who believe that the school is inherently a positive experience, and that its primary task is to empower us with appropriate knowledge, values, and skills. Indeed, here we are getting an insight into the darker side of the school: how, like the hospital or the prison, it cannot do without perpetual surveillance—given its notion of 'normality'; how, with time-tables and examinations, it restricts our movements and hierarchises us. The school is a disciplinary space—without any spontaneity or freedom. Or, as Foucault thought, the school ought to be seen as a site for the exercise of power: how the teacher exercises power over pupils; how power and knowledge are reconciled. Indeed, as Madan Sarup sees it, at a time when there is a 'tremendous growth of disciplinary institutions', Foucault's work deserves special attention.

It is, however, possible to argue that Foucault's work was based on the French experience and it may not be generalised. But what is more important is that Foucault's conclusions were absolutely of a pessimistic nature. While seeing the school as a disciplinary institution, he completely overlooked the possibility of *positive* discipline: discipline as an inner call, discipline born of an authentic dialogue between the teacher and the pupil, discipline as a beautiful way of relating to the world in an egalitarian/harmonious manner. Perhaps because of his notion of power (power is multiple and ubiquitous, power relations permeate every aspect of social life) he could not visualise the possibility of an alternative practice: the school as a place where the teacher and the taught are engaged in a reciprocal relationship. He could not give us the option to believe that the school—if we try—can be qualitatively different from the prison or the hospital. But then, the questions that Foucault raised are bound to sensitise us as we begin to strive for alternatives.

Dependence on Institutions and Expertise

There is no dearth of critical evaluation with respect to the meaning of school education. For instance, it has been argued that the school is an instrument of power not simply because it prepares one to accept the hegemony of the dominant class, but because it also causes excessive dependence on institutions and expertise. As a result, it denies one one's autonomy, one's faith in oneself, and one's ability to do things outside the institutional settings. It makes one terribly dependent on expertise. This, as Joel H. Spring puts it, is the meaning of schooling in our times. His observation is hardly surprising, because in our times the school tends to assume responsibility for teaching the child about everything: thinking, acting, dressing, playing, creating, and even leisure. And there are 'experts' for everything who define the 'proper' way of doing things. It seems that there is no escape from the culture of expertise. Spring narrates this frightening situation when he writes:

> This form of institutional dependence can potentially freeze and deaden all human activity. It is not beyond the realm of possibility, for instance, that sometime in the future people will not engage in sexual acts until 'properly' taught the most valuable response and the most important scientific method. It seems possible that in the current discussions in geriatrics there will develop techniques to help people die 'properly'. Death education and sex education will probably become important elements in our educational system if current practices continue. (Spring 1972: 152-53).

This is essentially the ultimate experience in alienation: something rooted in the logic of the prevalent technological civilisation. It is in this context that Spring refers to the French sociologist Jacques Ellul and argues that technology dominates the goals and aspirations of man. The chief goal of technology, according to Ellul, is not human emancipation, but its own perpetuation and expansion. Man becomes a 'thing' to be controlled for the benefit of the technological system. To live in such a society is to adjust to its logic: accept what the technical experts are saying, and repress your own likes and dislikes! This, for all practical purposes, has become the function of the school. For Ellul, children are educated so that they become precisely what the society wants them to become. They must have a social conscience that allows them to strive for the same ends as society sets for itself. For example, the much talked about 'vocational education' is seldom interested in the natural aptitude of the individual. Instead, its primary agenda is to nurture only those aptitudes which are essential to the needs of the technological system. 'The school', as a result, 'becomes a source of power for the technological machine' (Spring 1972: 161).

Hence, 'social adaptation', says Spring, is the chief purpose of the school. It is futile to expect that the school is creating a free/reflexive/imaginative mind. 'The only type of personality that the school can support and approve of is one that fits smartly into the institutional organisation.' (Spring 1972: 164). With schooling begins alienation (losing faith in oneself and the resultant dependence on institutions and expertise), and it is this alienation that defines the technological system.

True, not everyone would accept this 'extreme' viewpoint, because not everything about the culture of technology/ expertise is bad, and thereby, the school cannot be unduly blamed if it prepares one for that culture. Moreover, it can be argued that there may be counter-cultures in the school itself that can pose a challenge to the dominant technological ethos. Yet, the point that Spring and Ellul raise cannot be denied, because the power of technology, as we are realising in our own times, is irresistible, and it does shape the environment of the school; the way it defines the agenda of knowledge and socialisation.

IV
Search for Alternatives

As we are beginning to realise, it is not easy to escape the questions being raised by the opponents of the prevalent school practices. It is, therefore, not surprising that an attempt has been made—by educationists and social philosophers—to strive for and experiment with alternative schools: the schools based on freedom (not control), creativity (not a packaged curriculum causing alienation), humanism (not arrogance or submissiveness), and a reciprocal teacher-taught relationship (not the monologue of the teacher as a dictator). It is important to understand the social meaning of these alternatives.

To begin with, let us reflect on Ivan Illich—a radical educationist whose disillusionment with the school as a 'manipulative institution' was total. No wonder, Illich was not willing to remain contented with just moderate reforms in the school system. Instead, he pleaded for what appears to be impossible to many: 'deschooling society'. For Illich, the school evolves a logic of its own; it is not a 'dependent variable', it is futile to believe that a change in the politico-economic system would alter the function of schooling, because 'schools are fundamentally alike in all countries, be they fascist, democratic or socialist, big or small, rich or poor' (Illich 1984: 77). Hence, what is desirable is to appreciate the 'revolutionary potential of deschooling.'

Before we understand the meaning of deschooling, let us see why Illich debunked the school. The schooled mind, according to Illich, loses freedom, becomes alienated, and internalises the myth that knowledge is impossible without certificates. One is 'schooled to confuse teaching with learning, grade advancement with education, a diploma with competence, and fluency with the ability to say something new' (Illich 1984: 9). This 'hidden curriculum' is dangerous, because it leads to what Illich called 'physical pollution, social polarisation, psychological impotence and modernised poverty.' For example, with schooling begins the internalisation of a series of myths. One learns 'the myth of institutionalised values'. In other words, the school tells one that nothing exists outside institutions; knowledge is what 'certified' experts teach at school; there is no such thing as a self-taught man or woman! One also learns 'the myth of measurement of values'. One is told that everything, including one's imagination, can be measured, graded and ranked. There is nothing unique about a man who refuses to be measured and compared. 'In a schooled world', as Illich said, 'the road to happiness is paved with a consumer's index' (Ibid: 46). One also learns 'the myth of packaging values': how knowledge can be packaged in the form of a scientific curriculum. In fact, the school denies one one's creativity, hampers one's inner growth and deprives one of learning from the flow of life itself. To quote Illich:

> School makes alienation preparatory to life, thus depriving education of reality and work of creativity. School prepares for the alienating institutionalisation of life by teaching the need to be taught. Once this lesson is learned, people lose their incentive to grow in independence; they no longer find relatedness attractive and close themselves off to the surprises which life offers when it is not predetermined by institutional definition. (Illich 1984: 51).

Moreover, as schools tend to lay a total claim on the time and' energies of its participants, we witness how the teacher begins to dictate the reality of life. According to Illich, the schooled society turns the teacher into a custodian, a preacher and a therapist. And this is dangerous. Because this is a denial of the ethos of a liberal society—the spirit of freedom.

No wonder, this sharp critique led Illich to think of alternatives. The school system, he argued repeatedly, rests on illusions—say, the illusion that 'most learning is the result of teaching'. Illich fought this illusion, and asserted his conviction unambiguously.

> Most learning happens casually, and even most intentional learning is not the result of programmed instruction. Normal children learn their first language casually, although faster if their parents pay attention to them. Most people who learn a second language will do so as a result of odd circumstances and not of sequential teaching... Most people who read widely and with pleasure, merely believe that they learned to do so in school; when challenged they easily discard this illusion. (Illich 1984: 20).

In a way, what characterised Illich was this firm hope and conviction that there were multiple ways of learning, and that there was no reason for anyone to accept the monopoly of the school. He, therefore, sought to liberate the human mind from the burden of schooling. With deschooling, he thought, would begin liberation. One would be able to choose one's education outside institutions; one would acquire the confidence to gain education even without passing through the ritual of examinations, graded rankings, and school certificates.

Illich proposed four approaches for implementing the agenda of deschooling. First, he spoke of the necessity of reference services to educational objects. The goal was to enable anyone interested in learning to use the educational material—the material that could be stored by libraries, laboratories, museums, theatres, factories, airports and farms. In other words, this easy accessibility of educational material would enable the society to fight against the school monopolising the domain of education. Second, he spoke of skill exchanges—a situation in which interested people would be able to list their skills, and the conditions under which they are willing to exchange them. This, he hoped, would lead to an abundance of skills, because the school would no longer be allowed to equate skills with institutional requirements, thereby making them scarce. Third, he felt the necessity of a communications network designed to allow persons—who want to learn a particular activity—to describe their specific areas of interest so as to be able to find a partner who would be interested in their enquiry. This 'peer-matching' network would be easier to establish with the help of computers. Finally, he thought of reference services to educators-at-large. This would enable one to see beyond teachers and discover all those professionals, para-professionals and freelancers interested in engaging themselves with education as a communicative act. To conclude, Illich wanted a society in which education would no longer be confused with schooling, nor learning with teaching, or creativity with diploma. His was the vision of a society in which the trajectory of life would become free from bureaucratic/institutional control.

The points that Illich made are intensely enlightening. Yet, it should not be forgotten that the school has also a positive role to play. After all, the school, as we have already discussed, enables the child to come out of the protective context of family/kinship ties, allows him/her to experience the larger society, as well as to interact with the complex network of social relations. Moreover, the school, its limitations notwithstanding, may also prepare the child for organised learning, and which—even if it curtails the freedom of the creative genius—is not altogether meaningless for the majority of the learners. That is why, it would be wrong to remain blind to progressive changes/reforms/innovations in the school system. In other words, we need to focus not just on deschooling, but also on an alternative form of schooling: how new schools can operate and function with relatively enhanced innovation, creativity and egalitarian values.

Karl Mannheim, for example, saw the possibility of a more progressive form of schooling in tune with the process of democratisation of society. What he had in mind was the movement for progressive/child-centred schools that he saw emerging in the West at the beginning of the twentieth century. A major characteristic of progressive schools is that the teacher is 'gradually being turned from an authoritative and possibly authoritarian instructor into a guide who relies upon the initiative of the learner, and recognises that for good intellectual learning, a prior condition is emotional respect between teacher and pupil' (Mannheim and Stewart 1962: 28). In other words, the child ought to be seen as an autonomous person to be respected, not just coerced, disciplined, and moulded by the adult. This democratic process, Mannheim felt, could also be seen in the new form of learning. This meant that 'students are participating in the direction of their own learning, they are much more encouraged to discover for themselves through the use of libraries, laboratories, attendance at conferences and participation in committees and other forms of self-government' (Ibid: 31). As a result, subjects like art, music, crafts acquired importance. Besides, education became an experience of inner joy; it was not based on 'external rewards like marks, prizes, ranking' (Ibid: 32). In Mannheim, we saw the affirmation of optimism. In the movement for progressive schools he saw the possibility of freedom, the autonomy of the child and above all a 'broader and deeper' notion of education affecting the personality of the pupil at all levels.

In fact, the progressive movement made it clear that it was possible to have an alternative notion of childhood and childrearing practices. Before we understand this alternative, let us examine the dominant/mainstream form of schooling and the associated childrearing practice. It is true that 'organisationally, schools are still tailored to authoritarian, class-based impersonal forms of teaching, requiring both incentive and punishment as aids to control' (Schostak 1986: 58). Beneath this authoritarianism lies a particular image of the child—an image created by the doctrine of Original Sin, an image of the child as 'material to be moulded and finally treated... by the will of the adult.' (Ibid: 45). This only goes to show that the child has no autonomy, that it is the responsibility of the adult to 'discipline' him/her!

But the progressive tradition, as Schostak argues, has an altogether different notion of childhood and human nature. Its roots could be seen in Rousseau's thinking. Rousseau, we know, advocated a form of child centred curriculum which located the source of evil not in human nature but in society. Rousseau, therefore, pleaded for natural stages of development of the child. Education, it was thought, should not require much constraint, that is, the disciplinary gaze that coerces the child. Instead, it should rest on the child's natural growth. No wonder, John Dewey—another advocate of progressive education—spoke of a new teacher who 'reduces to a minimum the occasions when he or she has to exercise authority in a personal way.' For Dewey, the model for teacher-pupil relations is that of the 'well-ordered' family. The teacher, far from being a dictator, thinks and does what is good for the child. But then, according to Schostak, this progressive tradition is not sufficiently liberatarian, because it is not free from 'subtle authoritarianism: It is 'paternalistic'; it assumes that the adult knows the best. But in 'liberatarian traditions' Schostak sees the possibility of true emancipation.

The origin of the liberatarian tradition could be seen in Godwin—the great English anarchist thinker. Here the primary assumption is that individuals do cooperate even without being coerced. In other words, the child is inherently good, social, and cooperative. It is, therefore, better to have faith in the child's natural motivation for learning. The task of the liberatarian teacher is to respect this motive, not to hinder or pervert the child's natural inclinations.

Hence, although authoritarianism remains the dominant school practice, there have been attempts to strive for alternatives. And these alternatives—progressive and liberatarian traditions—seek to make the school a better place, with a relaxed environment conducive to the child's inner growth. Yet, one need not necessarily be happy even with this humanism. For example, the standardised Marxist critique is that this child-centred approach is romantic and conservative. It fails to realise that a class-divided/stratified/ unequal society cannot be altered merely by changing the individual's consciousness. In a way, it is an emotional turning away from the society. As Madan Sarup argues, 'the entire approach is just an alternative to the dominant practice, but it is not oppositional' (Sarup 1982: 11).

It is in this context that Paulo Freire's approach to liberatarian education would be appropriate. It is possible to have an affinity between Freire and the alternative tradition we have discussed, because Freire too disliked the monologue of the teacher, the reduction of the school into a disciplinary space that crushes the autonomy of the pupil. But then Freire—with his radical pedagogy—seeks to make the transformation possible: from an exploitative society to an egalitarian one.

Education, for Freire, acquires special importance, because it is through the prevalent system of education—or 'banking education'—that the 'culture of silence' is reproduced. This education is not liberating for the oppressed. It is, therefore, important that the oppressed have new education—or 'liberatarian education'—to emancipate themselves. Before we understand how Freire distinguishes his new pedagogy from the prevalent one, let us see how he views the relationship between the oppressor and the oppressed. He seems to be convinced that the power that the oppressors wield has already dehumanised them; that they cannot think of any emancipatory agenda. In fact, it is the oppressed who have the 'great humanistic and historical task' of liberating themselves as well as the oppressors. Because 'only power that springs from the weakness of the oppressed will be sufficiently strong to free both' (Freire 1972: 21). Yet, Freire reminds us, it is not uncommon that the oppressed take on the values of the oppressors. This is a tragic situation, because 'the oppressed, instead of striving for liberation, themselves tend to become the oppressors, or sub-oppressors' (Ibid: 22). This happens because of what Freire calls 'prescription'—a hierarchical mode of existence in which the oppressors impose their values upon the oppressed. As a result, the behaviour of the oppressed becomes a 'prescribed' behaviour; it follows the guidelines of the oppressor. It is in this context that Freire talks about the 'duality' of existence that characterises the oppressed.

> They are at one and the same time themselves and the oppressor whose consciousness they have internalised. The conflict lies in the choice between being wholly themselves or being divided; between ejecting the oppressor within or not ejecting him; between human solidarity or alienation; between following prescriptions or having choices; between being spectators or actors; between acting or having the illusion of acting through the action of the oppressors; between speaking out or being silent, castrated in their power to create and recreate, in their power to transform the world. This is the tragic dilemma of the oppressed which their education must take into account. (Freire 1972: 24-25).

It is in this context that Freire talks about the 'pedagogy of the oppressed'—the pedagogy that would enable the oppressed to overcome their dilemma, show them the road to salvation, and eventually make liberation possible. This pedagogy, according to Freire, has two distinct stages. First, the oppressed unveil the world of oppression, and through the praxis commit themselves to its transformation. Second, when the reality of oppression has been transformed, the pedagogy ceases to belong to the oppressed only; it becomes a pedagogy of all men in their quest for permanent liberation.

According to Freire, it is not impossible to find certain members of the oppressor class joining the oppressed in their struggle for liberation. There is, however, a risk involved, because 'they almost always bring with them the marks of their origin; their prejudices and their deformations, which include a lack of confidence in the people's ability to think, to want, and to know' (Freire 1972: 36).

In other words, they talk about the people, but fail to establish any meaningful communication with them. That is why, Freire makes it categorically clear that liberation is not a gift from outside; that the leadership cannot implant in the oppressed a belief in freedom; that it must emerge from their own 'conscientisation'.

> The only effective instrument is a humanising pedagogy in which the revolutionary leadership establishes a permanent relationship of dialogue with the oppressed. In a humanising pedagogy the method ceases to be an instrument by which the teachers (here the revolutionary leadership) can manipulate the students (the oppressed), because it expresses the consciousness of the students themselves. (Freire 1972: 44).

It is, therefore, obvious that the new pedagogy Freire is talking about restores the human agency. It strengthens the confidence of the oppressed, makes them believe that they matter and that it is possible for them to create a better world. With the liberatarian pedagogy, they become subjects as they resist the process of objectification. Authentic education, they realise, requires the active presence of the learner. That is why, Freire distinguishes his new pedagogy from what he calls a banking concept of education. Banking education privileges the teacher. It assumes that the teacher knows everything; that the student is merely passive; that there is no possibility of a creative engagement between the teacher and the student. As Freire sees it, the banking concept of education suffers from 'narration sickness'. The teacher talks about reality as if it were motionless, static and compartmentalised. He assumes that his only task is to 'fill' the student's mind with the contents of his narration. The banking concept of education is, therefore, 'an act of depositing, in which the students are the depositories and the teacher is the depositor' (Freire 1972: 55). In fact, in the banking concept of education, 'knowledge is a gift bestowed by those who consider themselves knowledgeable upon those whom they consider to know nothing' (Ibid: 56). This means that it is hierarchical; it perpetuates inequality and oppression. It is anti-dialogic.

But what characterises liberatarian education is its dialogicity. Here the teacher, Freire says, is not merely the one who teaches. For him, teaching itself is a process of learning. As he engages himself in a dialogic relationship with his students, he begins to learn. Likewise, in the process of being taught, the students teach the teacher. As Freire says, 'through dialogue, the teacher-of-students and the students-of-teacher cease to exist and a new term emerges: teacher-student with student-teacher' (Ibid: 53). In other words, unlike the banking education, Freire's 'problem posing education' rests on creativity. It assumes that the learner is active and capable of attaching his/her own meaning to the world. As a result, it resists the *status-quo*, and celebrates revolutionary transformations.

It becomes clear that Freire's educational philosophy has been heavily influenced by humanistic Marxism and existentialism. As a matter of fact, what distinguishes Freire is his faith in the power of dialogue. Because dialogue means faith in humanity. Dialogue means one's refusal to accept one's passive existence. Dialogue is a creative engagement with the world. It means love, reciprocity, mutuality. It is to overcome one's silence. Dialogue, Freire says, is an 'existential necessity' (Ibid: 61). That is why, he attaches supreme importance to dialogue. 'Without dialogue', Freire says, 'there is no communication, and without communication there can be no true education' (Ibid: 65). It is this dialogic education that Freire wants to be an important component of the revolutionary practice.

To sum up, as we reflect on our search for alternatives—from child-centred progressive education to liberatarian pedagogy—we see a new notion of learning emerging: learning as a process of inner discovery; learning as a creative process filled with immense joy and enthusiasm. We also see the assertion of a dialogic/reciprocal relationship between the teacher and the taught. This means a new way of looking at the school, which, far from manufacturing cogs of a vast social machine, stimulates one to assert one's subjectivity and agency, and prepares one for a world that is humane and egalitarian.

V
School Education in Contemporary India: Expectations and Anxieties

All that we have discussed so far helps us understand that the phenomenon called schooling has to be examined critically. In fact, it has become clear that one's perception of schooling is deeply related to one's socio-political imagination. For example, as we have seen, it was the vision of a stable social order that led Durkheim to see the school as a moral agent. For Parsons, the school must select the manpower for the workforce. But then, those who dislike the *status quo*—the capitalist society—evoke a critique of the school, the way it reproduces class inequality. And those who strive for a humane/egalitarian society restoring human agency, see beyond the 'disciplinary' logic of the school and speak of child-centred/progressive/dialogic education. In other words, in the divergent perceptions of schooling, we see a spectrum of worldviews: from the celebration of a modern/ industrial society to the critique of capitalism; from the postmodern critique of modernity to the romantic vision of a non-competitive, egalitarian society!

It is in this context that the debate on Indian schooling has to be located. Well, it may be argued that all that we have discussed so far has its origin not in India, but elsewhere. True, the theoretical debate that we have initiated cannot be isolated from the Western context: how the theory of schooling emerged in a modern/industrial/capitalist society. Yet, we insist, the theoretical insight—be it that of a French Bourdieu or an American Michael Apple—has given us the skill that we need to examine the sociology of schooling in India.

As we look at India, it is important for us to reflect on the following:

1. Here is a society that is experiencing massive social transformation. It is merging with the 'new' age: the age of modern science, technological development, and secular rationality. But, at the same time, it cannot forget the traumatic memory of colonialism: how the colonial West sought to demoralise it, and to undermine its traditional cultural knowledge and heritage.
2. Here is a society with its political agenda: the agenda of a modern nation striving for equality and democracy. In other words, the goal is to reduce societal divisions and disparities and to create a just society. A leading Marxist political economist speaks of what he considers desirable in the future:

> The three most important elements in future education policy should be (a) to make primary education not only available but also reached to and availed of by all children, so that at least in the next generation, we have a more educated, alive and alert population; (b) to focus on the education of women, and particularly female children, by reaching out to them; and (c) to make education worthwhile, and relate it to the actual needs of the people in terms of suitability of the education imparted for employment, for better skills, for a better

> understanding of health, education, environmental and other relevant issues. (Ghosh 1992: 680).

As a matter of fact, in our times, the school has often been seen as a major instrument for achieving these objectives. The school, it is argued, is a 'modern' institution. It cannot remain contented with traditional/religious knowledge; it must train children for the new age and equip them with techno-scientific knowledge.[6] It is also thought that with universal schooling, a society like ours would eventually move towards equality. Moreover, the school, it is hoped, would also decolonise the mind and retain the cultural spirit of India. Here, we see an optimistic perception of schooling. In fact, this optimism—high expectations from school education—can be seen in different education commission reports in post-Independence India.[7]

But this positive view—the school as a progressive institution leading to social transformation, or the school creating a just society—is not necessarily shared by all. We are also witnessing a sharp critique of the prevalent functions of the school.[8] This critique, to put it simply, seeks to make us aware of the fact that the school, far from creating an equal society, is reproducing the societal inequality; elite schools isolate the children of the privileged classes and take them to a world filled with arrogance, snobbery and contempt for the larger society. And schools for the masses somehow survive without creativity or inspiration. The critique also examines the politics of school knowledge and curriculum. It is also argued that the school, because of its close affinity with Western symbols, has failed to retain the spirit of decolonisation. It is, therefore, important to have new schools—schools that are in tune with India's cultural/spiritual tradition. Furthermore, the school has also been criticised for its conservative functions: the way it breeds competition, promotes conformity, suppresses the spirit of innovation, and renders the learning process bereft of any joy or creativity. It is, therefore, felt that we need new schools—schools that would be different from the 'mainstream' tradition and establish alternative values: cooperativeness, togetherness, child-centredness, holism, and affinity with nature. This alternative tradition draws its inspiration from the educational philosophies of Gandhi, Tagore, Sri Aurobindo, and Jiddu Krishnamurthy.

It is, therefore, possible to argue that there are conflicting views on the function of schooling in the Indian society: from optimism to despair, from an instrument of social transformation to a conservative machinery for reproducing social inequality, from a socialising agency preparing the child for the competitive techno-economic world to an emancipatory site for child-centred/progressive education in tune with India's culture and spirituality. Hence, we need to focus our attention—more seriously and rigorously—on the meaning of schooling in India: the debate on educational policies and practices, how a post-colonial society looks at education, how knowledge is produced and received, the social meaning of 'legitimate' school texts and curriculum, the kind of values/orientations children internalise in the process of school education, and how the dissenters imagine and strive for alternative education—its possibilities and contradictions. In the following chapters, we have tried to reflect on these issues with the hope that we would be able to get a better understanding of the kind of relationship that exists between the school and the society, politics and knowledge, ideology and curriculum, social imagination and educational practices.

Notes

1. Randall Collins (1979) has shown how in the modern societies, educational qualifications are being used to limit the supply of candidates for socially and economically advantageous positions, and to monopolise such positions for the holders of educational patents.
2. Durkheim and Parsons were the main champions of the functionalist orientation to education. But there are many others who too share a similar view. For example, David Hargreaves

derived his inspiration from Durkheim and argued that the school must fight excessive individualism, and restore the moral authority of the community. To quote him:

> The teacher's burden is to transmit to pupils the authoritative demands that group life makes on all, both teachers and pupils. The teacher is the instrument, not the author, of the moral power and authority that emanates from group life. (Hargreaves 1980: 193. Also see Hargreaves 1982).

Ralph Turner is another sociologist who sees a possibility in the school system of the United States. Everyone is treated equally and encouraged to strive for the elite status. There is no early elimination. As Turner argues, the twin problems of elite recruitment and the continued loyalty of the non-elite is thus ensured in the United States. The school system, therefore, promotes order and consensus. Turner, however, distinguishes the American system from the educational system prevalent in England. In England, as the practice of grammar schools suggests, the future elite are chosen by some select criteria when quite young. They are trained to believe that they should care for the rest of society. And non-elites are educated to accept their relative incompetence and station in life. For details, see Turner 1971.

3. See, for instance, Reynolds and Sullivan 1980.
4. Paul Wills, for instance, has spoken of the counter-school culture. His work is based on a case study of a group of twelve non-academic working class boys who attended a secondary school in a small Midlands town. Wills observes smoking, drinking, violence, vandalism and theft among these boys. In a way, they break the authority of the school, and distance themselves from normal social activities and attitudes. In this counter-culture Wills notices resistance or subversion of authority. Wills, however, argues that the pupils of the school counter culture readily move into unskilled and semi-skilled jobs. As a result, the continued enslavement of working-class people remains unaltered. For details, see Wills 1977.
5. It was Michel Foucault who gave us these powerful insights. For a lucid interpretation of Foucault's writings, see Sheridan 1980.
6. Yogendra Singh has spoken of this possibility. He has examined the dialectical relationship between the school as a modern

institution and a traditional society. (Singh 1967:52 71). Also see Kamat 1985; and Gore, 1994.

7. Perhaps the most illuminating illustration of this project can be seen in the *Report of the Education Commission 1964-66* (Ministry of Education, Government of India, 1966). The report which was titled 'Education and National Development' gave tremendous importance to the role of school education. To quote from the report:

   In our opinion, therefore, no reform is more important or more urgent than to transform education, to endeavour to relate it to the life, needs and aspirations of the people, and thereby make it a powerful instrument of social, economic and cultural transformation necessary for the realisation of our national goals. (p. 6).

8. In fact, in the new literature on the sociology of education in India, one can see the articulation of this critique. See, for instance, Kumar 1989; Kumar 1996; Shukla and Kaul 1998; and Ghosh and Zachariah 1987.

1

Education as an Arena of Struggle

Reflections on Policies and Objectives

Education, it is believed, is inseparable from our societal aspirations. As these aspirations/worldviews undergo a process of transformation with the changing times, so does the meaning of education. In ancient times, for example, there was a distinctive spiritual meaning associated with education. Education, as many would argue, was for the realisation of the Ultimate and the Absolute; it was to overcome the finiteness of existence: all earthly temptations and desires. But then, for a modern/technical mind, this preoccupation with supreme spiritual knowledge may not hold such fascination. In this case, the goal of education is essentially secular; it is primarily the acquisition of a technical skill needed to achieve excellence in the techno-economic world. Likewise, the political objective of education also changes. For example, for the colonisers, the goal of education was to establish the cultural/civilisational superiority of the West. But then, during the nationalist struggle for liberation, we could see an attempt to fight the colonial design and regain our indigenous symbols and aspirations. In other words, history teaches us a very important lesson: we have been debating on the societal meaning of education because we have been debating on our ideals, that is, what we are and what we wish to strive for.

It is in this context that this chapter acquires its relevance. It has two main objectives. First, it gives us a broad historico-philosophical orientation to the societal meaning of education—how it has changed from, say, ancient India to post-colonial times. Second, this historico-philosophical sensitivity helps us develop a critical consciousness. We become aware of the flaws in the existing system; we seek solutions from history and explore the alternatives. Eventually, this approach may help us evolve a new agenda for education.

I
Religiosity and Ancient Educational Ideals

To begin with, let us understand the spiritual ideal behind education in ancient India—the ideal that education is inseparable from the country's cultural traditions. Here, our objective is to take a brief look at the ancient educational system and identify its salient features.

Education as Spiritual Realisation

It was the supreme religious ideal that shaped the ancient educational philosophy. The ideal was the realisation of the Absolute—the knowledge of the *Atman.* The goal was to overcome all divisions and dualities, to transcend the finiteness of existence and to merge with the Infinite and the Eternal. Education, as a result, was a means to the highest end of existence, viz., *Mukti* or emancipation. There is a fundamental epistemological difference between the ancient educational philosophy and our recent preoccupation with objective knowledge, which is something that can be gained through sensory organs, something that is empirically demonstrable, that can be weighed, quantified and measured. It is the knowledge of the phenomenal world. But then, the ancient educational philosophy speaks of another domain that refuses to remain limited to the finite boundaries, that cannot be measured nor quantified, that requires the elevation of not just the intellect, but also intuition or the inner spirit. As Radha Kumud Mookerji (1969: xxiii) wrote, 'it is more concerned with the subject than the object, the inner than the outer world.'

There is another difference. As we see now, the goal of education is pragmatic and secular: acquiring a skill for practical intervention in the world. But, in the ancient system the goal of education was the emancipation of the soul. Not surprisingly, the *Upanishads* attached great importance to supreme knowledge or *para vidya*—the knowledge through which the Ultimate Reality is known. It was often extolled as *sarva-vidya-pratistha* the foundation of all arts and sciences; the final and highest stage of Vedantic education. Without the internalisation, realisation and intimate experience of this knowledge, everything else, as we were told repeatedly, would remain superficial and incomplete. In the *Chandogya* Upanishad, Narada acknowledged to Sanatkumara:

> I have studied, most reverend sir, the Rigveda, Yajurveda, Samaveda, the Atharvaveda as fourth, the epic and mythological poem as fifth veda, grammar, neurology, arithmetic, divination, chronology, dialectics, politics, theology, the doctrine of prayer, necromancy, the art of war, astronomy, snake-charming and the fine arts—these things, most reverend sir, have I studied; therefore am I, most reverend sir, learned indeed in the scriptures but not learned in the *Atman*. Yet have I heard from such as are like you that he who knows the *Atman* vanquishes sorrow. I am in sorrow—lead me then over, I pray, to the farther shore that lies beyond sorrow. (Quoted in Mookerji 1969: 110-11).

And Sanatkumara replied, 'Whatever you have studied is but words' (Mookerji 1969: 111).

Again, in the *Chandogya* Upanishad, it was shown how Svetaketu's rigorous study of all the Vedas for twelve years left him full of conceit and confidence in his study and wisdom. However, he was ignorant when it came to answering questions put to him by his father regarding the

One and the self-existent, through the knowledge of which everything could be known.

As a matter of fact, there was a continual reminder: true knowledge was not mechanical memorisation of the scriptures; it was essentially an experience of realising and living in the Brahman. True, as we could see in the *Rigveda,* recitation of the texts or the hymns was an important pedagogical practice. Great value was attached to the power of the very sounds of the letters and syllables by which the sacred words were uttered. But then, it should not be forgotten that the *Rigveda* emphasised the necessity of understanding and realising the deeper meaning behind the words.

> He who does not realise the ultimate truth behind the *Rik* and *Akshara* (word and letter) in which rest all gods—what will he do by merely reciting and repeating the Riks? (Mookerji 1969: 30).

or

> He is only the bearer of a burden, the blockhead, who having studied the Veda does not understand its meaning (like an ass carrying a load of sandal-wood whose weight it feels without enjoying its fragrance). (Mookerji 1969: 31).

In fact, the *Upanishads* mentioned the three steps that led to the acquisition of the highest knowledge—*Sravana, Manana and Nididhyasana. Sravana* was listening to words or texts as they were uttered by the teacher. It was to be followed by the process of *Manana:* deliberation or reflection on the topic. But this intellectual comprehension alone was not sufficient. What was further needed was the process of *Nididhyasana:* the realisation or internalisation of the Ultimate Truth. This step was often described as *Darsana* (seeing is believing).

Education as Inner Discipline

As the chief objective of education was human emancipation, it was important for the student to undergo a rigorous process of learning self-discipline. Discipline was necessary, but not because of the fear of an external authority; discipline was meant to evoke one's sensitivity and consciousness for the realisation of the Ultimate Truth. The *Rigveda,* for example, narrates the ideal of a *Rishi* absorbed in *tapas* so that he may transcend from the lowest form of being to the highest. It was like overcoming all earthly temptations and desires. As the hymn suggests, the Muni (or Rishi) becomes all-pervading like the *vayu,* the all-seeing like the *sun* and the equal of the gods by *sukriti* or pious deeds. It was this reference model that explained the importance attached to self-discipline that a young learner or a *brahmachari* ought to undergo in order to orient himself to true education.

We know that the pupil used to live with the teacher as a member of his family. The school was a natural formation; not artificially constructed. It was the home of the teacher. The pupil was required to imbibe the inward looking philosophy of the teacher; the spirit of his life and work. We also know that the pupil's daily duty was to first walk to the woods, cut and collect fuel, and fetch it to the teacher's house to tend the sacred Fire with. The pupil's next duty was to attend to the teacher's house and cattle. This was by no means a masochistic/submissive activity; it has to be seen as an exercise for attaining inner growth and a robust physique. In a way, this practice was also a great pedagogic ideal: learning through doing and overcoming the tendency to separate mental work from manual labour. The significance of yet another important duty of a *brahmachari* has to be understood. He was required to go out on a daily round of begging—not for himself but for the support of his school. In fact, it would not be wrong to say that begging was designed to produce in the pupil a sense of humility, humanity, and renunciation. It was meant to destroy all egotistic desires. Radha Kumud Mookerji wrote:

> ...the daily duty of begging makes the Ego less and less assertive, and, with it, all untruly desires and passions, which do not shoot forth, as their roots wither. (Mookerji 1969: xxx).

In fact, it was emphasised time and again that the acquisition of the highest knowledge was not simply a matter of study but of life. For a genuine learner, it was, therefore, necessary to overcome all desires in order to acquire the supreme knowledge of the *Atman*. Perhaps an ideal illustration of such a pupil could be found in the *Katha* Upanishad: Nachiketa approaching Yama for instruction on the nature of the soul and its destiny. In order to judge his sincerity and zeal in the pursuit of Truth, Yama offered him the most irresistible temptations that might divert him from his end —'sons and grandsons who shall live a hundred years, herds of cattle, elephants, gold and horses, sovereignty of the wide abode of the earth, fair maidens with their chariots and musical instruments, and control over death' (Mookerji 1969: 116). But then, nothing could divert Nachiketa. He answered like a true *Sannyasin:* 'Keep thou thy horses, keep dance and song for thyself. No man can be made happy by wealth' (Ibid: 116). And Yama admitted: 'I believe Nachiketa to be one who desires knowledge, for even many pleasures did not tear thee away' (Ibid: 116).

As a matter of fact, it was an ideal of studentship—an ideal illuminated by the ethos of *tapas, sannyasa* and *yoga*. Doubtless, this ideal is different from what we see in our own times, characterised by the increasing professionalisation/secularisation of education. Education, as a technical skill, does by no means require the annihilation of desires or the elevation of spiritual consciousness. Instead, it stimulates the desire—the desire for success, achievement and prosperity. In fact, the prevalent impersonal professional-client relationship is different from the ancient deep-rooted, spiritual bond between the teacher and the taught. It should not be forgotten that this relationship was marked by a religious activity called *upananyana:* 'The teacher holding the pupil within him as in a womb, impregnates him with his spirit and delivers him in a new birth.' The pupil was then known as a *Dwija,* 'born afresh' in a new existence, that is, 'twice born'. Not surprisingly, the responsibility of the teacher was tremendous. He was, after all, a Rishi. 'The truth is not grasped when taught by an inferior man', says the *Katha*

Upanishad. Likewise, the *Mundaka* Upanishad requires the teacher to be well-versed in the sacred lore and dwelling entirely in the Brahman. Moreover, it was the duty of the teacher to teach the pupil the truth without concealing anything from him. In other words, it was a sacred bond; learning was inseparable from the process of perpetual spiritual elevation.

Education as the Culture of Critical Enquiry

Another striking feature of the ancient system of education was its fairly advanced culture of debate and discussion. It was an exercise that involved perpetual contemplation and reflection on the meaning of the Ultimate Truth. Hence, apart from the teacher's home, there were institutions like the debating circles and parishads—institutions designed to satisfy those whose quest for knowledge did not cease with the completion of formal education. Such students used to improve their knowledge through mutual discussions or through instruction from renowned scholars and literary celebrities. In fact, there is an opinion that the *Upanishads* themselves are in a sense to be regarded as the record and outcome of such academic disputations; the transactions of the philosophical societies or circles of the literary celebrities of the times.

It has also been mentioned that there were occasions when a king would organise a conference or a gathering in which the representative thinkers of various schools would be invited to meet and exchange their views. One such Congress of Rishis was recorded in the *Brhadaranyaka Upanishad*. King Janaka Videha invited all the Brahmans of the Kuru-Panchala country and a special prize of great value (1000 cows with their horns adorned with gold) was offered to the wisest, the best read and the most learned person. Eventually, *Yajnavalkya* won this prize by responding to a series of complex questions concerning the rituals, the gods, the soul and the supreme cause of the soul (Mookerji 1969: 136-37).

The message is clear enough. The realm of higher learning was fairly conducive to the ethos of debate and discussion; the environment encouraged the spirit of keen enquiry and learning.

Education that is not Altogether Indifferent to Secular Pursuits

Doubtless, the main thrust of the ancient system of education was on religion/spiritually. Yet, there must have been a considerable amount of secular/non-religious education. A glimpse of it could be found in the *Rigvedic* hymn:

> We different men have different tastes and pursuits. The carpenter seeks something that is broken, the physician a patient, the priest someone who will perform sacrifice. (Mookerji 1969: 55).

A reference to divergent pursuits (not just religious/spiritual) could be found in another passage of the hymn. The author says that he is a poet, his father a physician and his mother a grinder of corn. This means that a Brahmin could practise medicine while his wife performed the ordinary household duties (Mookerji 1969: 152).

This, however does not mean that the Brahmins were normally agriculturalists or merchants. Essentially, the Brahmin represented the intellectual and spiritual interests of the community. Similarly, a Kshatriya's role was that of an administrator and a warrior. As a result, the Kshatriya was concerned with those subjects of study that would provide training in the occupations that he had to follow—like *Kshatravidya* (the science of the ruling class, of polity or administration) and *Dhanur-Veda.*

The *Vaisya* played a relatively small part in the Vedic literature. Not much information is available for us to know how he was educated. Similarly, there is hardly any record of the type of education that the *Sudras* received.

Yet, it would not be right to say that the Vedic education was essentially elitist. Look at this *Mantra* from the *Rigveda:* 'All classes have an equal right to study the Vedas.' (Mookerji

1969: 53). Furthermore, there was a striking presence of women in the domain of Vedic learning. From the *Rigveda,* we came to know of many learned Rishikas like *Lopamudra, Apala, Ghosa, Fuhu, Paulomi, Urvashi,Yami* and *Indrani.*

Continuity and Development of the Ancient Ideal

The fundamentals of the ancient system of education—as formulated in the *Vedas* and the *Upanishads*—reveal the supremacy of religiosity and spiritual awakening; the urge to transcend the parameters of 'objective knowledge' and its finiteness; and to realise the Absolute. It would, however, be interesting to observe the impact of the Buddhist intervention on these fundamentals. True, there were differences between the Buddhist and the Brahminical systems of education. For instance, in the Buddhist system, the primary centre for learning was the monastery, not the teacher's home. In fact, in the Buddhist system the learning process began with the severance of all domestic ties. Moreover, while the Brahminical system was based on the monarchical principle, the Buddhist system of education corresponded to the republican or democratic style of functioning. It should not be forgotten that the Resolutions of the Sangha had to be passed by the entire body in a meeting in which all members —seniors and juniors—had equal voting power. This democratic spirit could also be seen in its openness to all castes. To enter the order was to give up all the visible marks of the earlier life—the marks of caste as of clothes. Because of this debrahminisation, the Buddhist system gave an impetus to the study of the vernacular dialects of the country. Sanskrit was supplanted and superseded as a medium of instruction by the vernacular dialects.

These differences need not necessarily mean that there was no similarity between the two systems. As a matter of fact, the Buddhist system too, like the Brahminical system, aimed to create a mind free from all mundane desires. Its main focus was on non-violence, self-discipline, and spiritual growth. No wonder then, in the monastery, great importance was attached to chastity and living in poverty. Monkhood meant a dissolution of all blood-relations. The Buddha, after he became a monk, was addressed as Sramana by his son Rahula and not as 'father', and he hardly ever noticed his wife. Again, as living in poverty was an essential mark of monastic life, the Buddha was called a *Bhikshu, Bhikkhu,* or a *Beggar.* As we have already said, the urge to discipline/ spiritualise oneself and to realise the strength within was paramount. For example, during the probation period, the *Bhikshus* were forbidden to injure plants or vegetables, to store property, watch public shows (like theatrical representations, recitations, concerts, etc.), engage in games detrimental to progress in virtue, adorn their bodies, indulge in mean talk and so on. This moral discipline manifested itself in the pupil's whole-hearted devotion to the teacher. As Radha Kumud Mookerji wrote:

> The Buddhist system, like the Brahminical, enjoins upon the pupil the duty of serving his preceptor as a part of education. The pupil is to rise early from bed and give his teacher a teeth-cleanser and water to rinse his mouth with; then, preparing a seat for him, serve him rice-milk in a rinsed jug, and, after he drinks it, wash the vessel and sweep the place. Afterwards, he is to equip his teacher for his begging round by giving him a fresh undergarment, girdle, his two uppergarments, and his alms-bowl rinsed and filled with water. When he returns, the pupil must be ready with the necessary things and help him change his clothes. Then after serving him with some food, if required, he is to help him bathe by giving him cold or hot water, as may be desired .... (Mookerji 1969: 403-04).

This ideal of the self-sacrificing pupil was encouraged and cultivated by a similar ideal of the teacher. The teacher too was required to remain equally committed to his student. He had to give the *Bhikkhu* under his charge all possible intellectual help and guidance. Again, if the pupil fell ill, the teacher had to nurse him—even if it meant spending the rest of his life doing so—until the pupil recovered.

It should, however, be remembered that the Buddhist

idealism (spirit of equality/reciprocity/fraternity) was not always easy to practise. Women were not always seen as equal partners in the monastery. In fact, it was with considerable reluctance that the Buddha consented to admit women in his order. It was *Mahapajapati*—the sister of the Buddha's mother—who insisted and eventually succeeded in securing the deserving women's right of entry into the order. Yet, the nuns were kept in a condition of complete subordination to the monks. A *Bhikkhuni, even* of a hundred years standing, must look up to a *Bhikkhu* even if he is only just initiated. Despite these unfavourable conditions, there were some great women leaders like *Dhammadinna, Soma* and *Anumpama* who made their presence felt.

The primacy of spiritual education should not mean that the ancient system was altogether indifferent to practical education. In fact, the Buddhist literature, from the *Vinaya* texts downwards, conveys that there was a significant progress in medicine and surgery in ancient India. We cite the example of *Jivaka*—the most distinguished medical expert of the age—who went to Taxila to study medicine under a world-renowned physician who lived there. The course of medical studies, it was reported, extended to a period of seven years, on completion of which, a practical examination was held in order to evaluate the student's knowledge of botany or his first-hand knowledge of medical plants and their properties. From the Jatakas too, we learnt more about Taxila—its well-known schools of medicine, law, military sciences, and how they attracted students from distant parts of India: Benaras, Mithila, Ujjeni and Kosala. Benaras too was a great seat of learning for its school of music.

The progress in the field of education continued; its supreme manifestation, of course, was *Nalanda*—the great institution of higher learning—which, as we came to know from *Hiuen Tsang* who visited the place in the seventh century AD, attracted students from distant countries like China, Korea and Tibet. The courses of study offered by the Nalanda university included a wide spectrum of knowledge:

Brahminical and Buddhist, sacred and secular, philosophical and practical, and sciences and arts. The great teachers like *Dharmapada* and *Silabhadra* further enhanced the prestige of the university.

Besides Taxila and Nalanda, there were other important centres for learning like *Valabhi, Vikramsila, Mithila* and *Nadia.* Take, for instance, the tradition of Mithila. We came to know of its culture of learning—as promoted by the philosopher king *Janaka*—from the *Upanishads.* Again, Mithila as a centre for learning flourished during the 13th, 14th and 15th centuries. It was known for *Vidyapati*—the great poet. Likewise, *Nadia* became a great centre for Hindu learning and was well known throughout India during the period 1198-1757. Nadia too excelled in the study of *Nyaya* or logic.

An awareness of the traditional Indian learning will remain incomplete unless we look at the state of education during the Muslim period. The *Maktabs*—the centres of primary education—were attached to the mosques. The children in the *Maktabs* were acquainted with various subjects relating to religion and practical knowledge. The *Madrasas* were the institutions of higher Islamic learning. The course of study included grammar, rhetoric, logic, theology, metaphysics, literature, jurisprudence and science. The centres like Jaunpur in Agra and Gopama and Kharibad in Oudh were fairly well-known. What was striking about the Islamic education was the importance it attached to both religious and material needs of existence. Furthermore, the Islamic system, like the earlier ones, laid great emphasis on the necessity of moral discipline. The teacher or the *Ustad* occupied a place of reverence. It was his responsibility to see that his students learn morals and manners, sincerity and good habits.

II
Problematising Religious Education

We have talked about the emancipatory possibilities (ego-transcendence, humbleness, and inner realisation) inherent in the tradition of ancient/religious education. This does not, however, mean that this tradition was altogether free from its discontents. In fact, no meaningful understanding of ancient/religious education would be complete without its critique. The problems associated with the ancient system of education are as follows:

First, as contemporary sociologists would argue, the ideals of ancient/religious education do not fit in with the rationale of a modern/industrial society (see Singh 1967: 55-71). It is believed that much of ancient education was esoteric and sacred in nature. It was neither secular nor scientific. It remained contented with the interpretations of religious texts and scriptures. But now, the emphasis is on our need for problem-posing/problem-solving secular/scientific/ practical education. It is also thought that the traditional education saw teachers as charismatic gurus. But in modern societies, the process of secularisation would require professionals as teachers. In other words, this critique is centred on the sociological dichotomy: tradition vs. modernity, religiosity vs. secularity, subjective revelation vs. objective knowledge. In fact, in India we saw many modernists who apprehended the dangerous consequences of glorification of ancient/ religious education. As we would discuss subsequently, Raja Rammohan Roy—the renaissance man—did not like the promotion of Sanskrit, especially because he felt that modern English education would be needed to spread rationality and fight religious orthodoxy and superstition. And Jotirao Phule questioned religious education, because he felt that it could further revive the oppressive hierarchical culture of Brahminism and reproduce inequality.

Second, it is possible to sense a lower caste critique of ancient/religious education. Education cannot be seen in isolation. It is an integral component of one's worldview. And it is often felt that ancient education legitimatised a hierarchical culture, thereby degrading the lower castes, untouchables and the Sudras. In other words, ancient education is viewed as elitist and exclusivist. The roots of this hierarchy, as many contemporary scholars argue, could be seen even in the *Rigveda* (see Massey 1995). Two opposing forces could be seen in the *Rigveda:* first, the force on whose behalf the hymns are addressed to gods, and second, against whom they are addressed—i.e. the deva worshipping *Arya* as against the riteless *Dasyu* or *Dasa*. The *Dasyus* were contemptuously referred to as ritualless, inhuman, following alien laws. There are many who would like to believe that the origin of Dalits could be seen in these *Dasyus* whom the Aryans oppressed and marginalised. In fact, it would not be wrong to say that with the passage of time, an oppressive system of social hierarchy emerged that gave no space to the Sudras. Education was being monopolised by twice-born castes. Perhaps the *Manusmriti* was a logical culmination of this practice. One could, for instance, see the hierarchical form of the division of labour. The *Manusmriti* dictates, 'Among the several occupations, the most commendable are, teaching the Veda for a Brahmana, protecting (the people) for a Kshatriya, and trade for a Vaisya' *(Manusmriti,* X, 80). And let a Sudra follow 'those mechanical occupations and those various practical arts by following which the twice-born are best served.' (Ibid, X, 101). It is further added that 'the service of Brahmanas alone is declared to be an excellent occupation for a Sudra, for whatever else besides this he may perform will bear him no fruit' (Ibid, X, 123). Still further, 'A man of low caste who through covetousness lives by the occupations of a higher one, the king shall deprive of his property and banish' (Ibid, X, 96). Indeed, education was not for a Sudra. He could not imagine himself excelling in what Brahmins or other twice-born castes were engaged in.

No wonder, we could see a similar mindset in the *Ramayana*. In those days it was only the upper castes who were allowed to do *tapasya*. Yet, a *Sudra* decided to do penance in order to attain divinity, as a result of which, a 15-year-old Brahmin boy, so it is said, died. The bereaved father complained to Lord Rama, who after learning the cause of the death, went in search of the Sudra. On meeting him,

Lord Rama said to him:

> You are indeed blessed. Tell me in which caste you have been born. I am Rama, son of Dasaratha. Out of curiosity, I have asked you this question. Tell me the truth. Are you a Brahman, Kshatriya or a Sudra?

The ascetic replied:

> O king, I am born of the Sudra caste. I want to attain divinity by such penance. When I want to attain divinity, I won't tell lies, I am a *Sudra* by caste, and my name is *Samvuka*.

As soon as the ascetic uttered these words, Rama drew forth his sword and severed Samvuka's head.

Likewise, in the *Mahabharata*, there is a reference to the degraded status of the Sudras. The story of *Eklavya*, an indigenous boy, relates how he had to lose his right thumb because he had learned archery and was in no way inferior to Arjuna in his skill.

These are traumatic collective memories that remind the Dalits and the lower castes of their discontent with the ancient/religious system of education and its implicit civilisational agenda. No wonder, when B.R. Ambedkar burnt a copy of the *Manusmriti*, he conveyed a strong message: the doctrine of inequality at birth, on which the caste system was based, must be rejected. No emancipatory pedagogy is possible in a system that rationalises inequality.

Third, ancient/religious education would be riddled with problems if evaluated from the feminist point of view. It can be argued that ancient education was a part of the patriarchal system that refused to give space to women to flourish as autonomous persons. It is, however, important to recall, as historians tell us, that the position of women in the Vedic age was fairly satisfactory (see Altekar 1999: 49-71). Girls were educated and like boys, had to pass through a period of *brahmacharya*. Many of them became distinguished poets. Their marriages took place at a relatively advanced stage, that is, at the age of 16 or 17 years. There was no seclusion of women. They occupied a prominent position in social/religious gatherings. However, the later Hindu society failed to retain these Vedic ideals and consequently, women lost their earlier status. Gradually, pre-puberty marriages became the normal rule and women, having lost the status of a *dwija* or twice-born, came to be regarded as *Sudras.* And like the *Sudras,* they were declared unfit for reciting or even listening to Vedic hymns. In fact, *Manusmriti* created a theoretical basis for the legal and social subordination of women. Here are some illustrations:

> In childhood a female must be subject to her father, in youth to her husband, when her lord is dead, to her sons; a woman must never be independent. (*Manusmriti,*V 148).
>
> Though destitute of virtue, or seeking pleasure (elsewhere), or devoid of good qualities, (yet) a husband must be constantly worshipped as a god by a faithful wife. (Ibid, X, 154).
>
> She who, controlling her thoughts, words, and deeds, never slights her lord, resides (after death) with her husband (in heaven), and is called a virtuous (wife). (Ibid, X, 165).

The effect of Manu's injunction could be seen in the epics. Look at, for instance, the *Mahabharata.* The feminists want us to see the state of women in the epic (see, for instance, Jhanji 1996). Gandhari's act of blindfolding herself lights the enormous approbation associated with being a chaste and pious wife. The epitome of chastity lay in her unquestioning fidelity. It lay in her wilfully becoming a disabled equal to her blind husband. Madri expressed her fidelity by dying with her husband; Kunti by raising her children—the living memento of her husband—and finally retreating into the woods to do penance in order to join him. Draupadi achieved the same objective by her unflinching service to all her five husbands and by giving up all royal comforts.

The feminist critique of ancient/religious education and culture is strong and uncompromising. One can imagine the anguish of Pandita Ramabai:

> Those who diligently and impartially read Sanskrit literature in their original, cannot fail to recognise the law-giver Manu

> as one of those hundreds who have done their best to make women hateful beings in the world's eye .... I can say honestly and truthfully that I have never read any sacred book in Sanskrit literature without meeting this kind of hateful sentiment about women. (Quoted in Omvedt 1995: 27).

It is, therefore, not surprising why Lata Mani—a leading feminist scholar would not spare even Raja Rammohan Roy, who, his fight against *sati* notwithstanding, drew his inspiration from the religious scriptures, not excluding the *Manusmriti* (Mani 1989). And Uma Chakravarti saw a new possibility in Jotirao Phule who found patriarchy in Brahminism, fought against it, and gave new momentum to the project of female education (Chakravarti 1996).

All these three critiques are important. Yet, we would insist that there are certain emancipatory possibilities in some of the ideals of ancient education. These ideals are austerity, humbleness, ego transcendence and resolution of dualities.... That is why, ancient/religious education has its complexities. It can neither be glorified and nor can it be negated. The challenge lies in how to adapt its emancipatory potential to our contemporary sensibilities (a project to create a symmetrical/egalitarian society), and in how to form a critical/creative engagement with this tradition. As we would discuss later on in this chapter, Gandhi and Tagore—the two outstanding cultural innovators—were engaged in this project.

Furthermore, it is necessary to assert the worth of these ideals, because with the advent of colonial modernity, an attempt was made to demoralise us, and tell us that we were inferior: morally, intellectually and cognitively. In other words, to recall these ideals is to gain the strength to fight the colonial design. No wonder, the colonial era witnessed an interesting debate on the objectives of education. On the one hand, there were colonisers trying to hierarchise the cultures (colonialists as 'enlightened' educators teaching the 'ignorant' natives); on the other, there were dissenters recalling the worth of their culture and fighting the principle of domination. But then, the battle against colonial education, as we would argue, was not easy, because many educated Indians began to feel that an encounter with the Western civilisation would also mean an entry into the modern age, and modernity—for its secularity, rationality and scientificity—could not go ahead with what the ancient system of education emphasised: religious orientation to the world!

III
Colonialism and Education as a Principle of Domination

Colonialism is about power. It hierarchises the world. It privileges the coloniser; enables him to suppress the colonised. And this violence is not just physical; colonialism is inseparable from moral/cultural/symbolic violence. The colonised are generally a demoralised lot. It becomes difficult for them to have faith in themselves. They tend to think that they are inferior and they associate qualities like strength, courage, education and civilisation—in fact, all that is positive—with their colonial masters. Colonial education, needless to add, is an important component of this ideological apparatus. As one looks at the history of colonial education one realises how education played a key role in the process of this legitimisation. The meaning of English/modern education (a 'gift' from colonial masters) was primarily an exercise of cultural invasion. It condemned all our civilisational ideals and equated knowledge with Western ideas; it was not particularly sensitive to the history of our educational heritage. Besides, in a subtle way it legitimised colonialism, because the colonial masters looked like great school teachers (learned adults) from whom, as passive/ignorant children, we must learn the fundamentals of knowledge!

The arrogance that characterised colonialism was not surprising. In order to assert its 'civilising mission' it spoke of the 'dark age' prevailing in India. We can understand the falsehood implicit in the idea of the 'dark age', because, as we have already shown, India did have a profound tradition of education and learning. Not solely that; even the studies conducted by the British officials did suggest the widespread prevalence of the culture of learning in India at the time of colonial invasion. Take, for instance, William Adam's report (1941) in 1835-38 for the Bengal Presidency.[1] The report spoke of the general consciousness on the importance of education, particularly among the members of the upper strata of society. The importance and dignity attached to education became clear when Adam observed:

> The teachers and students of Sanskrit schools constitute the cultivated intellect of the Hindu people and they command that respect and exert that influence which cultivated intellect always enjoys. There is no class of persons that exercise a greater degree of influence in giving native society the tone, the form and the character which it actually possesses than the body of the learned. (Adam 1941: 274).

We also know from Adam's report that the indigenous elementary schools were of two kinds. The first derived their principal support from the patronage of a single wealthy family, and the second depended upon the general support of the community in the town or the village in which they were established. He had estimated that there were 100,000 indigenous elementary schools in the Bengal Presidency at the beginning of the nineteenth century (Ibid: 6). He came to the conclusion that there was, on an average, a village school for every 73 children of schoolgoing age and one for every 30 or 32 boys (Ibid: 6-7). To quote from the report:

> It will appear that the system of village schools is extensively prevalent, that desire to give education to their male children must be deeply seated in the minds of parents, even of the humblest classes; and these are the institutions closely interwoven as they are with the habit of the people and the custom of the country. (Ibid: 7).

Apart from these elementary schools—*pathasalas* and *madrasas*—there were several centres for higher learning in Sanskrit, Arabic and Persian, which flourished during the eighteenth century. The major centres for learning Sanskrit were Benaras, Ujjain, Tirhut, Nadia, Rajshahi, Tanjore and Trivandrum. For Islamic studies, the three important centres were Jaipur, Lucknow and Patna. According to Adam, Calcutta had 28 seminaries for learning Sanskrit and there were 173 scholars in 1818; Nadia had 31 seminaries with 747 scholars in 1801. In Rajshahi in (1834-35) Adam found 38 colleges for Sanskrit education, 19 for the Hindu law, 13 for general literature, two for logic and four for Vedanta, tantric, pauranic and medical learning' (Adam 1941: 175-83).

In this context, Dharampal's work on indigenous Indian education in the eighteenth century becomes quite relevant (Dharampal 1983). He concentrates on the reports/surveys as conducted by the British officials and personnel—mainly, Adam's reports on Bengal and Bihar, Munro's survey in the Madras Presidency and Leitner's findings on the state of education in Punjab. He has three points to make.

First, he seeks to refute the myth that the state of education in India was terribly poor when the British came to colonise us. Instead, he points out that in many respects, Indian schooling was much better than what prevailed in England. It is true that England had a rich tradition of learning during the 16th, 17th or the early 18th century. There were universities like Oxford, Cambridge and Edinburgh. Also, there were thinkers/philosophers like Francis Bacon, Shakespeare, Milton and Newton. And by the end of the 18th century, England had around 500 grammar schools. Nevertheless, as Dharampal asserts, 'all this considerable learning and scholarship was limited to a very select elite' (Dharampal 1983: 3). And what was the state of affairs in India during this period?

> The content of studies does not appear very dissimilar to what was then studied in England. The duration of study was more prolonged... School attendance... was proportionately far higher than the numbers in all varieties of schools in England in 1800... (Ibid: 14).

For Adam, there were 1,00,000 village schools in Bengal and Bihar in the 1830s. And for Munro, every village had a school in the Madras Presidency. Besides, as these reports suggest, the duration of study varied from a minimum of five, to a maximum of about 15 years. It was also confirmed that 'before the students attain their 13th year of age, their achievements in the various branches of learning are uncommonly great'. Furthermore, the schools functioned for fairly long hours; usually starting around 6 a.m.—followed by one or two short intervals for meals, etc.—and finishing at the time of sunset, or even later.

Second, Dharampal argues against the opinion that education in India was mostly limited to the twice-born amongst the Hindus, and that amongst the Muslims, it was only for the ruling class. The actual situation, however, was quite different. 'At least amongst the Hindus, the districts of the Madras Presidency (and dramatically so in the Tamil-speaking areas) as well as the two districts of Bihar, it was instead those termed Sudras, and the castes considered below them who predominated in the thousands of the then still-existing schools in particularly each of these areas' (Dharampal 1983: 14-15). For example, a surprising revelation of Adam's report was that there were 61 Dom, and 61 Chandal students in the district of Burdwan; their number was nearly equal to the number of *Vaidya* students.

Third, Dharampal wants us to reflect on the popular notion that education in India was largely religious/theological in nature; that it lacked in practical/technological instruction. In the documents that he relies on, there was much on the question of higher learning, especially in the field of Theology, Law, Medicine, Astronomy and Astrology. There was, however, scarcely any reference to training in the scores of technologies and crafts which existed in India. A possible reason could be that those who wrote on education—whether as government administrators, travellers or Christian missionaries—were not really interested in how such crafts were taught or passed from one generation to another. Moreover, as Dharampal sees it, most crafts were learnt in the home, and what was termed apprenticeship in Britain, was a more informal way of learning in India; the parents usually being the teachers and the children the learners. This could be another reason for the lack of information on the teaching of techniques and crafts.

Dharampal laments that most educated Indians remain ignorant of what India had to offer in the sphere of education two centuries ago. 'It [this ignorance] has induced a lack of confidence, and loss of bearing amongst the people of India in general' (Dharampal 1983: 79). It was indeed sad that colonialism, with its ideologues like Thomas Babington Macaulay, could undermine our heritage, demoralise us and establish the moral/cognitive superiority of the colonisers.

True, to begin with, the East India Company was not eager to spread modern/European education. Instead, it showed its willingness to support and promote the indigenous system of education. For example, in 1781, Warren Hastings established the Calcutta Madrasa and revealed his fascination for the Indo-Persian culture. The courses at the Madrasa included natural philosophy, Koranic theology, law, geometry, arithmetic, logic and grammar—all on Islamic lines. The medium of instruction was Arabic. Likewise, in 1784, Sir William Jones established the Asiatic Society of Bengal in Calcutta. As Jones put it, the urge was to know Asia: 'The nurse of science, the inventress of delightful and useful arts, the scene of glorious action, fertile in the production of human genius, abounding in natural wonders, and infinitely diversified in the forms of religion and government, in the laws, manners, customs and complexions of man' (quoted in Ghosh 1993: 177). The same story—unlocking India for Europe—continued when in 1792 Jonathan Duncan established a Sanskrit college in Benaras for preserving and cultivating the laws and literatures of the Hindus. Elphinstone did the same thing when in 1820, he founded a Hindu college at the city of Poona.

It is at this juncture that we need to raise an important

question: what was the deeper meaning of this *orientalist* approach? Was it merely an act of love and tolerance; a genuine urge to understand and respect the indigenous knowledge system? For some, this might be acceptable. Yet, the fact remains that beneath this orientatlist approach lay many political considerations. The East India Company was not yet certain of itself. As a result, the goodwill of the native elite was crucial. It was important to make them believe that the British were not cultural invaders. Moreover, as Aparna Basu has demonstrated, it was important for the East India Company to find 'Indian officers well-versed in Sanskrit, Persian and Arabic' to assist them in governing the country (Basu 1982: 1). In other words, even this involvement with the indigenous system of education was designed to control the Indian subcontinent politically.

Things, however, began to change. Not everyone was happy with the policy of encouraging oriental education. Instead, it was felt that English/modern education ought to be introduced in order to improve this 'decadent' civilisation. Charles Grant was indeed a turning point—a powerful force behind the promotion of the *Anglicist* policy. Grant, who had been associated with the East India Company's administration in Calcutta and London for nearly forty years, wrote his famous treatise *(Observations on the state of society among the Asiatic subjects of Great Britain, particularly in respect to morals; and on the means of improving it)* in 1792. Grant's document was not merely an educational agenda; it was primarily a verdict on Indian culture and civilisation. It revealed the arrogance of the colonial masters and their irresistible urge for cultural conquest. Grant charged the Hindus with dishonesty, corruption, fraud, mutual hatred and distrust. 'The Hindus err', wrote Grant, 'because they are ignorant' (quoted in Ghosh 1993: 179).

Not surprisingly, Grant was categorical in his critique of oriental education. The East India Company, he thought, was under no obligation to protect the creed of the Hindus which was monstrous and 'subversive of the first principles of reason, morality and religion' (Ibid: 179). For Grant, the answer was clear. India, he felt, needed Christianity, modern science and European literature. He wanted English as the official language, pleaded for the establishment of English schools under teachers of 'good moral character'. It was primarily because of Grant's appeal that a bill was introduced in British Parliament in order to send missionaries and school teachers to India for the ultimate conversion of Indians. But then, the Company officials felt that a move of this kind would cause political unrest in the country. They condemned the bill. And through some of their connections in both the Houses of Parliament, they managed to defeat it.

Yet, Grant's ideas were significant, because he was speaking the language of the changing times. To begin with, he was clearly aware of the emergent capitalist class in Britain and its economic interests in India. English education, Grant felt, would enable the natives to develop the taste for British goods. In other words, he was visualising a close affinity between commerce and education. It is equally important to realise that Grant belonged to the Age of Reason in which modern Europe was becoming increasingly certain of itself, its scientific achievements and its rationality. It was this certainty that led the colonial power to believe in its 'civilising' mission: the West—with its Enlightenment rationality and science—must educate the rest of the world! In other words, even after the bill was defeated, it was becoming increasingly difficult for the East India Company to resist what Charles Grant wanted: an educational metamorphosis and the resultant 'improvement' of the Indian civilisation!

For example, it was in 1813 that a clause was introduced in the Company's Charter which made it 'not obligatory but lawful' for the Governor-General to set apart for education a sum of not less than one lakh of rupees. However, even though it was mentioned that the money would be spent for the revival and improvement of literature and the encouragement of the learned natives of India, it was, at the same time, decided that a part of it would be spent for the introduction and promotion of the study of sciences among the natives.

This was also the time of the *utilitarians.* In 1817, James Mill—a noted utilitarian closely associated with the Company—published his *History of British India,* a work in which, like a real colonial master, he condemned Indian civilisation, its culture, religion and knowledge system. The presence of his celebrated son John Stuart Mill—another utilitarian—in the affairs of the East India Company further encouraged the idea of modern/European education in India. And things altered radically with the emergence of Thomas Babington Macaulay. Macaulay was a utilitarian; he was closely associated with the utilitarian Governor-General William Bentinck. In fact, he was a law member of Bentinck's council. Macaulay's faith in the supremacy of modern/English education was unshakable. Macaulay knew how to legitimise colonialism and to justify its 'civilising' mission. He was desperate to prove that modern/English education would be a gift from the British civilisation; a symbol of its humanism and political altruism.

It was on July 10, 1833 that he gave his famous speech in the British Parliament. He said:

> ...What is power worth if it is founded on vice, on ignorance, and on misery, if we can hold it only by violating the most sacred duties which as governors, we owe to the governed, and which, as people blessed with far more than ordinary measure of political liberty and of intellectual light, we owe to a race debased by three thousand years of despotism and priestcraft? We are free, we are civilised to little purpose if we grudge to any portion of the human race an equal measure of freedom and civilisation. (Quoted in Ghosh 1993: 183).

Bentinck knew that he could rely on Macaulay. The General Committee of Public Instruction, which was formed in 1823, was divided between the Orientalists and the Anglicists. Both sides appealed to Bentinck in January 1833. And Bentinck asked Macaulay, in his dual capacity as a law member and President of the General Committee of Public Instruction, to give his views. The result was his famous *minute of February 2, 1835.*

Macaulay, like Charles Grant, was an advocate of cultural imperialism. He did not have the slightest respect for our culture, religion or knowledge. He was against the continuance of the institutions of oriental learning, because, according to him, these institutions did not serve any useful purpose. He advocated that the printing of oriental books should be stopped, all oriental colleges, except those at Delhi and Benaras, should be abolished and all stipends should be discontinued. Macaulay was certain about the supremacy of English education. English, he thought, ought to be the medium of instruction, because

> ...the dialects commonly spoken among the natives of this part of India contain neither literary nor scientific information and are moreover so poor and rude that until they are enriched from some other quarter, it will not be easy to translate any valuable work into them. (Ibid: 183).

Macaulay did not have any knowledge of either Sanskrit or Arabic. Yet, he could arrogantly state that: 'a single shelf of a good European library was worth the whole native literature of India and Arabia' (Ibid: 184). English education, he felt, would serve a useful function. It would civilise and educate the Indians; they would act like mediators between the rulers and the ruled and subsequently spread knowledge among the masses. To quote Macaulay:

> We must at present do our best to form a class who may be interpreters between us and the millions whom we govern, a class of persons Indian in blood and colour, but English in taste, in opinions, in morals and intellect. To that class we may leave it to refine the vernacular dialects of the country, to enrich these dialects with terms of science borrowed from the Western nomenclature and to render them by degrees fit vehicles for conveying knowledge to the great mass of the population. (Ibid: 185).

Doubtless, Bentinck—with his strong utilitarian belief—was

happy with Macaulay's minute. Macaulay won the battle and Bentinck passed the following order on March 7, 1835:

> His Lordship is of the opinion that the great object of the British Government ought to be the promotion of European literature and science amongst the natives of India and all the funds appropriated for the purposes of education would be best employed on English education. (Ibid: 185).

Bentinck's order was in tune with the financial needs of the Company. He knew that the East India Company was passing through severe financial difficulty. One of his principal tasks was to economise. As one of the main items of expenditure was the high pay of British officers, he considered employing Indian subordinates in the judicial/revenue branches. It was necessary for these Indians to know English.

Macaulay's education policy, as we wish to argue, was a turning point. It legitimised the 'civilising' mission of colonialism, promoted the cultural hegemony of the West and, in the ultimate analysis, created a mind-set slavishly dependent on the West—its values, culture, and religion. In fact, Lord Hardinge was not wrong when he wrote to Queen Victoria in 1844.

> The literature of the West is the most favourite study among the Hindus in their schools and colleges. They will discuss with accuracy the most important events in British history. Boys of 15 years of age, black in colour, will recite the most favourite passages from Shakespeare, ably quoting the notes of the English and German commentators. (Quoted in Carnoy 1976: 101).

True, not everyone approved of Macaulay's condemnation of oriental knowledge. We know, for example, how the Wood's Despatch (1854) felt: that the oriental institutions were necessary for 'historical and antiquarian purposes'. The Despatch also emphasised the importance of the oriental languages for studying the Hindu and Muslim laws. The Hunter Commission (1882) too seemed to be in favour of the indigenous knowledge system. Yet, these 'concessions' notwithstanding, the fact was that the idea of cognitive superiority of modern/English education remained unchallenged. The Wood's Despatch too categorically declared that the nature of education was to be the 'improved arts, sciences and literature of Europe' and stated that the eastern systems 'abound with grievous errors' (Ghosh 1995: 74-75).

In fact, the lure of English education was difficult to resist; the educated Indians themselves wanted it. Raja Rammohan Roy—the 'renaissance' man—could not deny the inherent promise in English education. It should not be forgotten that in 1823, Roy protested against the establishment of the Sanskrit college in Calcutta. Roy, in fact, revealed the mood of the age. For the emergent middle class, English education was a source of mobility, an opportunity to experience modernity.

Poromesh Acharya has brilliantly illustrated how the Bengali *bhadralok* were engaged in an alliance with colonial masters for promoting modern/English education in nineteenth century Bengal (Acharya 1998: 25-38). For the *bhadralok*—the ambitious class lured by the 'promises' of the new age—the interests of the larger sections of society were not important. No wonder, as Acharya reminds us, they did not oppose Macaulay's elitist education policy. As a matter of fact, they opposed the attempts made by Governor General Mayo and Lieutenant Governor George Campbell to spread vernacular education among the masses. Be it Vidyasager or Rajendralal Mitra, Keshub Chandra Sen or Surendranath Banerjee—the story, according to Acharya, was the same. The Bengali *bhadralok* saw the affirmation of their class interests in English education. In order to retain their own interests, they overlooked the negative effects of this elitist education—its colonial character, its arrogance, and its indifference to the experiences of the larger community. Again, the majority of young Indians—particularly, in Calcutta, Bombay and Madras—saw in it an opportunity to get employment in various British establishments.

There are, however, three points to note:

1. The glamour of English education notwithstanding, it did not help the Indians to acquire the so-called techno-scientific knowledge which was necessary for the accomplishment of the industrial development project. This is because English education was primarily literary in character. For example, the curriculum for the first year class in the Hindu college, Calcutta, in 1832 consisted of English literature which included Shakespeare, Milton, Pope's Homer and Dryden's Vergil; history, mainly of Greece, Rome, England and modern Europe; mathematics and geography (see Basu 1978: 60). Hence, it was stated time and again that the curriculum ought to be altered to suit our practical needs. The Wood's Despatch spoke of the drawbacks of a purely literary character of instruction and emphasised the necessity of professional training in law, medicine and engineering. The Hunter Commission too attached great importance to vocational education. Likewise, the Calcutta University Commission (1917) urged the inclusion of applied science and technology in its courses. However, despite these recommendations, the techno-professional skills needed for a fruitful engagement in productive activities were not available to educated Indians. In fact, Martin Carnoy was not wrong when he said:

   > The British did not try to instil in the natives a deep grasp of the fundamental principles of economics, technology, science and politics; rather they were content to force their pupils to ape and recite English literature, philosophy and metaphysics in the most slavish, imitative fashion. (Carnoy 1976: 101).

2. Because of this excessive importance given to literary education, there was not much choice left for the educated Indians, who relied heavily on government jobs. Moreover, with the establishment

of the three universities in Calcutta, Bombay and Madras in 1857, the number of aspirants began to increase. This led to further scarcity of jobs and consequently, frustration amongst the educated youth. Not surprisingly, a movement sprang up in many parts of the country to fight the reduction of the maximum age from 21 to 19 at which one was considered eligible for the Indian Civil Service examinations. The British, needless to add, did not appreciate this political turmoil; this growing unrest amongst educated Indians. It was at this juncture that the Hunter Commission suggested that the Government must retreat from the domain of higher education. After all, Hunter himself believed that the same education, which the British gave to Indians, was becoming counter-productive. Hunter was indignant because, as he thought, Indians were revolting against those who taught them to see the world. As he saw it, they were revolting against the principle of discipline, of religion, and of contentment (quoted in Ghosh 1993: 192). The point we are trying to state is that for the colonial masters, it was a paradoxical situation. Grant and Macaulay had thought that they must 'educate' Indians. But this very act of education made them 'disobedient'! This apprehension made them exercise further control on education. It was in this context that Curzon's attempt to establish absolute control over education needs to be understood. Curzon felt that if not controlled, the Indian universities would develop into 'nurseries of discontented characters and stunted brains' (quoted in Basu 1982: 11). The fact, as we have already stated, was that colonial education could never be separated from the rationale of power. Its primary aim was not to create a sense of freedom and independence. It intended to colonise the mind. As a result, it could not tolerate even the slightest revolt.

3. It was no wonder then, that this system failed miserably as far as mass education was concerned. Well, there was no dearth of recommendations to salvage the situation. With its critique of Macaulay's 'filtration policy', the Wood's Despatch emphasised that vernaculars should be cultivated for the promotion of mass education. True, the Despatch suggested that the aid would be given to all schools imparting good secular education and government instruction. But, at the same time, it decided to levy fees from the students. As a result, it was only the more affluent who were able to organise and pay for their children's schooling. There was no way one could hide this failure in mass education. For example, the Hartog Committee (1929) stated that out of every hundred boys admitted in Class I in 1922-23, only 19 were found studying in Class IV in 1925-26 (Ghosh 1995: 151).

It was this story of failure that led the Sargnet Plan of 1944 to repeat the rhetoric: there should be a provision of free/compulsory education below the ages of 6 and 14 (Ibid: 167). This failure in mass education revealed once again what the colonial masters wanted. Collective empowerment was not the aim of the system of education they introduced. Time and again they spoke of their 'civilising' mission, their 'duty' to educate Indians. But seldom could they go beyond their commercial motives; they could not engage themselves whole-heartedly in universal primary education. Gokhale realised this bitter truth when in 1912, his bill—which he introduced in the Imperial Legislative Council for making elementary education free and compulsory throughout the country—was defeated!

To sum up, it can be said that colonial education created a small section of English educated babus (who came largely from upper castes) and that it failed miserably in the field of primary education. Yet, one may argue that not everything was bad about colonial education. After all, this familiarity with the West—its knowledge systems—did create a kind of a critical consciousness. As a result, Indian leaders—from Rammohan to Nehru—looked at their past, fought its pathologies, celebrated the new age of reason, and eventually fought against the British. However, it has to be realised that this project of decolonisation was never complete. Because even when they resisted the British imperialism, not all of them succeeded in emancipating their minds from the West, its colonial categories and assumptions.[2] In other words, for an educated Indian, the West was (and is) a permanent presence. It is certainly not an overstatement when Martin Carnoy writes:

> Even today it is very difficult for Indians to break this pattern. They feel much closer bonds with British professors than with Hindu peasants, to whom they are unable even to speak. (Carnoy 1976: 101).

The fact is that English education did severe damage to our collective psyche. We lost faith in ourselves; many of us failed to tap our own cultural resources. The colonial citizen, as Krishna Kumar has pointed out, became our educational ideal (see Kumar 1991). We began to speak the same language. In fact, according to Krishna Kumar:

> ... education became the symbol of a new kind of secular ethnicity. (Ibid: 39).

It meant 'salvation' and 'emancipation'. It meant an entry into an exclusivist elite club, isolated from the large section of 'ignorant' masses. Let us recall what W.C. Bonnerjee wrote from England in 1865:

> I have discarded all ideas of caste, I have come to hate all the demoralising principles of our countrymen. I have become an entirely altered man. (Quoted in Kumar 1991: 34).

That was it! Arrogance became the by-product of modern/ Western education. Like the colonial master, the educated Indian too thought that his countrymen were ignorant and superstitious, and that with Western knowledge, he must 'civilise' them and restore 'order' in society.[3] Macaulay did not remain a historical memory. He entered our souls. We allowed ourselves to be invaded. We unlearned our own ideals. And, ironically, the entire process was called education!

IV
Colonialism, Revivalism and Lower Caste Response

Not everyone could remain contented with the agenda of colonial education. Doubtless, there were dissenters. But before we know more about the story of dissent, it is important to realise that the possibility of some kind of revivalism had always been there while evolving a critique of colonial education, its implicit arrogance, and cultural domination. Revivalism, as we know, often meant the glorification of the Hindu past, the celebration of Hindu ideals for the restoration of an 'authentic' Indian identity which, it was feared, would be destroyed because of colonial invasion.[4] In a multi-religious society like ours, revivalism would always appear extremely hegemonic; it would like to destroy the identity of minority communities. In other words, it could prove to be a debacle in the freedom of the oppressed and marginalised sections of society.

This apprehension was not entirely unfounded, because there was indeed a revivalist current in the 'nationalist' pursuits. Moreover, the lower/oppressed castes needed their emancipation which, they might have felt, could be attained in a more conducive colonial state (with its modern legal system and liberal values) than what the nationalist elite could offer. Not surprisingly, the lower caste response to colonial education was complex. Instead of viewing colonial education as alien, it sought to see great potential and possibility in it for the emancipation of India's marginalised castes.

A careful look at Jotirao Phule's intervention in the domain of education would enable us to understand this complexity. The biographers of Phule tell us that he could not forget what his immediate ancestors experienced: discontent with the rule of the Peshwas (see, for example, Joshi 1992). This terribly autocratic rule negated justice and dignity. The Brahmins were the favoured caste, and merit was not the criterion when it came to giving them high posts. Besides, for many of their crimes, the Brahmins got away with milder punishment than what was stipulated by the law. No wonder, Jotirao saw a progressive possibility in the British rule. At least, the malpractices of the Peshwa regime were abolished. Moreover, there was no discrimination on the basis of caste under the British rule which, he felt, followed the principle that all human beings were equal. Furthermore, he was highly influenced by modern/liberal/Western values of freedom and equality. His own experience as a student in the Scottish Mission Secondary School, as M.S. Gore writes, exposed him to new ideas on science and religion (see, Gore 1989). The missionaries criticised Hinduism for its idol worship, for its pantheon of gods, its denial of the spiritual equality to all human beings, the tyranny of superstition, and rituals in daily life. It is possible that Jotirao took this critique quite seriously. Besides, he also read Thomas Paine's *Age of Reason* which shaped his consciousness (in fact, he later dedicated one of his books to Thomas Paine).

Hence, between the malpractices of the Peshwa regime and the progressive potential of the British rule, he chose the latter. This could also be the reason why Jotirao did not support the 1857 mutiny. Instead, he welcomed the victory of the British.

> If the British government had lost in the mutiny, then history would have repeated itself. The Peshwa regime of the Brahmins would have been resurrected. The Hindu culture of the scriptures, *Smritis* and *Puranas* would have regained strength,

> and the hope of emancipating the *Sudra* and the Ati-sudra masses—a hope born as a result of the advent of the British government—would have been lost forever... (Quoted in Joshi 1992: 86).

Phule was convinced that with the help of modern education, the common man could benefit from the legal system and scientific reforms of the British government, and regenerate himself. With this hope, Phule appealed to the colonial state time and again. For example, in his representation to the Hunter Commission in 1882, he argued that the government should not be under the illusion that people from the upper castes would spread education among the lower castes. He appealed to the colonial state to appoint teachers from lower castes, because he felt that the religious prejudices of Brahmin teachers would not allow them to mingle with children from the lower castes.

But then, Phule was not content with just the appeals. He was a man of action. He ventured into the domain of education and started his own schools. He felt that a true emancipatory agenda would require modern education and enlightenment of both the Sudras and the women from the Hindu community. With this conviction he could succeed in persuading his wife to get educated, and eventually both of them started a school in 1848—a school that was open to girls from untouchable castes such as Mahars, Mangs and Chamars. This was the time when Pune, in particular, was the bastion of ultra conservative Hindu ideology. Phule's endeavour was viewed as an offence against the *shastras*, religion and the society. Phule's determination, however, saw him through the difficulties and resistance from various quarters (even his father could not approve of his son's action). As a result, his innovations in the field of education continued. He started a second school in 1851; a third in 1859. The curriculum included reading, grammar, arithmetic, geography, history, map reading, etc.

Jotirao's schools were making a difference. They were shaping the consciousness of the new generation of learners.

For example, a fourteen-year-old girl from one of his schools for the untouchables wrote an essay in which she said:

> The Brahmins say that other castes should not read the Vedas; this leaves us without a scripture. Thus, are we without religion? Oh God, please tell us, what is our religion? God, by your Grace, you sent us the kindly British Government. This has brought relief and welfare. Before the British came, the Mahars and Mangs were beheaded when they committed an offence against the people of higher castes. Earlier we were not allowed to move about freely in the bazaar of Sultekadi; now we can. (Quoted in Joshi 1992: 12).

It ought to be realised that Phule's aim was not just to see positive/progressive features in the British rule. His vision was far deeper. Through his *Sarvajanik Satyadharma* he sought to construct a new society; a society that would be qualitatively different from the traditional/Brahminical/ hierarchical order; a society that would celebrate modern/ scientific knowledge as opposed to religious beliefs and practices; a society in which all men and women would enjoy equal rights, and occupations such as farming, artisanship and labour would not be allowed to degrade a man's dignity.

Jotirao Phule's project demonstrates that colonialism drew divergent responses, and the 'nationalist' project was not necessarily consensual. It is also important to remember that the lower caste response to the British rule does not mean that it always saw progressive features in the colonial state. Instead, it was engaged in an ambiguous relationship with the British rule. For instance, B.R. Ambedkar revealed time and again how the British chose to remain indifferent to the education of the lower castes, although, as he felt, great hopes were raised among the depressed classes by the advent of the British rule, because it was a democracy which, as he felt, believed in the principle of equality.

V
Voice of Dissent: Education as a Decolonisation Process

It is not difficult to understand the ambiguities inherent in the lower caste response to colonial education. But then, this does not mean that a critique of colonial education would invariably lead to revivalism or the assertion of orthodox Brahminical tradition. In fact, there were dissenters who, despite their critique of colonial policies and sensitivity to Indian educational ideals, were by no means conservative. Instead, they fought against militant revivalism; their educational ideals had many emancipatory possibilities which, as we would say, have not lost their meaning even in our times. Here we will concentrate on two such dissenters —Gandhi and Tagore.[5]

Gandhi, we know, fought colonialism and evolved an alternative worldview. He wanted us to see the evils of modern civilisation and appreciate the merits of a counter-culture based on non-violence, spirituality, austerity and man's harmonic relationship with nature. It was, therefore, hardly surprising that he was not comfortable with the premises of colonial education. His alternative propositions are indeed worth examining.

Gandhi resisted colonial education not just because it came from the West. Essentially, he disliked its inherent elitism, its irrelevance as far as the needs of India's rural/subaltern masses were concerned. Moreover, with his profound pedagogic sensitivity he could see the damaging effect of colonial education—how it hampered the integral development of the child. For example, it was difficult for him to accept English as the medium of instruction, because he felt that it had created a permanent bar between the highly educated few and the uneducated many (Gandhi 1951: 17).

Moreover, Gandhi felt that English made one a stranger in one's own land. Besides, with this kind of education, one could not appreciate the dignity of manual labour. In other words, one could not respect the worth of the toiling masses. Gandhi condemned this education as 'intellectual dissipation'. His anguish was clear:

> The young man who emerges from this system can in no way compete in physical endurance with an ordinary labourer. The slightest physical exertion gives him a headache; a mild exposure to the sun is to cause him giddiness . ...As for the faculties of the heart, they are simply allowed to run to seed or to grow anyhow in a wild undisciplined manner. The result is moral and spiritual anarchy. (Gandhi 1951: 11).

It is important to note that Gandhi attacked what Macaulay wanted to create: a class of people alienated from the pulse of their own country. Unlike many of his contemporaries who wanted more of English education (because they equated it with modernity and progress), Gandhi spoke the language of the labouring class; his horizon was that of the villagers, the toiling masses. Never did Gandhi hierarchise the different human faculties. He often asked:

> Why should you think that the mind is everything and the hands and feet nothing? (Gandhi 1951: 73).

Instead of this elitist/fragmented approach to education, he imagined an 'indivisible whole' that would integrate the body, mind, and the soul. That was perhaps the reason why Gandhi refused to remain contented with mere learning through books. Instead, he sought 'to impart the whole education of the body, the mind and the soul through handicraft.' For example, he chose *takli*—a handicraft which, according to him, could be found everywhere and lasted throughout the ages. And that was the most important component of his educational agenda. This, as he thought, would restore the dignity of manual labour, promote a profit-yielding vocation and make education relevant to the labouring class.

It should not, however, be thought that Gandhi's craft-centred education was narrow, merely instrumental and blind to the other important branches of knowledge. As a matter of fact, a careful look at Gandhi's *basic education* would suggest that it was not limited merely to the craft; through the craft, he wanted to impart knowledge on all important branches of learning: history, geography, science and arithmetic. For example, Gandhi visualised that learning the handicraft would invariably mean a course in mechanics—on how to construct the *takli*. It would also demand a knowledge of history.

> A brief course in Indian history, starting from the East India Company, or even earlier, from the Muslim period, giving them a detailed account of the exploitation that was the stock-in-trade of the East India Company, and how by a systematic process our handicraft was strangled and almost killed. (Gandhi 1951: 9).

It would 'also mean

> ....a few lectures on cotton, its habitat, its varieties, the countries and provinces of India where it is at present grown and so on. (Ibid: 9).

The point we are trying to state is that for Gandhi, the handicraft was the medium which, he thought, would enable the learner to relate ideas to practice as well as arouse his/her curiosity and enthusiasm in learning, because the 'lessons' would be rooted in the learner's vocation.

One knows that it was at the *Wardah Conference* in 1937 that Gandhi's principles of basic education were debated and discussed. The resolutions that the conference passed approved of Gandhi's proposals like free/compulsory education for seven years, mother-tongue as the medium of instruction, education centred around some form of manual/productive work and a self-supporting education in the sense that it would be able to cover the remuneration of teachers.

We also know that the Gandhian agenda did not succeed. The kind of education that prevails in India is a negation of the Gandhian project. True, it can be argued that, despite his critique of colonial education, Gandhi was not relevant in modern times. Moreover, in a technologically developed world in which the nature of knowledge is becoming increasingly complex, techno-scientific and professional, his scheme of basic education looks simplistic—an obstacle to progress!

But then, there are obvious limits to this kind of a critique, because modern education is not without its flaws. Moreover, there are possibilities in the Gandhian scheme that can always be explored and reformulated to suit our present needs. For example, the fundamental principle of learning through doing remains an attractive pedagogical proposition. It arouses the interest of the child, enables him/her to mediate between the concrete and the abstract; knowledge gets merged with the music of life. It is also possible to see how by giving legitimate space to manual/productive work, Gandhi radicalised the curriculum. He was attacking the unequal social order and trying to

> ...check the progressive decay of our villages and lay the foundation of a just social order in which there is no unnatural division between the 'haves' and 'have nots'. (Gandhi 1951: 51).

It is unfortunate that in post-Independence India his scheme was not taken seriously; the Wardah Conference remains merely a historical memory!

Like Gandhi, Tagore was another great dissenter. He was a great poet with extraordinary imagination and sensitivity. His willingness to transform the agenda of modern civilisation was remarkable. He wrote extensively on education. Besides, the poet was also an activist; a practical doer. He created his own educational institution. *Santiniketan* was a project through which he sought to accomplish his alternative educational agenda.

Tagore, needless to add, was critical of colonial education, its alien character, its remoteness from the rhythm of everyday life.[6] This critique manifested itself again and again in his vehement protests against English as a medium of instruction. Its unnaturalness, Tagore wrote with deep anguish, would damage the child's creativity. Knowledge acquired through a foreign language, he argued, could never become an organic part of the learner's personality. No wonder, he could see the unbridgeable gap between the book and life; the tragedy of the 'English educated' Indian—his/her inability to relate to people.

Tagore could not appreciate Macaulay's arrogance; his principle of cultural domination; his ruthless condemnation of Indian civilisation. Instead, with great humility, he could look at the past, reinterpret the ancient educational ideal, and derive his inspiration from it. In fact, the idea of *tapovan*—a sacred space amidst the abundance of nature in which the child acquires from the charismatic guru his knowledge, wisdom and spirituality did have a profound impact on Tagore's mind. He knew that there was no way one could go back to the past. But then, there were possibilities in this ideal that Tagore wanted to tap, and utilise in his educational project.

Tagore had never been in favour of the emerging trends in urban/ modern civilisation: the school cut off from natural surroundings—a closed space with a regimented system that restricts the spontaneity and freedom of the child. The idea of a school as a 'factory' manufacturing 'products' was something that he hated. Instead, Tagore pleaded strongly for harnessing the great possibilities in nature. He wanted his school amidst natural surroundings, for he believed that the child should feel like he is a part of nature; relate to it; learn from it. This intimacy with nature—an act of communion with the earth and the sky, the sun and the stars, the trees and the flowers, the rivers and the mountains, the silences and the storms which grow in the heart of nature—the poet thought, would open up the child's mind and help him gain not only in physical, but also in mental and emotional health.

Likewise, Tagore asserted the importance of the ancient ideal of simplicity. He saw the death of this ideal in a civilisation that was becoming complex, industrial and market-oriented. But he realised that an alternative educational agenda must begin with austerity; it would enable the child to overcome violent desires and impluses, and help him develop his innate strength. Because of this need for simplicity, Tagore was also against the unnaturalness of excessive learning through books. A system of education that relies heavily on books and forces the child to accumulate—almost mindlessly all that is written in books, Tagore wrote, is life-negating. It destroys the learner's confidence in his/her own experience. It intensifies complexity, destroys originality, and renders the process of education bereft of any joy or creativity. No wonder, he wanted to free the child from the burden of excessive academic pursuits. He wanted to draw all the resources from music, song, drama, dance and drawing, thereby enriching the child's life in every possible way.

For a poet like Tagore, who was gifted with an extraordinarily sensitive/spiritual mind, it was not easy to see the teacher as just another professional—a paid employee. The ideal of *tapovan*, as we have already said, inspired him. He visualised the teacher as a charismatic guru, gifted with the power of love, knowledge, wisdom, and the ability to educate/inspire the child through his own life-practice. Perhaps it would not be wrong to say that he saw limitations being imposed on the child's overall development through excessive professionalisation/secularisation of education.

In his writings and speeches, Tagore repeatedly reminded us of the message of India, the essence of her civilisation, her educational ideal. He was warning us of the dangers of aping the West. This, however, does not mean that he was a revivalist, or in his thinking he was an exclusivist. Never did he appreciate the doctrine of militant nationalism; his internationalist outlook was well-known. The ideal of education Tagore was affirming was not a sectarian dogma. It was emancipatory. He was fully aware of the role of reason and intellect. He welcomed with open arms the new movements of scientific thought which were gathering an increasing momentum in Europe.

In fact, there are two possibilities in Tagore's critique of colonial education and the alternative that he visualised and sought to practise.

First, since he strongly believed in child-centred/ emancipatory education, he was deeply concerned about the damaging effect of the modern system of education on the dignity and autonomy of children. For Tagore, we as adults do not have the right to rob the child of his fascination with nature in the name of teaching him geography, or to put curbs on his own language in order to teach him grammar; we can not deprive him of his taste for, say, an epic and burden him with chronicles of facts and dates. 'Should the child be blamed for not having learnt the problems of algebra before coming into the world?'—asked the poet. For him, the child is a natural born learner, and the process of learning ought to be filled with the spirit of joy, creativity and freedom. Second, his educational agenda—because of its close affinity with nature—was an affirmation of ecological values like harmony, intimacy, simplicity and austerity. In a way, this agenda has a tremendous potential in a civilisation that is becoming ruthlessly modern, consumeristic and ecologically destructive.

But then, the voices of dissent, as articulated by Gandhi and Tagore, were forgotten. To quote Poromesh Acharya:

> Unfortunately, the educational discourse in India was changed in the wake of the Nehruvian modernisation programme. Both Tagore and Gandhi lost their importance in the national discourse but were remembered more by street and 'bhavan' names. In every city we have streets in the name of Gandhi and a 'Rabindra Bhavan'. The national system of education, however, still remains the legacy of the colonial system, turning more and more segregative and bookish. (Acharya 1997: 601).

VI
Education for Modernity and Nationalist Aspirations

The way society formulates its educational agenda depends on its objectives and priorities. We, therefore, ought to know the nationalist agenda that India sought to evolve after Independence, because it is against the background of this nationalist project that the contemporary educational policies have to be understood. There are, primarily, two components of the nationalist project. First, it attaches great importance to modernity: the vision of a modernised and industrially developed new India. This means openness to science, technology, rationality and urbanisation. Second, it is deeply concerned with the unity of India as a modern nation. National integration means awareness of unity: overcoming all local identities and regional differences; realising our shared Indianness and strengthening the centrality of the new nation-state. Apart from these two primary objectives—modernity and national integration—we should also take into consideration some other important factors. For instance, as it is believed, it is important to be aware of our culture. Culture, as our shared memory, makes integration possible. Moreover, it is our culture that gives us a specific identity—an identity that a post-colonial society must retain in order to overcome the trauma of colonialism. In other words, the dream of a new India should be that of a strong, integrated, industrially developed, nation-state with a rich cultural heritage.

The ambiguity of this nationalist project—with respect to its equation with the West—is evident. Independence implies that we must retain our distinction from the colonial West; as well as our uniqueness and specificity, and protect our culture. But, at the same time, the West remains the positive reference point; it is the ultimate symbol of all that modernity implies: industry, technology, science, development and affluence. Not surprisingly, in this kind of a nationalist agenda we see a break as well as a continuity with the colonial worldview. There is a continuity, because it also privileges the West—its science, rationality and knowledge system. But there is also a break, because it seeks to retain our identity and protect our culture. Perhaps it would not be wrong to say that these nationalist aspirations were strongly articulated in the Nehruvian agenda of nation-making. In a way, Nehru was the child of modernity. He believed that India must modernise herself, overcome her fixation with the past, and enter the new era. He disliked the glorification of the 'golden' past. Because such a 'foolish and dangerous pastime' (Nehru 1983: 81), as he thought, would take us nowhere. 'India', he argued, 'must break with much of her past, and not allow it to dominate the present' (Ibid: 509). Nehru was known for his celebration of the 'scientific temper'. 'The scientific approach and temper', he stated passionately, 'should be a way of life, a process of thinking, a method of acting and associating with other fellowmen' (Ibid: 512). His vision of modernity was essentially Western, with emphasis on industrialisation, secularisation and material well-being. As a result, Nehru did not always feel comfortable with Gandhi—his critique of modernity, his religious language, moral obsession and simplicity. For instance, he was absolutely critical of Gandhi's *Hind Swaraj*. It was 'wholly at variance with modern ideas and conditions' Nehru 1984: 510); it was an 'utterly wrong and harmful doctrine' (Ibid: 510). In *Hind Swaraj* he saw nothing but 'the praise of poverty and suffering and the ascetic life' (Ibid: 510). His goal was, therefore, clear: 'We cannot stop the river of change or cut overselves adrift from it; and psychologically, we, who have eaten of the apple of Eden cannot forget that taste and go back to primitiveness' (Ibid: 511).

But then, Nehru was not free from ambiguities. Despite being a modernist celebrating radical social transformation, he was not altogether indifferent to the cultural tradition of India.

> We can never forget the ideals that have moved our race, the dreams of the Indian people through the ages, the wisdom of the ancients, the buoyant energy and love of life and nature of our forefathers, their spirit of curiosity and mental adventure, the daring of their thought, their splendid achievements in literature, art and culture, their love of truth, beauty and freedom, the basic values that they set up. (Nehru 1984: 509).

For Nehru, it was important to take pride in that heritage. Because 'if India forgets them (the ideals) she will no longer remain India and much that has made her our joy and pride will cease to be' (Ibid: 509). In other words, in the Nehruvian agenda we could see precisely what we have been talking about: an attempt to reconcile *science* (for development and progress) and *heritage* (for retaining the cultural uniqueness of a post-colonial society).[7]

It is this agenda which, as we would see, shapes our educational policy. A careful look at the reports of different education commissions reveals the following:

Science as Supreme Knowledge

We see the importance attached to science, because science is the language of modernity. For a new nation seeking to be modernised, science must become an integral part of its education. Not surprisingly, the *Radhakrishnan Commission* (1949) put great emphasis on science and technology. It was also felt that science and technology, as the two important tools of modernity, would be able to reconstruct our rural/agrarian society. The Commission, as a result, was in favour of the idea of setting up rural universities to meet the needs of rural reconstruction in industry, agriculture and various walks of life. Likewise, the *Kothari Commission* (1966) emphatically articulated the need of scientific education for modern India. Science, the Commission argued, was needed for productivity, self-sufficiency in food, economic growth and employment. Moreover, the Commission attached great importance to the quality of science education. Science should be taught in such a way that it enables the learner to understand its basic principles; to develop problem-solving analytical skills and the ability to apply them to the problems of the material environment and social living; it should promote the spirit of enquiry and experimentation.

The story repeated itself in the *New Education Policy (1986)*, which also stressed the necessity of promoting technical/management education for the growth of the industry.

> The curricula of technical and management programmes will be targeted in current as well as the projected needs of the industry or user system. Active interaction between technical or management institutions and industry will be promoted... (*The New Education Policy* in Shukla 1988: 21).

In order to respond to the changing times, the policy also spoke of the importance of computer education.

> As computers have become important and ubiquitous tools, a minimal exposure to computers and training in their use will form a part of professional education. Programmes of computer literacy will be organised on a wide scale from the school stage. (Ibid: 19).

Hence, the new education that post-Independence India has visualised is science and technology oriented, because science is endowed with a positive meaning; science promotes technology, and technology means development; science means rationality and critical enquiry; science education is practical, problem-solving and development oriented!

Unity as a Nationalist Project

We see the importance attached to national integration. The report of the Mudaliar Commission (1953) emphasised the role of education in promoting national integration. An attempt was made to see the nation as a cohesive whole. All local/regional identities were seen as something negative, destabilising to the unitary vision. Education, it was felt, should promote our shared Indianness. It should create loyal/ responsible citizens. For the Kothari Commission too, social and national integration became an important agenda of education, because, as the Commission felt,

> ...the growth of local, regional, linguistic and state loyalties tend to make the people forget India. (Government of India 1966: 2).

The Commission suggested:

> The deepening of national consciousness can be fostered specially by two programmes: (1) the understanding and re-evaluation of our cultural heritage, and (2) the creation of a

> strong driving faith in the future towards which we aspire. The first would be promoted by the well-organised teaching of the languages and literatures, philosophies, religions and history of India, and by introducing the students to Indian architecture, sculpture, painting, music, dance and drama. ...Faith in the future would involve an attempt as a part of the course in citizenship, to bring home to the students the principles of the Constitution, the great values referred to in its preamble, the nature of the democratic and socialistic society which we desire to create. (Ibid: 16-17).

In other words, an attempt was made to make the learner feel proud of our cultural heritage: the heritage that gave us the strength to survive, to fight colonialism and exist as a nation. This unitary vision of culture could be seen in the New Education Policy too. When it visualises the national system of education, it speaks of the *common core curriculum*.

> The common core will include the history of India's freedom movement, the constitutional obligations and other content essential to nurture national identity. These elements will cut across subject areas and will be designed to promote values such as India's common cultural heritage, egalitarianism, democracy and secularism, equality of the sexes, protection of the environment, removal of social barriers, observance of the small family norm and inculcation of the scientific temper. All educational programmes will be carried on in strict conformity with secular values. *(The New Education Policy* in Shukla 1988: 4-5).

The point we are trying to state is that education has been viewed as a vehicle for promoting national values and restoring unity and order.

Equality as a Secular Aspiration

What is equally striking is the importance attached to equality. There are two reasons. First, it is believed that democracy is impossible without education and literacy. Second, in the new era, education—acquisition of knowledge, information and skills—is seen as a great resource for the enhancement of one's life-chances. Education is seen as a right, not a privilege. Education for all—or universal education—becomes an important agenda of a modern/ democratic society. It was no wonder then that the Kothari Commission recommendations began with a radical statement:

> The destiny of India is now being shaped in her classrooms. (Government of India 1966: 1).

Moreover, it was felt that the vision of an integrated/ egalitarian society could not tolerate the dual system of education:

> ...the minority of private, fee-charging, better schools meeting the needs of the upper classes and the vast bulk of free, publicly maintained, but poor schools being utilised by the rest. (Ibid: 10).

In order to eliminate these evils, the Commission proposed a *common school system* of public education. The idea was that a system of this kind would be open to all children irrespective of caste, creed, community, religion, economic conditions and social status. As no tuition fee would be charged, it would meet the needs of the average parent. Moreover, it would meet the required standards; one would not feel the need to send one's children to expensive schools outside the system. It was this egalitarian urge—the urge to fight educational inequalities—that could be seen even in the New Education Policy.

> The nation as a whole will assume the responsibility of providing resource support for implementing programmes of educational transformation, reducing disparities, universalisation of elementary education, adult literacy, scientific and technological research, etc. (*The New Education Policy* in Shukla 1988: 5-6).

In order to remove the prevalent disparities, the policy spoke of a scheme called *Operation Blackboard*—a scheme designed to improve primary schools all over the country. To quote from the policy:

> Provisions will be made of essential facilities in primary schools, including at least two reasonably large rooms that are usable in all weather, and the necessary tools, blackboards, maps, charts and other learning material. (*The New Education Policy* in Shukla 1988: 12).

The message it conveyed was clear enough. Despite our democratic aspirations, crude inequality exists in the realm of education. But it is high time we fought this inequality.

Cultural Sensitivity as Unique Identity

It would, however, be wrong to say that the national policy on education is mainly about modernist objectives—science education, consolidation of the nation-state, and democratic equality. What is equally noticeable is the importance it attaches to India's identity. To protect this identity is to protect India's culture, her moral/spiritual ideas, her ancient wisdom. In other words, modernity is good, but it does not mean the denial of our own traditions; both can coexist. Education must create the mind-set that is open to such a noble synthesis. The Radhakrishnan Commission, despite its strong recommendations for science/technology education, suggested the courses on the central problems of the philosophy of religion. Likewise, the Kothari Commission, all its radical pronouncements notwithstanding, could not forget India's cultural/spiritual heritage. True, the Commission accepted the gains of European scientific knowledge. But, at the same time, we were asked not to forget our own contributions.

> Atom and Ahimsa, or, to put it differently, man's knowledge and mastery of outer space and the space within his own skull, are out of balance. It is this imbalance which mankind must seek to redress... India has made many glorious contributions to world culture, and perhaps the grandest of them all is the concept and ideal of non-violence and compassion sought, expounded and lived by Buddha, Mahavira, Nanak and Kabir, Vivekananda, Ramana Maharshi and Gandhi in our own times, and which millions have striven to follow after them. (Government of India 1966: 22).

It was this spiritual awareness that led the Commission to suggest that education ought to cultivate one's religious sensitivity. Secularism, the Commission felt, should not mean hostility to religion. Instead, what is important is the 'eternal quest of the spirit.'

That is why, as the Commission felt, it is important for one to understand the common truth behind all religions.

> We suggest that a syllabus giving well-chosen information about each of the major religions should be included as a part of the course in citizenship or as part of general education to be introduced in schools and colleges up to the first degree. It should highlight the fundamental similarities in the great religions of the world and the emphasis they place on cultivation of certain broadly comparable and moral and spiritual values. (Government of India 1966: 21).

The Commission also showed its sensitivity to the Gandhian conscience. It attached great importance to work experience, because work experience could make the distinction between intellectual and manual work less marked, as also the social stratification based on it. In other words, what we are witnessing is the concern with culture—its role in developing the mind and the spirit. The New Education Policy too shared the same concern.

> The preoccupation with modern technologies cannot be allowed to sever our new generations from the roots in India's history and culture. De-culturalisation, de-humanisation and alienation must be avoided at all costs. Education can and must bring about the fine syntheses between change-oriented tendencies and the country's continuity of cultural tradition. (*The New Education Policy* in Shukla 1988: 23).

VII
Prevalent Reality: Education as Reproduction of Inequality

There are many ways of looking at the nationalist policy on education. For example, it is possible to see its 'Western' bias—the way it privileges science and technology, and attaches 'instrumental' meaning to knowledge. It is possible to think that this policy is not particularly eager to tap the traditional knowledge system and reformulate it for contemporary purposes. It is also possible that it has not learned sufficiently from dissenters like Gandhi and Tagore.

For instance, although the recent document *National Curriculum Framework For School Education: A Discussion Document* (NCERT 2000) has reaffirmed the same nationalist ideals and spoken almost a similar language, it has, nevertheless, expressed some kind of fear: the fear of losing indigenous knowledge. It speaks of the necessity of an 'indigenous curriculum' that would celebrate the ideas of 'native thinkers such as Aurobindo, Gandhi, Tagore and Krishnamurthy' (Ibid: 10). To quote from the document:

> Paradoxical as it may sound, while our children know about Newton they do not know about our own Aryabhat, they do know about a computer but do not know about the concept of zero. Mention may also have to be made, for instance, of Yoga and Yogic practices as well as Indian systems of medicines like Ayurvedic and Unani forms which are being recognised and practised all over the world. The curriculum shall have to correct such imbalances. (Ibid: 10-11).

In other words, it is feared that the existing education policy, because of its modernist orientation, is not always sensitive to our cultural heritage. As a remedial measure, the document imagines 'a fine synthesis between change-oriented technologies and the country's continuity of cultural tradition' (Ibid: 9).

In this context it would not be inappropriate to mention that the critique of the prevalent educational agenda may also lead to a counter-ideological propaganda—the way the triumphant Hindu Right has been trying to intervene in the domain of education and textbook writing in recent times and showing its clear-cut departure from the Nehruvian brand of secularism.[8] In other words, the debate on the objectives of education, as we are witnessing, can take many forms like, (a) education as inculcation of 'progressive' ideals of the Nehruvian agenda of nation-making; (b) education as an emancipatory experience as visualised by Tagore and Gandhi; and (c) education as yet another ideological hegemony in order to assert the pride of Hindu India and counter the imbalances caused by the politics of 'pseudo-secularism'!

But then, even those who agree with the nationalist policy would admit that there is a vast difference between the ideal and the real. The policies, as formulated in different commissions and reports, have not necessarily been implemented. For example, the idea of equality—education for all, removal of disparities and equal access to quality education—is negated every day. According to the Acharya Ramamurti Committee report (A *Perspective on Education*, New Delhi, September 1990), India ranks 115th in the world with regard to its expenditure on education as a percentage of the GNP. As a result, even though the number of primary schools in the country has increased considerably, inequality is rampant in the domain of education. If we take the help of a somewhat old document (National Institute of Educational Planning and Administration, *Education for All by 2000*, New Delhi, March 1990) there were 2,628 primary schools without any teacher, as many as 1,48,033 primary schools with but one teacher; the two categories together accounting for 28.5 per cent of all primary schools. Furthermore, nearly a third of the primary schools had only two teachers each. It should also be noted that 7 per cent of the primary schools had to function out in the open; about 20 per cent had either thatched or *kutcha* buildings or functioned from tents. More particularly, basic amenities like drinking water, bathrooms, playgrounds were absent in most schools. Even blackboards were missing in most primary schools. This pathetic state of affairs continues, with the simultaneous growth of 'private schools'—the schools that boast of their success in terms of five star facilities: air conditioned buses, swimming pool, and continual supply of Bisleri water!

This dual system of education remains a grim reality—elite/exclusive schools for the children of the affluent, and poor quality government schools for the rest. What characterises these elite schools, as Krishna Kumar points out, is the process of 'early selection' through which the children of the affluent are separated from the rest and trained in a manner that further assures their success in life (see Kumar 1987: 27-41). This is nothing but 'sponsored upward mobility'!

These schools are *exclusivist* in nature. There are two reasons: First, the heavy tuition fee that these schools charge significantly cuts down the number of potential clients. Indeed, the economic status of the parents is a major determinant of selection in these schools. Second, the selection process takes into account another kind of exclusivity which comes from 'merit'. Merit, however, is judged in terms of etiquette and certain kinds of skill—a sort of a cultural capital—that only the children of the affluent are gifted with. This inherent elitism cannot be overcome merely by a symbolic equaliser like 'mass examination'. True, mass examinations tend to give the impression that status can be achieved through competition. But the fact remains that there is no 'fair' competition, no 'equal' race. The children of the dominant classes, because of their exclusivist schooling, have already won the race! The message that Krishna Kumar seeks to convey is that the kind of education that prevails is not conducive to the aspirations of a democratic/egalitarian society. Instead, it breeds elitism, reinforces/reproduces the existing inequality.[9]

This dual system of education has another major implication for the children of the down trodden. There is not much in the prevalent system of schooling that can sustain their interest, and bring education closer to their life-situations. For them, poverty remains a major obstacle. It means continual hunger, malnutrition and illness, which interfere with their regular attendance at school and their ability to learn. For many of them, school knowledge appears to be irrelevant to their needs. This perhaps explains, as innumerable sociological works have demonstrated, the drop-out phenomenon (see, for example, Acharya 1987; Chitnis 1987). Moreover, school knowledge is often biased; it favours the cultural capital of the urban/upper caste/class; it perpetuates symbolic violence amongst large sections of agrarian/subaltern masses. It makes their failure inevitable.

Indeed, as Poromesh Acharya has pointed out, the problem of non-participation in the existing system of education is crucial (Acharya 1994: 27-30). An important reason is that the existing education alienates the children from labouring classes, from the culture of labour, and as a result complicates their problem further, thus reducing their employability.

> Toiling people in less advanced rural situations may not find any use of the existing elementary education. The culture content of the elementary programme may also act as a deterrent. It may make children shy of soiling their hands. On the other hand, landholding employers may not like to employ educated labour as they create labour problems by asserting their rights. (Ibid: 28).

Talib is not wrong when he says that school texts alienate the children from the marginalised section of society (Talib 1998: 199-209). The words, images and themes in these texts make the gulf between the high and low, the privileged and the toiling, seem natural. A striking example of the naturalisation of inequality is the way these texts reinforce the superiority and the efficacy of the mind and intellectual labour over manual labour. 'To those who were born and brought up to do menial tasks', says Talib, 'these stories at best inspired awe and at worst instilled a sense of inadequacy in the self' (Ibid: 204). In other words, as we have already discussed, failure or non-participation for the poor and the oppressed is rooted in the very rationale of the existing education.

Despite the growth in the school-going population, we have failed miserably by not being able to bring about egalitarian values in the field of education. The problem is not only that education remains inaccessible to many. The problem lies also in the very *meaning* of education. What kind of education are the 'lucky' ones getting? First, education, as it exists, does not unite; it divides and separates. One who gets education begins to consider oneself superior—morally and intellectually—to the rest of society. This problem becomes rather acute in elite schools. These schools create their own symbols, imageries and behaviour-patterns that make it difficult for a 'successful product' to merge with the rhythm of the larger society. Second, this kind of education cannot be sensitive to our own culture. Perhaps one 'studies' culture, but such culture is merely textual, rather than something that is a part of people's everyday life. If there is no relationship with people, there cannot be any living bond with their culture. Moreover, even in the post-colonial times, the West remains the primary reference point; it further alienates one from one's own cultural tradition. Third, barring some rare exceptions, the prevalent pedagogical practices are not conducive to creative learning. Be it an elite school or an ordinary government school—the emphasis is on rote memorisation, examinations, and on fixed syllabus with associated written texts. With school becoming a burden, there is not much space left for the elevation of the other important human faculties like creativity, criticality and moral/spiritual responsibility. Furthermore, as education is being seen as a utilitarian proposition, the meaning of knowledge changes. For example, for school-going children, science is not for rigorous critical enquiry; science becomes merely a means to enter the technological world. Science is lost amidst techno-economic priorities.

To conclude, education, as it exists, neither serves the intended nationalist ideal, nor does it conform to any alternative tradition, say, the dissenting tradition of Gandhi. Gandhi's educational agenda, as we have already stated, was in tune with the needs of the labouring class. It sought to reduce the gap between mental and manual labour. But in contemporary educational practices, we see its negation. Education, because of its urban/metropolitan bias, fails to reach the labouring class. It creates a mind-set that abhors manual labour and breeds elitism.

This education seems to have wiped out the memory of our ancient educational ideals such as austerity, humbleness, ego-transcendence, rigorous search for truth and discipline of the body and the mind. Instead, it stimulates the *desire* and inflates one's ego. It is not for the realisation of the Ultimate Truth; it is for immediate/temporal/material pursuits. This education is not spiritual; it is technical.

And perhaps this education is modern only superficially. It desires the success of modernity without, cultivating—critically, creatively and rigorously—its foundations of knowledge. Perhaps the prevalent educational practices continue to bear the legacy of Macaulay, because we see in them the reproduction of a mind-set that is elitist and indifferent to collective emancipation.

When will we realise that a departure from these discriminatory educational practices is in order; that there are possibilities if we dare to deviate from the beaten path; that a journey to an alternative system of education could help us find solutions.

Notes

1. The implications of this report have been studied by contemporary historians. See, for instance, Panikkar 1995: 47-53.
2. Ashish Nandy has written about the damage that colonialism did to our psyche, how its 'secular hierarchies', its ideals of 'development' and 'progress' wounded our self-pride, how we internalised the West, and sought to speak the language of the colonial master. See Nandy 1983.
3. This paternalistic attitude, for instance, was reflected in Keshub Chandra Sen's educational venture. Sen—the noted Brahmo Samaj reformer—intervened in the domain of popular education. For the neo-literate readership consisted of artisans, petty shopkeepers, people engaged in menial occupations, and

workers employed in the new industrial establishment, Sen started publishing a broadsheet called *Sulabh Samachar* in 1870. In fact, as Sumanta Banerjee has argued, it was an educational venture that, far from creating an egalitarian ethos, retained the hierarchical separation between the teacher (English-educated, civilised *bhadralok)* and the taught (uncultured/immoral masses). Moreover, as Banerjee argues, the readers of the *Sulabh Samachar* were often reminded of their 'low' status; they were asked not to become ambitious; instead, they were told to remain confined to their traditional occupations. The task, for them, was to alter their behaviour, learn the 'virtues of self-help' and improve their lot. (See Banerjee 1998).

4. For instance, we can recall the Arya Samaj endeavour in the domain of education. Whereas the moderate group led by Hans Raj and Lajpat Rai developed a chain of 'Dayanand Anglo Vedic' colleges, the more openly revivalist and militant Gurukul function founded by Lekh Ram and Munshi Ram started the Hardwar Gurukul in 1902 (based on the principles of *brahmacharya* and Vedic training). Within both these groups, as it is argued, there was an extraordinary emphasis on Hindu consciousness which, as it could be argued, was often openly communal and anti-Muslim.
5. This emphasis on Gandhi and Tagore does not mean that there was no other great educationist. In fact, Sri Aurobindo was a remarkably original thinker whose educational ideals were anti-colonial and emancipatory. In Chapter 4 we will discuss Sri Aurobindo's educational philosophy.
6. For understanding Tagore's contributions to education, I have relied on his Bengali essays. Rabindranath Tagore, *Shiksha* (Visva-Bharti, 1397(BS)).
7. For a more elaborate understanding of Indian Modernity, see Pathak 1998.
8. For further elaboration, see Pathak 1999.
9. In this context we can be reminded of Krishna Kumar's brilliant reflections on the educational experience of the subaltern class. Kumar has augured how history, as it is taught at schools, silences and degrades the cultural/religious experience of, say, the tribes. In other words, the knowledge that these texts embody asks the tribal child to accept his 'backwardness' and the 'superstitious' character of his group. He is asked to see the 'superiority' of the dominant class. This is like learning to be backward! (See, for details, Kumar 1989: 59-77).

2

Sociology of School Knowledge

Texts and Ideology

The texts that school children study—particularly those that are regarded as 'legitimate knowledge'—are worth examining, because in the prevailing system of education textbooks have acquired widespread legitimacy, and neither the teacher nor the taught can escape their influence. A critical enquiry into the sociology of these texts is important. There are two reasons.

1. It is desirable to free ourselves from the notion of 'objective' truth, because the world can be perceived, comprehended and known from divergent angles. Instead of thinking in terms of 'objective'/ 'disembodied' truth, it is better to see—as Karl Mannheim's contributions to the sociology of knowledge have taught us—the possibility of multiple perspectives.[1] As the horizons of the 'knowers' differ, there are many representations of the world. And each perspective, rather than being absolutely true or false, is a segment of truth or, to use Mannheim's words, a kind of 'total ideology' which is 'situationally determined' and 'relational' in character. It is, therefore, obvious that the knowledge that school texts contain can also be seen as a

perspective, a way of seeing the world from a particular vantage point. It need not be seen as something 'given' and 'eternally defined.' Instead, it is possible to critique school texts, and as Michael Apple suggests, problematise the content of knowledge itself (Apple 1979).

2. Not all perspectives get the same kind of status/legitimacy in human society. In a stratified/unequal society, it is the perspective of the dominant class that tends to acquire greater legitimacy and power. It seeks to project itself as 'true' and 'objective.' Its close affinity with the politico-economic establishment enables it to silence other views. It is, therefore, possible to argue that school texts, particularly the 'official' variety, may privilege the perspective of, to use Piere Bourdieu's words, the 'cultural capital' of the dominant class (Bourdieu and Passeron 1977). In other words, school knowledge may be perceived as an effective means for establishing the ideological hegemony of the dominant class. No wonder, the marginalised/oppressed groups, in the process of their struggle for liberation, may come forward with alternative texts that seek to challenge the prevalent hierarchy of knowledge.[2] In other words, school knowledge, far from being a doctrine of eternal truth, is a form of an ideological representation.

It can, however, be argued that in natural sciences or abstract disciplines like mathematics, it is possible to be free from ideological biases. But then, not everyone would agree with this, because science too can be seen as a social practice; and it is possible to see its politics. In other words, science is not necessarily different from or superior to ideology.[3] But then, here, we are not concerned with a debate of this kind. The only point we wish to emphasise is that the critique of the 'objective truth' that we are evolving becomes more meaningful in the sphere of social knowledge.

This becomes clearer when, for instance, we begin to

reflect on the knowledge of India as represented in school texts, the reason being that there are divergent viewpoints when it comes to seeing or representing India. Let us take a look at some examples: India as a *tolerant Hindu civilisation* may not necessarily be appreciated by non-Hindus; for them the experience of living in India, it can be argued, is synonymous with marginalisation, insecurity and communal hatred. Likewise, the vision of India as a *modern/secular/ industrially developed nation* may not be appreciated by the victims of history who experience poverty, alienation and homelessness. Therefore, in the context of the conflicting versions of India, it is important to know how India is projected/represented in school texts. Whose India is it? Is it the India of the upper caste/upper class elite? Or is it the India of the subaltern masses—dalits, adivasis and other marginalised people? A critical enquiry into the nature of India as projected in school texts is bound to make us see the significance of the politics of knowledge: the relationship between knowledge and power, ideology and curriculum.

There is yet another reason why this discussion on knowledge of India is important. We cannot escape our engagement with India. Be it a civilisation or a nation or a combination of multiple nations, India gives us our identity. Despite the anger, frustration, and sometimes the feeling of hopelessness, all of us, in our own way, wish to see or create our own India—a Utopia of our dreams. There are many projects, and as many conflicting perspectives. As children grow up, they too begin to identify themselves with these possible projects. However, the nature of their engagement, to a significant extent, would depend on their knowledge of India. School texts, needless to add, play an important role in the construction of this knowledge.[4] It is, therefore, obvious that school texts cannot be altogether free from the politics of this representation, that is, how India is being seen and perceived.

Even though India can be seen in all possible texts—from science to poetry—we would concentrate on *history* and *civics texts* for a more specific focus on the topic under discussion. These texts, because of their very nature, deal with the issues relating to India: its past, present and future. We have decided to concentrate primarily on the *NCERT* and *Eklavya* texts for Classes VI, VII and VIII,[5] because we believe that a careful reading of these texts—or the two approaches to the understanding of India—would enable us to realise the significance of the social construction of knowledge: the relationship between ideology and curriculum. Moreover, at a time when an attempt has been made—particularly by the proponents of *Hindutva*—to alter the existing NCERT texts, a study of this kind would also enable us to evaluate their strengths and weaknesses, and give us sufficient insight to participate in the ongoing debate on the politics of school knowledge and curriculum.

I
NCERT Texts and Social Construction of India

To begin with, we wish to concentrate on the NCERT texts.[6] These texts have been written by eminent scholars and historians and have gained widespread legitimacy. Romila Thapar has written the texts for Classes VI and VII, which deal with the history of ancient and medieval India (Thapar 1993a & 1993b). Arjun Dev and Indira Arjun Dev have written the history of modern India for Class VIII (Dev and Dev 1993). A look at these texts suggests that an attempt has been made to make the child aware of the rich history of India. The child is expected to absorb bundles of information: The Indus Valley Civilisation; The Vedic Age; From the Mauryan Empire to the Age of the Guptas; The Delhi Sultanate; The Mughals; The Rise and Growth of British Rule in India; Religious and Social Reform Movements;The Growth of Indian Nationalism; and The Achievement of Independence.

Yet, it has to be realised that history is not just bundles of information. History is also written in order to convey messages. Historical data need not exist as 'pure'/'neutral' facts as facts are often mingled with values. It is not impossible to see how historical writing privileges some facts and disregards others; how it praises, condemns, valorises things. History, in other words, is not just an 'objective' description of what happened. History is also about ideas, values and politics. Hence, from the huge stock of information available in these three texts, we wish to identify the messages, the values and the preferences through which history, as a body of school knowledge, seeks to influence the mind of the child.

History as an Ideology of Secular Nationalism

In fact, as we would demonstrate, the NCERT history texts project the ideology of secular nationalism. We would like to point out that this ideological preoccupation does have a significant impact on the way the past has been seen and constructed. Perhaps it would not be wrong to say that the NCERT has not tried to hide its ideological preference. For instance, in the foreword to Romila Thapar's text on medieval India, P.L. Malhotra has written:

> The National Policy of Education has stressed the importance of core curricular areas, along with a national curricular framework, in building the National System of Education. Many of the core curricular areas and the values that they are visualised to promote are directly related to the study of history. This relationship is obvious in the case of objectives such as promoting knowledge and understanding of India's common cultural heritage. It is no less important in its relationship with other objectives of the core areas such as the inculcation of scientific temper, and egalitarianism, democracy and secularism, equality of the sexes and removal of social barriers. It is also of crucial significance in combating obscurantism, religious fanaticism, superstition and fatalism.

The ideology of secular nationalism can be understood if we carefully look at what the following mean:

Avoiding the Glorification of the Hindu Past

What is striking here is a cautious/careful attempt to avoid the glorification of the Hindu past. For example, in the chapter on the Vedic age, there is no valorisation of the Vedic time. Not much has been written that characterises the philosophic depth of the Vedas or the cultural life of the people during that period. Instead, the historian seems to have relied heavily on the 'neutrality' of science or the 'objectivity' of information: how the Aryans came as pastoral nomads and how they took to agriculture and began to settle down in villages; how the cow was the pride of the place among the animals because people were dependent on the produce of the cow and how, for special guests, beef was served as a mark of honour. To put it in a nutshell, it would seem as though an attempt has been made to demystify/ demythologise the Vedic age. Not just that; the text wants the child to remember the story of power and conflict, not the Vedic hymns pleading for spiritual knowledge and the realisation of the Self. That is the reason why it speaks so clearly about the conflict between the Aryans and the Dasyus:

> The Aryans, when they settled in various parts of north India, were hostile to the indigenous people whom they referred to as 'Dasas' and 'Dasyus.' The Dasas and Dasyus did not worship the same gods as the Aryans and spoke a language which was different from the Vedic Sanskrit. Some Dasa chiefs were treated with great respect, but many of the Dasa people were enslaved so that eventually the word 'Dasa' came to mean slave. Thus Dasas who were enslaved had to do the most difficult and lowly work and were not treated kindly. (VI: 41).

No wonder, the text highlights the limitations of the Vedic religion, the irrationality of the caste system. Instead, it sees Jainism and Buddhism as egalitarian religions. For example, the projection of Buddhism as a more egalitarian religion and hence more sensitive to the needs of the subaltern classes becomes clear when it mentions:

> The Buddha too did not favour the Vedic sacrifices and the many rituals which people had to perform. He objected to the importance given to the *varnas* because those who belonged to the lower *varnas*, the *shudras* and others, were ill-treated by the

> upper *varnas*. Buddhism and Jainism had followers among the craftsmen, traders, and peasants because they felt that these religions were not difficult to practise. The *Brahmans*, on the other hand, had made their religion difficult to practise because of many ceremonies and rituals. Buddhism in those days was opposed to elaborate ceremonies because not only were they expensive but they also encouraged superstition. (VI: 56-7).

This urge not to glorify the Hindu past can also be seen in the narration of the age of the Guptas. True, the text tells us about divergent achievements of the Gupta period—the development of trade within India, western Asia and South East Asia; the great literary creation, particularly the genius of Kalidasa; progress in the field of science, mainly through the work of Aryabhatta, or the discovery of the decimal system and the concept of zero. The descriptions of these achievements notwithstanding, the text does not forget to remind the child of a major contradiction of the Gutpa period: the practice of untouchability.

> Society was divided into castes, most of which lived in harmony together. But there was one group in the towns which was badly treated—the untouchables. They had to live outside the town, separate from the rest of the townspeople. They were regarded as so impure that high caste people could not even look at them. This certainly does not speak well of the Gupta society. So much unkindness to other human beings was a serious flaw. (VI: 97).
>
> Even the achievements could not be seen in isolation. Because some of these had begun to mature in an earlier period. In evaluating classical Indian culture these earlier achievements have also to be considered. It was in part the prosperity of the earlier period which encouraged many arts and sciences in the Gupta period. (VI: 103).

The message is clear: before you begin to speak of the 'glorious' Hindu past, you ought to be humble. You ought to understand its limitations, contradictions and paradoxes.

Emphasising the Ideals of Tolerance and Harmony

Not surprisingly, what one witnesses is a parallel search for ideals—ideals that can educate the child and teach him/her values like equity, harmony, justice, and tolerance. What is strikingly visible in these texts is the identification and celebration of these ideals. To begin with, look at what history has to say about Ashoka—'the most famous of the Mauryan kings, and one of the greatest rulers India has ever had' (VI, pp. 60-61). The child is told about Ashoka's great transformation: the way the battle of Kalinga made him realise the futility of war and the way he became a champion of peace, love and harmony. Moreover, the text praises Ashoka's openness, his vast horizon, his tolerant attitude to all religions.

> Ashoka was a Buddhist and wanted to make Buddhism popular. But more than that he believed in high ideals, which could lead men to be peaceful and virtuous . ...Ashoka wanted all the different religious groups to live together in peace and tolerance . ...The important thing was not the differences but the unity within the empire. (VI: 62-64).

Furthermore, the text also hints at Ashoka's subaltern heart. The fact that Ashoka used Prakrit (not Sanskrit) to spread his message showed his closer relationship with the masses.

> This (Prakrit) was spoken by the common people, whereas Sanskrit was spoken by the educated upper castes . ...Because Ashoka wanted to explain his ideas to the ordinary people, he used the language which they would understand. (VI: 62).

Besides, the text reminds the child, Ashoka looked after his people in various ways. He built good roads; along the roads he planted shady trees to keep away the hot sun; he opened medical centres where sick men could be brought for treatment. In other words, in Ashoka, the text wants the child to see all that is positive, great and ideal.

Likewise, there was another great ideal—Akbar.

> Akbar was a great ruler not because he ruled a vast empire,

> but because of his concern for the country and the people .... In many ways Akbar had the same ideas about ruling as did Ashoka. Ashoka says in one of his edicts 'All men are my children.' If Akbar had known about this he would have agreed with it. Akbar's great dream was that India should be united as one country. People should forget their differences of religion and think of themselves only as the people of India . ...Akbar had one great quality. He was fearless. He showed boldness and courage in physical feats when he rode and tamed angry elephants or swam across rivers in full flood. He also showed courage when he opposed those who used their power and orthodoxy in trying to keep back new ideas and preventing changes from taking place in Indian society and Indian thinking. It was a fearlessness which was rooted in honesty and this is a rare quality. (VII: 94-95).

The chapter on Akbar is about his greatness. It is not just about his administrative skill; it is primarily about his accommodative spirit, his religious tolerance. It is mentioned how Akbar encouraged the translation—into Persian—of important works in Sanskrit like the *Ramayana* and the *Mahabharata,* and how this spirit of composite culture could also be seen in the architecture. For example, the architecture at Fatehpur Sikri is an excellent blend of Persian, central Asian and Indian styles. And the text also reminds the child of the rationale behind Akbar's new religion, i.e. *Din-i-Ilahi.*

> He felt that every religion pointed towards God. And therefore he wondered why it was not possible for people following different religions to live peacefully with one another. He also wanted a way which would be common to all religions and would unite all people . ...He suggested a new religious path. This was based on the common truths of all religions and a few rules taken from all religions. (VII: 93).

Perhaps this idealisation of tolerance means that history should not overstate the examples of hatred and antagonism—particularly, the extraordinarily sensitive issues relating to religious conflict and division. No wonder then, while an entire chapter has been written on Akbar, not much has been written about Aurangzeb. The section on Aurangzeb gets only two paragraphs. And here too one sees a certain restraint: a tendency not to overemphasise his intolerance or his hostility to other religious communities. Instead, there is an implicit attempt at blaming those who revolted against him.

> Aurangzeb's troubles arose mainly out of the fact that people in many parts of his empire were in revolt. (VII: 104).

In fact, the text has exercised restraint when it comes to writing about those who revolted against Aurangzeb. For example, as one reads the section on Shivaji, one realises that there is no glorification or idealisation of someone who was generally perceived as a great warrior. Instead, Shivaji has been depicted as a 'clever' and 'ambitious' ruler who was determined to 'harass' the Mughals! Unlike what has been written about Ashoka and Aurangzeb, no positive adjective has been used to designate Shivaji as a hero or a patriot.

Perhaps the idea is to allow the child to see the culture of tolerance; to let the child see the Mughals as insiders and not as alien intruders. This becomes fairly clear when the Mughals are compared with the Portuguese. The Portuguese, the text suggests, never wanted to make India their home.

> They wanted to convert as many Indians as possible to the Roman Catholic form of Christianity. They were intolerant of the existing religions of India and did not hesitate to force people to become Christian. (VII: 83).

But then, the story of the Mughals, the child is told, was entirely different.

> A bigger difference was that the Mughals made India their home. They settled here and became a part of the Indian population. They were concerned with the welfare of India. Nor were the Mughals interested in converting large numbers of Indians to their religion. (VII: 83-84).

This is a clear manifestation of the history of *Hindu-Muslim Unity*. The chapter on the life of the people during the period of the Sultanate, therefore, gives great importance to the *sufi/bhakti tradition*. For example,

> The *sufis* did not try to convert Hindus to Islam but advised Hindus to be better Hindus by loving the one true god. (VII: 53).

Likewise,

> The *bhakti* teachers also taught that the relationship between man and god was based on love, and worshipping god with devotion was better than merely performing any number of religious ceremonies. They stressed the need for tolerance among men and religions. (VII: 54).

In a way, the child is asked to study and appreciate the history of Muin-ud-din Chishti, Baba Farid, Nizam-ud-din-Auliya, Chaitanya, Kabir, and Nanak; not that of Mahmud of Ghazni or Mohammad Ghori!

Privileging Congress Nationalism

This emphasis on tolerance, unity and composite culture, it should not be forgotten, is also a historical necessity. It is important for the consolidation of modern nationalism; for promoting the vision of a united India. Hence, the depiction of the history of modern India means two things: (a) critique of colonialism, and (b) distinguishing nationalism from communalism. Colonialism is exploitative, communalism is divisive, and nationalism is progressive; it is about unity and emancipation. As a result, the Class VIII text on the history of modern India tells us about the exploitative character of colonialism, and divergent protests/revolts against it. What is, however, interesting to note is the *meaning* it attaches to nationalism. It is secular because it does not privilege any particular religion. It is based on unity and composite culture. That is why, the text asserts very forcefully, the distinction between nationalism and communalism.

> While the nationalist movement stood for the reconstruction of Indian society on the basis of equality of all Indians, the communal parties were opposed even to social reforms. According to them, the interests of all Indians were not common. That is why, instead of fighting for independence,

> they concentrated their energies on getting concessions from the British government for their respective communities. ...The activities of the communal parties took a dangerous turn when they started saying that the Indian people were not one nation. They advanced the theory that there were two nations in India, the Hindus and the Muslims. While the nationalist movement united the people on the basis of their common aspirations to take India on the road to progress, the communal parties questioned the very basis of Indian nationhood. As you have read in your books on ancient and medieval India, the Indian people, through the centuries of their history, had developed a rich common culture. It was rich because of its variety. The Indian nation consisted of people who followed different religions, spoke different languages and practised different customs. This richness has been a source of pride to the Indian people and is something to be cherished. The communal parties tried to divide them. (VIII: 239-40).

The text also makes it clear that it is essentially the Congress that symbolises the spirit of nationalism. The Congress—with its nationalist zeal—has been separated from the communal organisation, like the Hindu Mahasabha and the Muslim League.

> From its inception, the Congress stood for the unity of the people, irrespective of religious and other differences. (VIII: 175).

> The Congress during the first 20 years of its existence had helped to unite the people for common national aims. In the following years, this unity was further strengthened and the aims became clearer. From a movement in which only small sections of the society were active, it became a movement in which millions participated with the aim of attaining freedom. (VIII: 180).

While the Congress was for national unity, the Muslim League, for example, propagated the two nation theory. The Muslims, who wanted the unity of the nation, as the text suggests, were with the Congress.

Mohammed Ali Jinnah, who in the early years of the 20th

> century had been a nationalist leader, later became one of the most prominent leaders of the Muslim League. The Muslim League claimed that it was the sole representative of the Muslims. The British Government agreed with this and, thus, promoted the Muslim League. ...The demand for a separate state was opposed by large sections of Muslims. In the struggle for independence, Muslims, along with the people belonging to other communities, had participated and, like others, they also had suffered from the repressive measures of the British government. They were in the Congress in large numbers. (VIII: 240).

All this implies that the Congress is being projected as the primary agent of the nationalist struggle. That is why, in the four bulky chapters on the nationalist struggle, there is a prominent presence of the Congress—its origin, its development through the different stages, and its maturation through Gandhi and Nehru. No doubt, the text does talk about the alternate voices—say, the voices of Chandra Sekhar Azad, Bhagat Singh and Subhash Chandra Bose. The text also reflects on the movements of the depressed classes—the movements led by leaders like E.V. Ramaswamy Naicker and B.R. Ambedkar. Yet, what is striking is the overwhelming presence of the Congress in the text—the Congress as the primary agent, or Gandhi as the ultimate authority. Therefore, while writing about Ambedkar—and Ambedkar does not even get a full paragraph—the text does not forget to talk about 'the great importance which Gandhiji attached to the eradication of the evil of untouchability' (VIII: 242). Not just that; Gandhi's integrationist view is preferred to the politics centred primarily on caste identity.

> In 1932, the British government announced separate electorates for the so-called untouchable castes, like they had done in the case of Muslims and Sikhs. The nationalist leaders opposed this as they suspected that this was a part of the British policy of 'divide and rule.' Gandhiji, who was in jail at that time, went on fast unto death against this decision. He said, 'what I want, and what I am living for, and what I should delight in dying for, is the eradication of untouchability, root and branch.'

> Separate electorates for Harijans, he thought, would harm the cause of reform. Finally, an agreement was reached by which the decision to introduce separate electorates was withdrawn. At the same time, it was ensured that the people of the so-called untouchable castes would get adequate representation. (VIII: 242-43).

The point we are trying to make is that the text seeks to take Congress nationalism for granted. It does not problematise it. Furthermore, the nationalist movement has been shown in a positive light. The text highlights its 'secular' character, its 'socialist' objectives, its tolerant/'internationalist' outlook.

• • •

A careful look at the NCERT history texts, therefore, suggests the following:

1. The needs of the present shape our ways of looking at history. And it seems that modern nationalist pursuits—i.e. creating secular/united India—did shape the writing and interpretation of history.
2. The trauma of partition, the virus of communalism, the fear of religious fundamentalism—these anxieties did explain the priorities/preferences/biases in historical writing.
3. No wonder then, there is an attempt to resist the temptation of glorifying the Hindu past (the fear is that it might help the assertion of Hindu fundamentalism); there is a conscious effort to assert primarily the stories of Hindu-Muslim tolerance (the anxiety is that the history of intolerance might prove to be an obstacle to the growth of nationalist unity); there is an identification and celebration of the ideals of tolerance (the hope is that these ideals would help us strengthen the unity of the nation).

   In fact, this official nationalist agenda—a secular mission to rewrite the history of India—is manifest in the presidential address to the Indian History Congress of 1964.

> We must get to the spirit of the movement and the soul of India with an approach that will help surmount the danger of communal, regional, linguistic and class hatreds that beset history writing. History has a mission and obligation to lead humanity to a higher ideal and nobler future... The historian cannot shirk this responsibility by burying his head in the false dogma of objectivity. History must not call to memory ghastly aberrations of human nature, of dastardly crimes, of divisions and conflicts, of degeneration and decay but of the higher values of life, of traditions of culture and the nobler deeds of sacrifice and devotion to the service of humanity. The facts of Indian history and the process of its march have to be judged by the criterion of progress towards liberty, morality and opportunities for self-expression... The reason for omission is that such things bring in unhealthy trends which militate against the course of national solidarity or international peace. (Quoted in Sen 1973: xxii).

4. It is this urge to marginalise the voices of religious fundamentalism or communalism that leads to the projection of nationalism—as a broadly consensual experience. Not much has been written about the way the Congress nationalism as projected and celebrated in the text—has been questioned, interrogated and contested. 'Progressive' nationalism—with its 'secular'/'socialist' ambitions—has been set apart from all 'divisive' forces!

This celebration of Congress nationalism is not surprising, because if we look at this historiography closely, we can understand its ideological inclination. Bipan Chandra—a distinguished exponent of this kind of historiography—has expressed it without any ambiguity:

> In my view, the Congress was the leader of the popular anti-imperialist movement of the Indian people; and its activities in the main constituted this movement . ...Despite its many weaknesses, the Congress became, and remained until independence, the symbol as well as the chief vehicle and

> organiser—and representative—of the anti-imperialist or national liberation struggle. The movement led by the Congress was, with all its positive and negative features, the actual, historically existing anti-imperialist movement of the Indian people. It was in this movement that the historical energies and genius of the Indian people were incorporated, as is the case with any genuine mass movement. (Chandra 1988: 1-2).

Celebration of the State as an Agent of Development

These nationalist objectives become clearer when we look at the NCERT civics texts—the texts that, we would say, seek to teach the child about 'secular'/'socialist'/'democratic' intentions of the nation-state.

There are three texts. The text for Class VI is written by D.S. Muley and A.C. Sharma (Muley and Sharma 1987). Its primary objective, it seems, is to teach the child about rural development—the kind of transformation that Indian villages are undergoing because of community development programmes and panchayati raj institutions. It also makes the child familiar with the functions of municipalities and district administration. The text for Class VII is written by D.S. Muley, A.C. Sharma, and Supta Das (1988). Its central focus is on the Indian constitution—its ideals, its components: fundamental rights, duties and directive principles, the functioning of the Parliament, the judiciary and the executive. The text for Class VIII, written by D.S. Muley, Supta Das, Ramesh Chandra and Manju Rani (1989), seeks to familiarise the learner with the problems confronting India. It tells the learner about the problems related to casteism and communalism; about population growth, beggary, and drug addiction. And it stresses the need for national integration and democratisation of the larger society.

These three texts, as is obvious, carry loads of information. But then, there is a way of presenting information. Ideologies, values, preferences and choices—as we have stressed—are often mixed up with facts. As we look at these texts, we find that there are three primary concerns/preferences/desires that have shaped these writings.

State as an Emancipator

What comes through clearly in these texts is a *paternalistic* attitude. In other words, a hierarchy; active agents working on behalf of the passive objects waiting to be 'developed' and 'emancipated'! The former are either, (a) the modern state (which is projected as secular, progressive and socialist), or (b) enlightened urban upper caste/class people. They act. They work. And 'ignorant'/'superstitious' villagers or oppressed people are supposed to learn the lessons of emancipation from them.

Let us begin with Chapters 2 and 3 of the Class VI text. In these chapters, the child learns about the 'backwardness of the villages: This 'backwardness' is seen as an obstacle to modernity and progress. Let us take a look at this 'backwardness'; the way it has been described here in clear/ unambiguous terms.

> The main problems of our villages have been poverty, illiteracy, diseases and superstitions. These have proved to be the main obstacles to their development (VI: 6-7)
>
> Various social evils, e.g. dowry and extravagance, add to the difficulties of the rural people. They spend a large amount of money on occasions like marriages, births and deaths and so many peasants have become bankrupt because they have to borrow large sums of money (VI: 12).
>
> The rural society remains backward because of illiteracy and ignorance. Due to ignorance some people oppose good programmes such as family planning. Nutritious food and good education cannot be given to the children if their number is large in a family. Many villagers consider diseases to be the curse of gods and goddesses and try to get them cured by village witch-doctors (VI: 12).

What the child sees here is an image of a *dark village* refusing to alter its ways; a superstitious/illiterate villager unable to appreciate the gains of development. But then, there is an 'emancipator'—a modern/post-colonial state—which is determined to deliver the goods and change the face of the villages. The state with its Five Year Plans and Community Development Programmes—is making change possible.

> The aim of these plans was to bring about an all-round development of these villages. In these plans, provisions have been made for the health care of villagers; making drinking water available for them; increasing the yield of the fields; making arrangements for irrigation, supplying good quality seeds, manures and tools, removing illiteracy by opening schools; establishing hospitals, post offices and for developing the means of transportation. (VI: 7).

What is noticeable here is the positive agency attached to the state. The noble intentions of the state have been taken for granted. The only problem, as the child learns from the text, is the inertia of our rural population. It is their illiteracy and backwardness that causes obstacles. At times, they oppose family planning; they fail to take advantage of child care programmes organised by the Primary Health Centres; they do not like to send their daughters to school.

In other words, the state—as the enlightened tutor—is always right; the problem lies with the backwardness of the villagers. That is why, there can not be any dialogue between the state and the villagers. They do not choose, create and organise their own development. Instead, the state always advises them, trains them. This paternalistic attitude can be seen clearly in the following text:

> The Village Level Worker or the Gram Sewak holds the key position in the village development programme. He tells the villagers how to improve agriculture, how to utilize manures properly, and how to identify improved seeds. He advises them on the methods of keeping their cattle healthy. He also advises them on questions related to their health. (VI: 14).

The message is clear: there is nothing in the life-history of the villager that can be considered desirable or important.

He has nothing to offer. His passive/empty/illiterate mind has to be filled up by the enlightened tutor—the state, and its agents. Development, in other words, is a gift from outside; it is not a creation of collective struggle and endeavour.

This paternalistic attitude can also be seen in the way the social/cultural reform has been depicted. For example, in the battle against casteism/untouchability, it is primarily the story of forward caste reformers that has been emphasised. Take Chapters 4 and 5 from the class VII text. While the text emphasises the role of Gandhi in his fight against untouchability, it remains silent about the movement that emerged from within: how the oppressed castes themselves gained their agency, overcame their silence and fought the caste system. Nothing has been written about, say, Jotiba Phule and Ambedkar.

Constitution as the Truth

There is also a consensual view of the socio-political reality. We see the manifestation of this consensus in the projection of the state as the emancipator. There is no critique of the state, its policies or endeavours. That explains why so much importance is given to *cooperation* and why a good citizen has been described as a *disciplined* one following the prevailing rules and regulations.

> ...For the protection and progress of human life many institutions are needed. Institutions like the family, the school, the local bodies, the central and the state governments, all work for the improvement of civic life. ...It becomes our duty to have faith in these institutions. For this, discipline is the most essential factor. In our personal life as well as in civic life we should observe discipline. ...Discipline means strict observance of rules and duties. ...It is through discipline alone that we can give our maximum cooperation to these institutions. (VI: 50-51).

Hence, it is important to understand that the institutions have been taken for granted. The assumption is that there is absolute consensus on the validity and functioning of these institutions. The problem, if there is any, arises mainly because there are people who are not disciplined enough. As a result, the possibility and potency of protest/ rebellion has not been explored. Instead, there is a tendency to generalise and negate the language of protest as irresponsible behaviour.

> Why do some people indulge in the destruction of public property? There can be various answers to this question. Some people steal national property for their selfish interests. Some derive peculiar pleasure in acts of destruction because of their personal frustration. Some people have been found indulging in acts of violence for securing the acceptance of their demands. Factory workers, office employees, school and college students organise movements and strikes for the acceptance of their demands. During such movements they are led away by their emotions and thus damage the public property. (VI: 47).

It is to be noted that no attempt has been made to understand the positive meaning of protest, how people's movements can alter the *status quo* and create a better society. The text fails to create meaningful space that can enable the child to see that the act of rebellion, far from being destructive, can be profoundly creative and constructive. It does not want the child to know the positive meaning of protest, because its primary presupposition is the consensual view of the socio-political reality. As a result, it thinks that protest is inherently pathological. An ideal citizen is essentially a *good citizen.*

> A good citizen accepts responsibilities and obeys the laws of the land . ...He knows that the interests of the nation are much more important than his own (VII: 48).

Hence, the assumption: the laws of the land are perfect and the Constitution represents the collective will of the nation.

We see the celebration, idealisation and glorification of the Constitution. To begin with, the learner is told about the three noble objectives of our Constitution: democracy, secularism, and socialism. However, what is important to note is that not much effort has been made to enable the child to see the gap between the ideal and the real, and the resultant conflict in society. Instead, the text seeks to convey the message that the state is essentially sincere in implementing these noble ideals. Take, for instance, the chapter on Fundamental Rights (Chapter 4, VII). It informs the child of the right to equality, the right to freedom, the right against exploitation, the right to freedom of religion, cultural and educational rights and the right to Constitutional remedies. But the text largely remains silent on the violation of these rights. Well, as an exercise, the text gives a problem to the child:

> Give two examples of discrimination against weaker sections of society which you have noticed in your locality.

Apart from this particular example, there is not much in the chapter that can be said to be critical in spirit; that can reflect on the violation of these rights, and speak of conflict, domination and violence in our society. Perhaps this implicit tendency to hide the element of conflict means that the state is to be seen primarily as a responsible agent committed to the welfare of the people. The genuineness of the state is not questioned even when it speaks of the Directive Principles (free and compulsory education for all children up to the age of 14 years, adequate conditions of work, assuring a decent standard of life to all the citizens of India). The child is expected to see how 'eager' our governments are to fulfil the Directive Principles!

Development as Salvation

True, there are instances when one gets a glimpse of the reality, especially when it is argued that without a social democracy—i.e. real equality in the social sphere—political democracy would remain a myth. In other words, the constitutional guarantee alone is not sufficient; what is important is an active intervention in the social sphere. As a result, instead of writing in a consensual tone, the text makes the child think:

> Do all people in our country really enjoy freedom? Our society is unfortunately divided between various castes. Many of our people are considered to be belonging to the so-called lower castes. People belonging to these castes are generally poor and illiterate. They are exploited by other sections of our society. They are discriminated against in many respects. It is true that our Constitution and Government have made many laws to end this discrimination. Have we been able to abolish all discrimination in reality? Unless we are able to provide equal opportunities to all sections of society, we will not be able to achieve true democracy. True democracy means that every individual has freedom and equal rights. It also means that we have such conditions in the society that all sections are able to enjoy this freedom equally. This is social democracy. If we do not have social democracy, political democracy alone will not be successful in taking the country on the road to progress and prosperity. (VIII: 6).

Likewise, this critique can be seen in the way the text speaks of the prevalent economic inequality. For example, while analysing the problem of unemployment, it hints at the flaws in the existing pattern of development (how, excessive use of machines in industry and agriculture result in surplus labour). It also talks about price rise and how it intensifies economic inequality. Moreover, as we see in Chapter 8 (VIII), the text seeks to engage the child in a critical enquiry. Instead of remaining contented with the stories of progress, the child —as some of the exercises suggest is expected to reflect on conflict and inequality. Here are the examples:

> Have you noticed any person or family living below the poverty line in your neighbourhood? Find out the conditions in which that person or family lives. Discuss this in your class. (VIII: 50).

or

> Find out from your teacher the prices of various commodities e.g. notebooks, textbooks, pencils, vegetables, etc., twenty years ago. Compare them with the prices of today. (VIII: 52).

It is also possible to see gender sensitivity in the text. For example, Chapter 6 (VIII) talks about the position of women in our society, and the need for equality between the sexes. It informs the child of the divergent 'progressive' measures adopted by the state to improve the condition of women. However, it does not fail to point out:

> In spite of the constitutional guarantees, enactments of so many laws, efforts of governmental or voluntary agencies, the status of a woman in India is definitely not at par with that of a man. Women are still neglected and kept behind men in social, political, economic and educational spheres. (VIII: 33).

In fact, the text, through different examples, seeks to stir the child's imagination and encourages him/her to visualise a new society in which 'men and women will be accorded equal treatment in the real sense' (VIII: 34).

Likewise, the chapter focuses on other major problems —beggary, drug addiction, dowry, and communalism. As we have already said, here is an attempt to arouse the critical consciousness of the child, to make him/her see the darker side of India, and inspire him/her to create a new social order.

Yet, as we would argue, this criticality is partial. Essentially, the text gives its consent to the master narrative of 'development' and 'progress.' Hence, it speaks of agricultural modernisation; of how, with the help of the modern implements—tractor, trolly, thresher and sowing machine—'we have mechanised our agriculture and introduced intensive cultivation' (VIII: 56). It also informs us why 'our farmers have to be educated about the use of scientific method in agriculture' (VIII: 57).

It is this fascination with techno-economic development that can be seen in the discussion on India's magnificent progress in industrial production. Besides, for promoting industrialisation, the text glorifies the consumption-oriented living.

> Due to industrial growth a number of consumer goods have come in the market. Transistors, TV sets, watches, electronic gadgets, soaps, detergents, etc, are being widely used by the Indian people today. This has helped in improving the standard of living of the people. (VIII: 61).

The point that we are trying to make here is that 'modernity' or 'development' has been depicted as inherently progressive and desirable. The text refuses to problematise modernity. Modernity need not necessarily be beneficial to all sections of society. For example, as Krishna Kumar has noted, agricultural modernisation has benefited primarily the rich farmers and big landowners; it has also undermined the Gandhian scheme of 'basic education' which, according to him, was more sensitive to the needs of the subaltern section of Indian society (Kumar 1998: 79-98). Likewise, industrial development—or the form of living that it glorifies—has got its negative points. Apart from its elitist bias, it leads to greed, consumerism and environmental disaster. As Jeremy Seabrook has written with great sensitivity:

> All over the world, more and more people are being disadvantaged by a version of development, which, even as it creates wealth, leaves them with a sense of loss and impoverishment. ...Among the people marginalised in this way are many indigenous communities; the inhabitants of forests and uplands, evicted by loggers and mining companies; those forced from ancestral lands, who have no choice but to live in squalid city slums. There, they die of grief for their defunct way of life, or they destroy themselves with the destructive consolations of alcohol and drugs, which industrial society offers them for their loss. Nomads, pastoralists, fishing communities, those ousted from subsistence or self-reliant farming, are seen as obstacles to development, as indeed are the urban poor themselves. ...Upheaval, displacement and endless moving on are part and parcel of processes which have at their heart the subversion of self-reliance, the undermining of sufficiency, the destruction of satisfactions, which are found outside an expanding global marketplace. (Seabrook 1993: 7-8).

No effort has been made to make the child aware of the adverse outcome of industrial development. In other words, the text speaks the language of those for whom development is beneficial. Shalini Advani has argued brilliantly that the child reading these texts fails to see the costs of modernity —social, economic and ecological. In the process, textbooks blind the middle class students to whom they address themselves. They know nothing of the price of development —the dispossessed peasants, the children who labour in factories and the poor who have no access to the open markets thrown open to international capital. In other words, Advani problematises the projection of urban industrialism as a virtue in school texts (Advani 1996).

• • •

It is, therefore, clear that the primary objective of the NCERT civics texts is to inform the child about modern India's 'nationalist' aspirations and achievements: how a 'secular' nation state with its 'progressive' Constitution is creating a new India—modern, industrially developed and egalitarian. In other words, the NCERT texts—civics as well as history—support the ideology of the modern nation state. It is this official ideology of nationalism that becomes an important educational agenda. In fact, it can be said that the NCERT endeavour is closely related to what we have already discussed in Chapter 1: the educational agenda of the post-colonial state—an agenda that gave great importance to modernity, secularism, development and national unity. In a way, the NCERT project was a child of the Nehruvian vision of nation-making and modernity. Although, with the passage of time, the Nehruvian vision has experienced multiple challenges, the NCERT project, as Arjun Dev once told me, remains committed to that grand vision.[7]

It is this relationship between knowledge and politics that helps us demystify the 'objectivity' of school texts and enables us to realise that education is a field of conflict, and that there may be a scope for alternate educational ventures.

II
India Reinterpreted: Meaning of EklavyaTexts

The official language of nationalism or, say, the Nehruvian brand of modernity—need not necessarily be interpreted as 'real' and 'true' by all. To the victims of history, that is, the marginalised people, tribes and subaltern castes, India need not necessarily mean a 'secular'/'progressive'/'united' nation. On the contrary, it may be perceived by them as a conflict-ridden, exploitative, divisive and unequal society. Moreover, their vision of a good society need not necessarily be the same as that of, say, the urban, English educated 'nationalists.' Ranjit Guha, for instance, has spoken of the 'failure of the Indian bourgeoisie to speak for the nation' (Guha 1982: 5). For Guha, the poverty of 'bourgeois/ nationalist' historiography is obvious; it gives no space to the 'autonomous domain' of the 'politics of people'; it fails to even acknowledge, leave alone interpret, the contribution made by the people on their own, that is, independent of the elite, to the making and development of this nationalism (Ibid: 3). It is, therefore, important to see whether there are alternative texts that portray an altogether different perception of India—a perception that is sensitive to the experiential knowledge of the subaltern masses. It is in this context that a critical reading of the *Eklavya* texts becomes relevant, because *Eklavya*[8]—a voluntary organisation based in Madhya Pradesh—seeks to intervene in the domain of education. What distinguishes *Eklavya* is its departure from the dominant/mainstream pattern of education, its active involvement with the marginalised and the subaltern masses, its urge to alter the curriculum, and make knowledge accountable and meaningful to the experiential reality of the oppressed.

History as an Assertion of Subalternity

To begin with, we would look at the *Eklavya* history texts for Classes VI, VII and VIII—the texts which have been written in Hindi by a team of scholars, not specific authors.[9] What strikes one immediately is the style of writing. Unlike what one sees in the NCERT texts, it is written in a child-centred language; its dialogic form makes the texts more personal and arouses the imagination of the child. History, as a result, does not become a burden for the child; nor does it remain merely a chronicle of facts and events. Instead, it is presented in the form of *narratives*—narratives that take into account the child's (or the learner's) experiences and enable him/her to see history as the history of the people. In fact, *Eklavya* has described its agenda as follows:

> The textbooks of this programme seek to bring children close to experiencing the life and circumstances of people, including those in other times and places, by creating stories and case studies. They give space to the realistic experiences of people from all walks of life, viz. farmers, labourers, artisans, tribals, traders, rulers, etc. (Eklavya 1999).

Indeed, a striking feature of these texts is that *social history*—the history of the subalterns—has acquired great importance. Perhaps it can be said that the texts have been written from the perspective of the subaltern child. In a way, it is a significant departure from the mainstream trend. It invites the marginalised, and tells them that school knowledge need not be alienating; it may prove to be meaningful to their experiences. True, the texts do contain the important events of history—the Indus Valley Civilisation, the arrival of the Aryans, the Hindu Kingdoms, the challenge of Buddhism, the story of the Emperor Ashoka, the Gupta Empire, the arrival of Islam, the story of the Mughals, the colonial invasion and the freedom struggle. Yet, as we have already indicated, beneath these facts or events lies the history of common people.[10] An attempt has been made to sensitise the child, to awaken his/her critical consciousness. The meaning of this critical consciousness becomes clearer if we understand the following:

Debunking Grand Ideals: Seeing Conflict in History

There is no valorisation of the Aryan civilisation; its cultural practices, its religion, or the epics. Instead, the child is invited to see the reality of the social conflict—how the Aryans, to begin with, were engaged in a conflict-ridden relationship with the non-Aryans. It is also mentioned how the Aryans—primarily because of their material interests—often quarrelled among themselves. War or violence, as a result, was a primary feature of the Aryan culture. In fact, as mentioned in Chapter 5 (VI), beneath the origin of the Rig Vedic hymns (or prayer to, say, *Indra)* lay the desire to be victorious in war, acquire wealth and become prosperous!

The hierarchy in the Aryan civilisation becomes clear in the text. The child gets to know that not everybody was equal, that there was a dividing line between the king and the householder, the householder and the servant. The child also gets to know how the king used to extort wealth (in the form of cows, crops, etc.) from ordinary householders. The text suggests that this hierarchical/oppressive order was legitimised by the caste system. Each caste was assigned its specific role, its *swadharma.* The message that the text seeks to convey is that the caste system was designed to serve the interests of the priest and the king; it was an attempt to restrain revolt, and to allow the ruling order to perpetuate its dominance (Chapter 6,Vl).

In fact, the story of this alliance becomes clear when one looks at Chapter 3 (VII)—the chapter that deals with small kingdoms and their rapid growth in India from 400 AD to 1200 AD. These smaller kings—essentially, the rich people in specific regions—needed legitimacy. And, as the chapter suggests, the Brahmins helped them accomplish this hegemonic goal. They came forward, certified that the kings had a rich, ancestral heritage and made people believe that these kings were destined to rule. No doubt, the Brahmins were duly rewarded!

This critique comes into sharp focus when the text narrates the miserable conditions in which the poor people lived. In this context, it would not be inappropriate to recall a revealing example through which the text seeks to sensitise the child. This is the story of an upper caste/rich woman (Videhika) and her maid-servant (Kali) (Chapter 8). For a long time, Kali used to think that Videhika was a soft, kind, gentle lady. But then, she felt that she must verify whether Videhika was really so good. So, one day, she got up late. Videhika was angry. The next day, Kali got up late again. This time, Videhika was intolerant and rebuked her. Kali was, however, determined to know Videhika's real self. So, once again she got up late. And this time, Videhika—the soft, kind, gentle, rich upper caste woman revealed her true self; she became terribly violent and began to beat up Kali with an iron rod. Indeed, a story of this kind—a significant experiment with the form of history writing—debunks the greatness of the Aryan civilisation. It sees history from the perspective of the subaltern masses. In our 'golden' past it sees hierarchy, exploitation, violence, conflict, and war!

This intense criticality can be seen even when the text deals with an 'ideal' character like Akbar. A look at Chapter 1 (VII) suggests that Akbar was presented primarily as an Emperor who was clear about his hegemonic interests, who knew that India could not be ruled merely by force. In other words, his 'tolerant nature' (the way Akbar was often idealised in history) was not really an indication of his kind heart. Instead, all that he did—his alliance with the Rajputs, his marriage with a Hindu woman, and his dialogue with different religions—in fact, everything that he did, the text suggests, was designed to win the hearts of the Hindus so that he could rule. Here, one sees an attempt to project Akbar as a ruler with a perfect sense of diplomacy—not necessarily with a pious/idealist soul.

Likewise, because of the secular interpretation of history, the text refuses to see Aurangzeb as merely a 'Muslim' ruler. In fact, it argues that the reason for Aurangzeb's 'anti-Hindu' policy was not religious. At a time when, because of innumerable revolts, his empire was in turmoil, he needed the cooperation of the Muslim clergy in order to consolidate his position. Moreover, Aurangzeb, the text elaborates, was not intrinsically anti-Hindu, because, as the examples of Jai Singh and Jaswant Singh suggest, he was closely associated with the Rajputs. Many Hindus occupied important positions in Aurangzeb's empire. In other words, the message that the text seeks to convey is that it is essentially politics—or secular/

material interest that should be seen as the governing principle for evaluating the role of historical figures like Akbar and Aurangzeb.

In addition, in its characteristic style, the text carries a chapter (Chapter 3,VIII) on the state of rural life during the Mughal period. It shows how the peasants were often tortured/harassed, and taxes were forcefully collected from them. It also depicts the story of revolt—how this oppressive policy led to unrest, and eventually the peasants began to revolt against the Mughal Empire.

As a matter of fact, it is this subaltern history that distinguishes the *Eklavya* texts. No wonder, instead of celebrating the 'ideals' of kings/emperors, the texts depict the history of ordinary people—the phenomenology of their everyday existence. Look at, for instance, the projection of *Shivaji*—a character that, for, many, was an embodiment of intense patriotism and idealism. The text (Chapter 4, VIII), no doubt, speaks of Shivaji's courage, his warrior instinct, his determined will not to bow down before Aurangzeb. Yet, what is significant is that it also reminds the child of the price the poor peasants—had to pay to support the establishment of Shivaji. In fact, as the text mentions, Shivaji needed sufficient wealth to retain his huge army. This led him to demand taxes from poor peasants not just from his own kingdom, but also from those who belonged to other kingdoms. And the peasants were harassed, tortured, if they failed to pay the taxes.

Looking Beyond the Congress: Giving Agency to the Subaltern Masses

As is obvious, the history of the freedom struggle acquires a new meaning in the *Eklavya* texts. For instance, here we see not just the history of the elite—the way the English-educated Indian middle class led by the Congress engaged in the nationalist struggle for liberation. Instead, due importance is given to the history of the subaltern people—the way the tribals, peasants and workers contributed to the freedom struggle. In fact, there are three long chapters on this subaltern history (Class VIII), while only one chapter covers the role of the middle class, or the Congress in the freedom movement. What is really important to note here is that the text aims to make the child aware of the fact that the subalterns were not just silent masses; that they had their own historical agency; they participated in the struggle and broadened the meaning of freedom. For them, freedom meant not just the freedom from the British rule, it also meant freedom from the enemies within: the landlords, upper caste oppressors and the emergent industrialists.

Not surprisingly, a chapter on *New Thinking and Social Reform* (Chapter 7) gives importance to this emancipatory consciousness. It explains to the child the meaning of new thinking in the endeavours of Rammohan, Pandita Rambai Saraswati and Jotiba Phule. It talks about how Rammohun attacked Hindu superstitions and orthodox religious practices, defeated conservative priests and scholars (like Tarklankar), and eventually succeeded in forcing the British Government to ban *Sati*. This gender-sensitivity can also be seen in the projection of Pandita Rambai—a character that the text depicts with great zeal and enthusiasm. Rambai, the text states, could overcome the restrictions associated with being a woman; she chose her own life-project and inspired the Indian women to stand for their own rights. Another example of this emancipatory ideal was Jotiba Phule—the way he fought Brahminism, organised the subaltern castes, started educational institutions for them, and inspired them to overcome their silence and participate in the process of creating an egalitarian society.

This involvement with the subaltern sensitivity can also be seen in Chapter 8 when the text narrates the historic role the Indian peasants played in the freedom struggle. For example, it explains the significance of the peasant revolt of Bardauli in 1926. It tells the child that the peasants were active participants in the freedom struggle. They fought against the exploitative/anti-peasant policy of the British Government.

They organised themselves, and with their determined will forced the British Government to rethink its earlier policy. Likewise, the text gives an account of the Telengana movement—of how, in 1946-47, the peasants of the Telengana district of Andhra Pradesh, under the leadership of the Communist Party became aware of their legitimate rights, organised themselves and revolted against the landlords. Similarly, Chapter 9 talks about how the tribals, under the British rule, began to lose their rights in the forests. Hence, it is obvious that if a tribal child reads the chapter, he would get the message: his ancestors, far from being passive, were active agents of history, and played an important role in the struggle for liberation. The chapter talks about tribal revolts against the British rule, and makes it clear that a heroic figure like *Birsa Munda* deserves an important place in history. Moreover, Chapter 10 is equally vocal in narrating the experiences of the working class, their struggle and revolt.

Yes, after this sharp focus on the subaltern history, the text narrates the role of the middle class; the mainstream history of the nationalist struggle led by Gandhi (Chapter 12). The child learns about Gandhi's tremendous contribution to the freedom struggle. What is interesting, however, is that the text, with its characteristic style, raises critical questions, and inspires the child to question even the Mahatma's greatness. For example, it draws attention to the fact that Gandhi was not particularly sympathetic to people's revolt against the internal enemies—Indian landlords, industrialists, etc. Gandhi, as a result, could not appreciate the necessity of violence in people's struggle. This led Gandhi to interfere, time and again, in these resistances and to curb them. In other words, the child is asked to take note of the contradictions in the doctrine of truth that Gandhi considered so important.

Narratives of Struggle and Conflict

This intimacy with the subaltern experience can also be seen in the *Civics texts*. What is significant is that the people's experiences/voices have been given adequate representation in these texts. As a result, instead of just talking about the state or the government or constitutional norms, these texts succeed in narrating the contemporary socio-political life through the eyes of the subaltern masses.

Primacy of Social Reality

It is, of course, true that the civics texts, because of their very nature, deal with a wide range of issues: from the village panchayat to district administration; from agrarian transformation to industrial policy; from the Indian Constitution to divergent state-sponsored endeavours for the alleviation of poverty. Yet, never do these texts burden the child with information. In keeping with this trend, the socio-political knowledge has not been projected as hard data; as something disembodied, cold and impersonal. Instead, as we have already mentioned, an attempt has been made to sensitise the child through narratives —narratives born of people's struggle and aspirations; their experiences with the state, the Constitution and the government projects.

Take, for instance, the opening chapter of the text for Class VI. Far from creating a hierarchy between the town and the village ('developed' town versus 'backward' village), it builds on their inter-connectedness. It is a story of mutual dependence. In other words, the rural population, primarily because of its agricultural produce, contributes to the life of the city, while on the other hand, it depends on urban centres for its requirement of industrial goods. The focus on this inter-dependence, we wish to point out, rescues the rural life from becoming obscure. For a rural child, this chapter, as a result, becomes meaningful; it assures his/her presence in the country's social affairs.

In fact, the visible presence of rural life is a striking feature of this exercise. It can be seen quite clearly—in the chapter on the village panchayat (Chapter 3, VI)—how the panchayat functions, its difficulties, and contradictions. As a matter of fact, the presentation of real/concrete life situations in rural

India can be seen yet again in Chapter 5. It tells the child about the reality of hierarchy/stratification in Indian villages. The child is told that the Indian peasantry is not a homogeneous group; that the village society does not constitute a cohesive community. Instead, there are rich peasants, middle peasants, small peasants and landless peasants. Their life-situations, experiences and interests differ. Whereas rich peasants—with a lot of land, tractors, fertilisers and improved seeds—symbolise power and wealth, small or landless peasants continue to live with terrible survival anxiety.

In a way, divergent interests and the resultant social conflict become an important component of contemporary existence. What is revealing is that no attempt has been made to hide this reality from the child. The texts, as a result, are simple and bold; they depict how people experience conflict, violence and exploitation. For example, Chapter 5, on municipalities, begins with the scarcity of water in the town. As the chapter progresses, the conflict between common people and 'elected' members of the municipalities becomes obvious. The common people experience the scarcity of water, whereas the leaders remain somewhat distant and indifferent.

Likewise, Chapter 7 (VII) on bidi workers is about the way these workers are exploited, and the miserable conditions in which they have to work. This is yet another example of the prevalent social reality, its fragmentation, division, conflict and exploitation. No wonder, even the chapter on State Government (Chapter 11), while dealing with elections, narrates the same story. Instead of depicting elections as modern rituals for democratic governance, it, in fact, reveals the reality of manipulation: rigging, false voting and booth capturing!

Assertion of Criticality

It should, however, be recalled that the *Eklavya* texts are not indifferent to the nationalist aspirations: the aspirations embodied in the Constitution. They seek to make the child aware of the fundamental principles of the Constitution and also of India's agrarian/industrial policies as well as different social welfare schemes undertaken by the state. But then, the striking feature of these texts is that an attempt has been made to outline the problems associated with these aspirations and objectives. In other words, in the context of the prevalent social reality—with its divisions/hierarchy/ inequality—the 'ideals' have been examined and questioned. No wonder, the child is perpetually reminded of the possible conflict between the ideal and the real; between constitutional provisions and actual social practices.

For example, while discussing the Fundamental Rights in the Constitution, the text (Chapter 5, VIII) also asserts how these rights are often violated; how, because of their economic exploitation, the oppressed are often deprived of their basic rights. Let us reflect on one of the illustrations of this violation of rights. In 1982, during the Asian Games, a large number of workers from Bihar, Madhya Pradesh and UP were brought to Delhi for construction work. They were not given their due wages and were exploited. When a group of human rights activists appealed to the Supreme Court, the Court gave a positive verdict, and accepted that the rights of the workers were being denied. In fact, an example of this kind —a real life incident—gives a new meaning to the text. The Constitution is not seen as something sacred/unproblematic. Instead, it is seen from the perspective of the common man.

It is true that the texts reflect a positive orientation to modernity or techno-scientific development. This becomes clear in Chapter 7 on the agrarian policy and Chapter 8 on industrial development. Chapter 7 speaks of the Green Revolution, the increasing rate of agrarian production and the steps taken by the government to modernise India's agriculture. Yet, it should not be forgotten that, instead of looking at the Green Revolution from a purely economistic/ technical point of view, the text reflects on the inherent contradictions implicit in agricultural modernisation. The child is made aware of the fact that the Green Revolution has also increased the already existing socio-economic differences in the society. For example, the Revolution did not have much of an impact on small and middle peasantry. Unlike the rich peasantry, they could not have complete control over the technologies that made the Revolution possible.

Likewise, Chapter 8 has depicted the story of industrial development and how it has failed to resolve the problem of unemployment. As a matter of fact, this critical consciousness is obvious in Chapter 9—the chapter that discusses the different poverty alleviation programmes undertaken by the government. To begin with, it speaks of the incompleteness of the land-reform scheme: how, for example, the lands distributed to Harijans and landless peasants in Bihar caused social unrest; how big landlords eventually killed 122 Harijans for possessing the lands they had lost. In other words, the power of the big landlords and the state's unwillingness to show firmness over the issue of land reform/ distribution have made it difficult for Harijans and landless peasants to improve their life-situations. Similarly, while talking about the Community Development Programme, the text reveals how, at many places, the scheme has been utilised by the rich and not by those who need it, that is, the Harijans, tribals, landless peasants, etc.

III
Towards an Emancipatory Pedagogy

As a careful look at the NCERT and Eklavya texts suggests, the meaning of what we call 'knowledge' is not something constant and eternal; it varies and keeps changing. Moreover, these multiple meanings have to be related to the diverse ideologies/concerns that provide the background for writing these texts. As we have seen, it is primarily the ideology of nationalism (India as a modern/united/secular nation) that explains the content of the NCERT texts. This means that the state has been viewed as the primary agent of social transformation. It also implies that there is a broadly positive/ consensual orientation to the culture of the nation: its unity, its Constitution, its aspirations and its leadership. Perhaps it would not be wrong to say that these texts reaffirm the grand Nehruvian optimism or the agenda that manifested itself in different education commission recommendations. It is possible to see a meaningful relationship between the 'official' dream of the post-colonial Indian state, and the knowledge of India that the NCERT texts popularise. But then, as any intelligent student of contemporary Indian society knows, the grand Nehruvian consensus is in crisis today (for instance, see Pathak 1998: 64-71). As the conflicts and contradictions have become the order of the day, and the hitherto silent sections of society have begun to assert themselves, we are witnessing a critique of the official ideology of nationalism, and subsequently a desire for change. Perhaps the Eklavya texts have to be given a serious thought in this quest for alternatives. No wonder, here we see the experiences of the subaltern masses—the stories of their exploitation and misery, their conflicting relationship with the dominant sections of society. Whereas the NCERT texts take the spirit of the nation state for granted, the Eklavya textbooks tend to problematise it. Here we see a shift of focus from nation to people, from state to the masses, from consensus to conflict, from the narrative of progress to real life-situations of exploitation. As a matter of fact, we realise how ideology shapes the content of school knowledge. This seems to be the reason why different governments—from the Left Front in West Bengal to the BJP led government in Uttar Pradesh—take special interest in the rewriting of school texts, and altering the structure of knowledge. However, our main concern here is to respond to a series of critical issues that a comparative study of the NCERT and Eklavya texts have led us to.

Multiple Perspectives and Relativism

If the meaning of knowledge changes to suit the context, does it then mean that there is no escape from *relativism*? And if we accept relativism, the authenticity of knowledge—it may be argued—would erode. But, at the same time, if we continue to think that the truth is singular, we lose our critical faculty, and fail to problematise it. In other words, we find ourselves in a situation where we either remain terribly uncertain, or else we lose our criticality. In fact, this dilemma haunts the educationists, teachers and textbook writers. What would they teach? The truth, as viewed from the perspective of a section of society, or the conflicting perspectives and viewpoints? This dilemma leads to yet another kind of a problem. If we tell our children only one side of the story as the truth, we tend to make them conditioned, uncritical, non-reflexive. But, given the mental/emotional/cognitive stage of children, is it possible for them to deal with the multiple, conflicting viewpoints? Would this not confuse the tender mind, make it cynical and uncertain? These are complex problems to which there is no easy solution.[11] Perhaps for a meaningful curriculum, educationists, teachers, textbook writers have to continually go in for rigorous self-introspection. They have to examine their biases, try to overcome them and evolve a perspective that is more accommodative, balanced and integral.[12] Because, as we see it, the goal of education ought to be the creation of a new mind-set: open (not exclusivist), critical (not cynical), and tolerant (not uncertain). It is in this context that we wish to reflect on two other important issues relating to school curriculum/knowledge—the meaning of India, and of conflict/unity in social life.

People, State and Civilisation

It goes without saying that children must know about India. However, as there are different perceptions of India, it is quite possible that, because of the influence of the dominant classes, the 'official' perception, as our study of the NCERT texts suggests, may get more importance than other possible readings of India. This is dangerous for two reasons: First, it alienates the larger section of society for whom the official reading of India is incompatible with the reality of their lives. Texts, as a result, become distant, remote and alienating. Second, even for the children of the dominant classes, this limited view of India is harmful. They are not encouraged to move beyond their privileged circle or to look beyond their horizons. As a result, they too remain alienated from the kind of life as experienced outside the boundaries of the upper caste/upper class/urban/industrial India.

It is in this context that the *Eklavya* texts emerge as a powerful reminder, a necessary corrective. Because, as we have already said, here we see sensitivity to the language of real life—the experiences of the subalterns: tribals, peasants, workers, and the oppressed castes. In other words, the meaning of India takes on a broader prespective: India, not just as defined and seen by the planners, officials and main-stream nationalists, but India as experienced by the people.

This, however, does not mean that there is no truth in the official projection of India. Because the post-colonial state—guided by the liberatarian ethos of the freedom struggle—has its own project: the project embodied in our Constitution and in the nationalist aspirations. And school children must know about this project, its historical background, its objectives, achievements and failures. This is particularly important to remember because in our times, we are witnessing organised political violence or some kind of cultural narcissism that is destroying the dreams of the freedom struggle.[13] We also see a critique of the nation-state and nationalism and a tendency to debunk the very notion of India. Instead, there is the celebration of fragments, differences and communities.[14] But, as we wish to stress, children should be told that India, despite the differences, exists, and the nation-state, despite its failures and contradictions, does have an agenda for the larger collective. In other words, the centrality of India in our existence—India's civilisational ideals as developed over centuries, the freedom struggle and its mission to unite, the welfare state and its developmental endeavours—ought to be told to children with depth, rigour and seriousness.[15] It is in this context that the NCERT textbooks acquire relevance. In fact, as we wish to argue, we can learn from both the NCERT as well as the Eklavya texts, and evolve a broader perspective of India.[16] Let the children learn about India: India as a civilisation, India as a nation-state, India as experienced by people. Let this comprehensive understanding of India inspire them to relate —creatively/critically—to India!

There is another important point to note. It is true that the state plays a very important role in our lives. And it is also true that the nation-state embodies the spirit of modernity: the ideal of techno-scientific development. Yet, as we would argue, children should also know—and know honestly—about the people's agency and their dissenting voices; because if the state is placed above people, and the narcissism of the nation-state remains unchecked, there is a danger of authoritarianism,[17] as this would negate critical thinking and lead to violence. Take, for instance, the way the nuclear explosion—or the brute technological power—has been celebrated as a victory of the Indian nation-state! Hence, we wish to argue that critical consciousness should be an important component of school knowledge. Let children learn that the nation without its people, or the state without society, becomes oppressive. Let them learn that in the ultimate analysis, it is people who make the state great; not the other way round.

Conflict, Unity and the Art of Living

It is also important to know how we can tell our children of the reality of conflict in our society. It is true that there is a school of thought that likes to look at the society as a cohesive whole; a consensual/harmonious system; a living organism. And it is argued that when children imbibe the values of this consensual order, they become 'disciplined' and 'motivationally trained' to adjust to the system. But we also know that this functionalist/consensual approach has been challenged.

Here we can make two points. First, a consensual view of society may serve the interests of the dominant class; it may also restrict the perspective of the children of this class and deprive them of seeing how life is lived by the oppressed/marginalised sections of society. Second, it undermines the role of conflict as a pedagogic tool, because it fails to see that conflicting perspectives enable children to find their space, intervene in the process of learning, and bring dynamism and creativity to the entire exercise. Herein, we believe, lies the importance of the *Eklavya* textbooks.

But then, it is equally important to realise that conflict is not the only truth about human society. What make human history rich and colourful are those innovative attempts that seek to reduce suffering and exploitation, restore the spirit of human unity, and strive for egalitarian ideals. In other words, in human history/society we can see these noble actions when selfish interests are overcome, and the unity of the larger collective becomes important. We must relate these great stories and experiences to our children, because if they learn only of conflict, division and hierarchy, we would be doing a great damage to their consciousness. We would make them cynical, deprive them of visualising the possibility of overcoming conflict, and bringing about unity.

Take, for instance, the story of Gandhi. It is possible to tell the child that Gandhi, because of his caste/class interests, could not represent the voices of the oppressed castes/classes. In other words, it is possible to make them see the wide gap between the Gandhian spirit of nationalism and the experiences of the subaltern masses. Yet, it is important to note that this story, although relevant, is essentially partial. Because what was striking about Gandhi was his relentless urge to overcome conflict, and embody the spirit of oneness. It could be seen in his dialogue with Harijans and women, his conversation with Islam and Christianity, and in his merging with the heart of the Indian peasantry. Gandhi became a force and represented the nation precisely because of his mission to unite, his ability to overcome the class divide, and take the entire society with him. He did not escape the prevalent conflict. He transcended it by evolving an alternative practice of living.[18] This story is equally important, and children ought to know about it: its spirituality and the associated possibilities.

The point we wish to make here is: let the children learn about conflict, and also about attempts to transcend conflict. These attempts could be seen in religious movements (say the bhakti/sufi tradition), in nationalist aspirations (the Gandhian/anti-colonial struggle for liberation), and even in the policy of the welfare state (its intended objective to create a just society).

India, we know, is a vibrant society; full of diverse interests and conflicting viewpoints. But India is also our collective aspiration, an ideal of unity, an experience of belonging and togetherness. School texts must tell this story to the child and inculcate in the tender mind a sense of faith and optimism which is so essential to the child's creative development. From conflict to unity—let the children learn how to undertake this historic journey!

Notes

1. For Karl Mannheim, the principal thesis of the sociology of knowledge is that there are modes of thought which cannot be adequately understood as long as their social origins are obscured. In other words, there are social and existential determinants of knowledge. The fact that knowledge is inseparable from the social experience of the knower means that there is no singular truth; there are many perspectives, many ways of seeing the world (see Mannheim 1960).
2. In this context it would not be inappropriate to recall how Antonio Gramsci asserted the need for creating a counter-hegemony on the part of the subaltern classes to fight the ruling class hegemony. In this struggle for liberation, alternate ideas and education—according to Gramsci—play a key role (see Gramsci 1971).
3. In fact, the sociology of science, as developed by a large number of thinkers, shows the social character of science. Not solely

that; there are critical thinkers—from Feyerabend to Lyotard—who question the 'objectivity' of science as 'pure' knowledge. For an insightful summary of this debate on the cognitive status of science, see Richards 1987: 197-224.

4. It should, however, be remembered that there are limits to the legitimacy of school texts. The real world—its conflicts and contradictions—that children experience may lead them to delegitimise and interrogate these texts.
5. There are two reasons for choosing the texts of these three classes. First, it is important to focus on the select texts and study their meanings rigorously. Second, these three classes are important because at this formative period children begin to develop and internalise many ideas and evolve a way of seeing the world.
6. The NCERT was set up in 1961. It was a period when the Nehruvian agenda of nation-making was the dominant worldview. As Arjun Dev—a senior professor of the NCERT—told me: in the 1960s came the recommendations of the Kothari Commission. Perhaps it can be said that one of the major objectives of the NCERT was to concretise the recommendations of the Kothari Commission, or what we have already said in Chapter 1, the post-colonial agenda of education. The NCERT as a result, intervened in the process of writing the texts for school children. For example, the first edition of the history texts for Classes VI and VII were written in 1966 and 1967 respectively. The text for Class VIII was written in 1970. And the civics texts were written in the 1970s. These texts, needless to add, have gained widespread legitimacy and acquired a pan-Indian character.
7. But then, with the changing political equations in the country the NCERT too, as many suspect, may have to alter its agenda and articulate a different worldview which need not necessarily coincide with the gospel of Nehruvian secularism. In fact, the process has already begun. It leads to what is being regarded as 'saffronisation of education'.
8. The history of Eklavya has its roots in the Hoshangabad Science Teaching Programme (HSTP) which was started in 1972 by two voluntary organisations—Friends Rural Centre, Rasulia and Kishore Bharati, Bankheri. This programme was based on the concern for inculcating a scientific outlook in society and

improving science education in schools. In 1978, with the permission of the Madhya Pradesh Government, HSTP was expanded to all the middle schools of the Hoshangabad district. During the course of this expansion, various questions were being discussed by the group: Can there be any improvement in science education without a change in the totality of school education? Can one hope to sustain a school programme which questions the prevailing principles of hierarchy and knowledge-construction without attempting to change these in the social domain outside the school as well? From these discussions emerged a group of people who committed themselves to work towards social change through education. Eklavya was registered as a society in 1982. Eklavya focuses on creating alternatives in education and development with the active participation of the people. For more details, see Eklavya 1999.

9. In fact, Eklavya has combined history, civics and geography in a single text. For these three Classes VI, VII and VIII—there are three texts on social studies. The texts are the following:
   SamajikAdhyayan,VI (Bhopal: Madhya Pradesh Pathyapustak Nigam, 1995).
   Samajik Adhyayan, VII (Bhopal: Madhya Pradesh Pathyapustak Nigam, 1994).
   Samajik Adhyayan, VIII (Bhopal: Madhya Pradesh Pathyapustak Nigam, 1994).
10. These texts have been written in Hindi. While giving the examples from these texts, I have tried to capture the essence and present it in English.
11. There are sociologists of education who would, however, assert that children are deeply aware of social conflicts, and they must get the opportunity to discuss and reflect on social conflicts. In other words, it is argued that alternative pedagogic practices must encourage children to learn from the awareness of these conflicts. See Kumar 1996.
12. In this context it would not be inappropriate to recall what Karl Mannheim—the great sociologist of knowledge—expected from the intelligentsia. Mannheim spoke of multiple perspectives. But then, he sought to overcome relativism. He thought that it would be possible for 'free-floating' intellectuals, because of their criticality, education, and ability to come out

of the limited horizons of their classes, to evolve an integral and broader understanding of social reality (Mannheim 1960).

13. For instance, the assertion of *Hindutva* as a major socio-political force seems to have damaged the liberal/secular ethos of the Nehruvian era. True, the critique of the Nehruvian brand of secularism is possible. But then, the way the cultural narcissism of *Hindutva* seeks to destroy the pluralistic ethos of our culture is dangerous. It is authoritarian. And it can be seen in the way this political force is intervening in the domain of education, and trying to alter its agenda.
14. Indeed, the new subaltern studies, as developed by Partha Chatterjee and others, are heavily oriented to postmodern thinking. The proponents of this approach criticise the Enlightenment agenda of modernity, its 'rationality,' 'science,' progress,' and the gospel of 'national unity.' Instead, it celebrates differences, privileges local/indigenous/ communitarian knowledges and traditions. Not everyone can, however, appreciate this thinking. For example, it is feared that this attack on the secular, liberal nation state as a Western imposition may be appropriated by the Hindu Right. It is sad that the critique of bureaucratic rationalism of the Nehruvian era has gone to such an extent that words like 'secular,'' rational,' or 'progressive' have become terms of ridicule. No wonder, we are also witnessing a sharp critique of the new subaltern studies (see Sarkar 1997: 82-108).
15. It is important to assert the centrality of India. Because, despite differences, there is a civilisational unity. Take an example. The Adi Sankaracharya established four *Maths* in all the four corners of India more than one thousand years ago. And it has been the wish even of the illiterate traditional Indian women to go on pilgrimage to all the four Dhams which are located in the extreme east, west, north and south of India. Likewise, people from all parts of India congregate in their millions at specific times for events such as the Kumbha. This has been so at least from the time of Harsh, some fifteen hundred years ago. Moreover, the diversity of local cultures is also characterised by linkages and shared commonalties of culture traits, rituals, beliefs and customs. For instance, studies of folk culture across regions, as distant as Uttar Pradesh from Rajasthan, have shown remarkable similarity in the ritual styles, songs and their

central themes and symbols. That is why, we wish to argue that the centrality of India should not be missed even when we talk about local cultures and traditions. Education should enable one to mediate between the local and the national. For further elaboration on the kind of civilisational unity we are talking about, see Deva and Shrirama 1999; Singh 2000.

16. In this context an observation made by Arjun Dev acquires relevance. According to him, the centrality of India is the focus of the NCERT texts. And the Eklavlya texts, as he sees, have done a great job as far as local/culture-specific issues are concerned. But then, as he sees, there are limits to this fascination with the local. The child must know about the local as well as the national. That is why, as he thinks, the Eklavya texts can be supplementary to, but cannot substitute the NCERT texts.
17. Rajni Kothari seems to be extraordinarily sensitive to this problem. He reminds us that it would be dangerous if we place the state above people, the security of the nation-state above people's security, or if we think that the removal of real or imaginary threats to the state are more important than persisting threats to the masses and their survival. Moreover, the state, because of its obsession with 'technological modernisation,' often fails to cope with the needs and aspirations of the poor. According to Kothari, the challenge is to create a viable state and a democratic social order (Kothari 1988).
18. For an understanding of the deeper meaning of the Gandhian practice, see Pathak 1997: 122-31.

3

Looking Beyond Texts

Culture of Schooling and Formation of Consciousness

As we have already discussed, it is important for school children to remain sensitive to emancipatory values so that their relationship with their surroundings becomes truly meaningful. Perhaps it would not be wrong to say that the school texts, despite their contradictions and limitations, do try to articulate these values. For example, in our times we are witnessing the assertion of 'environmental studies'; even small children of Class III or Class IV are told that it is important to understand the emergent environmental crisis, and hence it is desirable to do what is necessary to protect our environment. In a way, a major lesson of environmental studies is the affirmation of what Tim Hayward would regard as 'core ecological values' like (a) live in harmony with nature, (b) overcome anthropocentric prejudice, and (c) recognise intrinsic value in beings other than humans (Hayward 1994). Take, for instance, a chapter entitled 'Care and Protection of Plants and Animals' from the NCERT textbook for Class IV (Bhattacharya, Khaparde, Rastogi and Sharma 1988: 20-29). The child is told why it is important to live in harmony with plants and animals. The chapter focuses on the devastating consequences of the large-scale destruction of forests. The importance of 'social forestry programmes' is asserted. And the text is categorical in giving the following messages to the child:

- avoid thoughtless cutting down of trees.
- protect forests from fire.
- protect plants against diseases.
- plant more trees.

In fact, there are many other examples that demonstrate how school texts seek to teach emancipatory values like holism, togetherness, and solidarity.[1] But then, the success of these noble objectives depends, to a great extent, on actual school practices: how teaching takes place, how knowledge is received, and how meanings are attached to the objective of education. Perhaps the accumulation and consumption of knowledge as 'course material' (for passing the examination, and acquiring the certificate) trivialises these emancipatory values. The result is 'book knowledge', which cannot be related to the actual life-practices of the child. The absence or devaluation of *experiential* knowledge is perhaps a major crisis of contemporary school education. Furthermore, the goals of school education need not necessarily be what the texts portray as 'noble' values. In fact, there may be *hidden* objectives rooted in actual school practices.

It is, therefore, important to go beyond what is written in the texts (although viewing the written words as 'legitimate knowledge' has its own significance), and examine the overall culture of schooling.[2] Because schooling is more than the huge stock of information and knowledge that the children acquire. Essentially, schooling tends to create a mind-set: a way of seeing, thinking and relating to the world. This does not mean that the other agencies—say, family and neighbourhood are unimportant in shaping the mind of the child. In fact, it is possible to imagine a situation in which the consequences of schooling get neutralised because of other socially relevant experiences. Yet, as we have repeatedly stated, the role of schooling can hardly be overlooked in modern times.

Our objective in this chapter is to examine what schooling

does or can do to the consciousness of our children in terms of their ways of seeing and relating to the world. Although there are multiple schooling systems in India, it is not difficult to identify the salient features of the *dominant/mainstream* pattern of school education. We would examine how this mainstream culture—with its characteristic hierarchy and inequality, pedagogy and curriculum—tends to shape the consciousness of young learners. It is important to see whether this schooled consciousness is conducive to the cultivation of truly democratic/egalitarian/humanistic values.

I
English is Power

Schooling, as it exists, perpetuates the societal inequality. In fact, it intensifies the existing divide between the elite and the masses. As a matter of fact, there are two kinds of schooling. To begin with, let us talk about the the *English-medium* schools. English, it has to be understood, is not just another language of communication. In a society like ours, English is the language of domination.[3] English is power; it symbolises one's status and privileges. Hence, the meaning of 'English-medium' schools needs to be explored.

These schools, because of their very nature, are exclusive. They exist only for the elite—those who can afford to think of isolating their children from the *mainstream*, from the reality of poverty and backwardness. As a result, the nature of socialisation in these schools acquires an altogether different meaning. One learns not just 'better' English, Physics, Mathematics and History, but something that is even more important. One learns how to feel different/superior; how to stay separate from all that is 'ordinary'. One learns that one is intelligent and hence privileged; that success is one's natural right and one is, therefore, destined to rule! Studying in English-medium schools is like joining an exclusive elite club with its distinctive symbols—music, hobbies, jokes and style of pronunciation!

And the schools where the medium of instruction is not English, tell an altogether different story. There is no trace of power or privilege; failure is all around. The funds are inadequate; the teachers are not stimulated to teach; the students are already demoralised, and parents too do not hope for much. There is no sincere effort to abolish this dual system of education.[4] It has been taken for granted that inequality should begin right from childhood!

The consequences of this duality are bound to be negative. Apart from the perpetuation and legitimisation of inequality, this dual system of education is detrimental to the pursuit of truth and knowledge. English, as we have said, has ceased to be the language of communication. English is the language of power and privilege. Not surprisingly, knowledge itself tends to be equated with English. English is knowledge. Knowledge is English! This explains why ambitious/mobile parents prefer to speak English and only English with their children, and why these schools do not encourage the use and promotion of Indian languages. In fact, in many 'good' schools in Delhi, Hindi is being treated as a second language. The general impression is that English is the only way through which one can attain the truth. This is damaging. It creates a negative orientation towards major Indian languages. Because of their excessive dependence on English material, children from English-medium schools are not encouraged to tap the abundant cultural resources stored in the Indian languages. This alienation is essentially their alienation from the larger collective—its experiences, victories, struggles, sufferings. The 'knowledge' they acquire does not help them relate to the larger society; it makes them outsiders, colonisers. English, as it is practised, does not unite; it alienates, separates, and brutalises.

But then, things are no better in schools where the medium of instruction is some Indian language. As we have already said, these schools are not sufficiently equipped to create a healthy pedagogical environment. Moreover, as the students are asked to resign themselves to the fact that they have to accept defeat right from their childhood, they grow up with a terrible inferiority complex. They fail to pose any meaningful challenge to the world the English-medium schools create. Instead, they begin to fear English; they feel jealous of those whose English assures success.[5] Or else, they spend their time and energy coping with English, or 'learning' English. In other words, English remains their only obsession: Fear it. Hate it. Or emulate it. Where is the time to do anything else? That is the ultimate irony. Even in a post-colonial society, despite the warnings given by visionaries like Tagore and Gandhi, we have allowed English to do what Thomas Babington Macaulay wanted!

II
Knowledge is Oppressive

What one learns at school through its texts and curricula is regarded as true/legitimate knowledge; everything else acquires a secondary status. In other words, schooling has became synonymous with *legitimate knowledge.* The success of schooled consciousness lies in one's ability to internalise this rationale. The child begins to believe that knowledge is what is acquired in the classroom, what is written in the prescribed text, and what the teachers think is important. This realisation leads the child to separate 'work' from 'play', 'real' texts from 'imaginary' stories. To make matters worse, the child is expected to concentrate on what is considered really 'worth-doing': mathematics, history and science, as taught at school. Everything else is regarded as 'extra-curricular', something that is merely symbolic having no substantial meaning for evaluating the child's performance. Schooling, as a result, tends to cultivate one— and only one —ambition: to gain complete mastery over legitimate knowledge. 'Good'/'disciplined' students are those who are willing to achieve this goal at any cost—even at the cost of missing out on all good and meaningful things of life during their growing years.

The consequences of this burden of legitimate knowledge are worth examining. First, its monopolistic tendency denies all alternate sources of knowledge and learning. It limits one's possibilities, restricts one's horizon; it stunts one's creative growth. For instance, a child is trained to believe that history is what is written in history textbooks; there is no history in his grandmother's experiences. Or literature means only those select pieces of poetry and prose, not his grandmother's folk songs or folk tales! In other words, schooled consciousness means arrogance; it refuses to give legitimacy to alternate forms of knowing.[6]

Second, the chronic anxiety to gain complete mastery over legitimate knowledge denies one the joy and aesthetics that are a part of the process of learning. As knowledge gets reified in the form of printed textbooks, human experiences are forgotten. Read poetry, but don't be poetic in life and practice. Read the history of the freedom struggle, but don't cultivate the emotional intensity needed to participate in the struggle for liberation. In other words, legitimate knowledge is something to be 'covered'; it need not be discovered, experienced and realised. Herein lies the relevance of what we have already stated. The instrumental orientation to knowledge (consume it for the examination, and then forget it) disregards what is really needed for authentic learning: life-experiences!

Third, legitimate knowledge is essentially a mechanism for reproducing social inequality. This is important to understand. If we examine carefully the construction of legitimate knowledge, it would reveal how it privileges the societal experiences of the elite. Let us take an example. Legitimate history, as taught at school, is more often a celebration of the active agency of the elite; seldom does it narrate the history of the subaltern people—tribes, lower castes, peasants. This kind of legitimate knowledge would make the marginalised people feel inferior. The implicit message is that there is nothing in their history that is worth knowing.[7] Moreover, what is important is to realise that the acquisition of legitimate knowledge requires special training—an orientation, an aptitude. This *cultural capital* is not everybody's privilege. For instance, a child in a lower middle class family, who does not have any skill of spoken English, would never be allowed entry into any 'good'/ 'prestigious' school. This is because legitimate knowledge—as defined by such schools—implies the possession of a skill (or cultural capital) that only the children of upper class families have: the ability to communicate in English and familiarity with, say, the nursery rhymes like 'Pussy Cat, Pussy Cat...'/'Mistress Mary, quite contrary...'/ 'Jack and Jill went up the hill...', and so on.

In fact, the neutrality of a 'good' school is a myth; its curriculum, its definition of knowledge, its mode of evaluation—everything is designed to suit the cultural capital that the privileged classes are gifted with. The reproduction of social inequality is the inevitable consequence of schooling. All this does not suggest any mechanistic/ deterministic relationship between schooling and the dominant class hegemony. Often, there is resistance; lower caste/class children refusing to accept the validity of school knowledge; imaginative teachers creating space for multiple interpretations. Yet, what cannot be denied is that the general impact of the burden of legitimate knowledge is not very positive; it is not expected to create free/imaginative/creative thinking.

III
Dialogue is Missing

Meaningful learning is dialogic; it unites the teacher and the taught. It means reciprocity, mutuality, and continual growth. It makes the teacher humble; he realises that knowledge is not his monopoly, and teaching is primarily a process of learning. It ensures the student's active participation in the learning process and makes him realise that learning is not passive consumption; it is active involvement. Dialogue means that knowledge is an ongoing process, not a finished product. Dialogue creates the space needed for multiple interpretations and contestations. But ironically, schooling, as it exists, has no room for dialogue. There are primarily four reasons for this.

- School teachers are not involved in the preparation of the curriculum; seldom do they write the texts they are asked to teach. Look at the NCERT textbooks for school children. These books have been written mainly by the renowned professors of Indian universities. Here, we are not challenging the quality of these books. What we wish to point out is that the professors who write these books are not directly involved with children, and without this association it is not easy to understand their minds, their confusions, their aspirations. But ironically, those whose daily occupation is teaching, remain alienated from this exercise of writing the material for school children. In fact, everything is imposed on the teacher, be it the curriculum; the syllabus or the textbooks. This alienation deprives him of his agency, and tends to kill his personal interest. He does not feel involved. He becomes more of a functionary; he does his job and draws his salary. He is not expected to cultivate the intense imagination needed for dialogic education.[8]
- The teacher too has been trained to believe that nothing exists beyond legitimate knowledge. He is not expected to challenge this belief, nor to question it. Between him and his students lies the authority of the texts. There is no way he can escape being dictated by them. This situation does not leave any room for a dialogue.[9]
- Time is money, and every fragment of it ought to be utilised for the 'right purpose'. And the 'right purpose' has already been defined: there is the annual examination; the texts have to be covered; legitimate

knowledge has to be memorised. Given these constraints, who has the time or the inclination to question the text? Besides, going beyond the text and seeing multiple possibilities in it requires a relatively free and relaxed mind. But freedom and the ritual of examinations cannot go together. Hence, dialogue remains a distant dream.

- Dialogue means that the teacher should be prepared to learn from conflict. It means that the child should be allowed to articulate his doubts or the conflict he sees between legitimate knowledge and his experiences, between what is written in the text and what he sees in the real life situations. But more often than not, conflict is feared, repressed and denied.[10] Let us take an example. After the demolition of the Babri Masjid, I asked a group of students of a reputed Kendriya Vidyalaya in Delhi whether their teacher, particularly the history teacher, had talked about the incident. They told me that nothing of that sort was discussed or even mentioned in the classroom. The students might have read from their history/civics books that ours is a secular state and Hinduism is a religion of tolerance. Yet, the all pervasive communalism/intolerance might lead them to question the validity of such legitimate/ bookish knowledge. In fact, this sense of conflict alone can lead to multiple interpretations of a given situation, thereby opening up the possibility of dialogue. A teacher ought to encourage this dialogic spirit. But often, his enthusiasm to do so is suppressed in order to retain the sanctity of legitimate knowledge. Hence, he does not allow any dissent.

The consequences of non-dialogic education are disastrous: schooling becomes an alienating experience; it becomes a burden. Knowledge is seen as something that is fixed, codified, handed down—not a process of mutual discovery and growth. The child feels that his own experiences, his own judgement have no place in the learning process. Education denies him his agency, his reflexivity. It reduces him into a passive receptacle of knowledge. This is the beginning of blind obedience: don't question! There is only one interpretation that matters—the interpretation that the teacher provides. That is the paradox. We need democracy in the larger society; but democracy seems to have no value in the classroom.

IV
Examinations are Threatening

Examinations, it is argued, are important. Without regular examinations, it is difficult to evaluate students. And evaluation is necessary, because schooling is not just about the distribution of knowledge; nor is it just about teaching/learning/sharing ideas. One important function of formal schooling is that it certifies; it quantifies one's level of achievement, one's cognitive skills and even moral conduct. Examinations are, therefore, necessary. It is also believed that this compulsion—the necessity to face examinations—helps students take their studies seriously and work hard. In other words, examinations 'discipline' them?

These manifest functions of examinations are often talked about. But what is equally important is to understand their *latent functions.* To begin with, examinations make objectification (of students) possible, because the 'neutrality' of examinations—their 'coldness', their 'impartiality'—does not see a student as an autonomous person with his/her specific needs, tastes, and demands. In the ultimate analysis, grades, percentage of marks define them. Their qualitative experiences, biographies, and their unique ways of knowing/comprehending, are all forgotten. What is recognised is their position in the hierarchy. This objectification is also an effective way of controlling them; of telling them that they are destined to be hierarchised, graded, quantified. They get the message: they have to realise/accept their powerlessness.

No self-evaluation or dialogue with the teaching community is possible. There are legitimate authorities, bureaucratic boards (CBSE, etc.) that would certify them, define their life-projects, shape their careers. The meaning is clear: Authority cannot be challenged!

Examinations give yet another signal: there cannot be any equality in society; hierarchy is inevitable. There is poverty. There is unemployment. But then, it can always be argued that poverty or unemployment exists because one is not sufficiently educated; one has not done well at school, etc. To put it otherwise, the lack of 'talent' (and examinations judge one's talent) explains one's unhappy existence. The deeper reasons for social inequity (private property, institutionalised exploitation) are forgotten. Schooled consciousness (I deserve everything good in life because I have passed the examination and done well; or I am useless because I have not done well at school), therefore, hides the real contradictions. It legitimises inequality. It makes inequality scientific!

Another important message: Examinations recognise success. Success is valued. Success is celebrated. It is through examinations that one gets to face the reality—that there cannot be any symmetry between success and failure. Failure is the negation of all that success implies: intelligence, hard work, talent, merit. Failure is condemned. This *success-anxiety* (or the fear of failure) is the substance of the exam-centred pedagogy. It is this chronic anxiety that leads to aggressive individualism.[11] To reach the top, one must monopolise knowledge; one should not share it. An urge to share or learn collectively is seen as a 'soft' quality. Softness does not count in a hard/competitive world. Examinations breed competitiveness, they adore success, condemn failure, and promote individualism.

In fact, schools do not prepare nor encourage one to accept and respect a humane/egalitarian milieu. On the contrary, schools make it easier for one to conform to the prevailing social order with its hierarchy, inequality, competitiveness and individualism. Moreover, as success (one's grade point indicates the degree of one's success) is what matters—and creative learning is not considered important—one is left with no choice but to evolve a strategy that would assure success. Private tuitions, notebook culture—these are not aberrations; they form an integral part of the system![12]

V
Technology is Colonising

We live in an age in which technology is allowed to lure us. Technology performs miracles. Technology promises development and growth. Technology is power. This great demand for technology shapes our educational priorities. The material power of technology is also its cognitive power. Not surprisingly, we experience the hierarchy of knowledge. Whatever is related to technology or helps one join the technological empire is considered. valuable, desirable, important, relevant. A clear illustration of this hierarchy is seen in the distinction between 'science' (Physics, Chemistry, Mathematics, Biology) and 'humanities' (Literature, History, Political Studies, Sociology). In fact, growing up in a school means the internalisation of this distinction and hierarchy. Almost every school student tends to accept that science subjects are challenging and worth doing. Science, it is believed, calls for intelligence, merit, hard work. But history or literature, it is thought, is not so important; it is merely a narrative, a fiction. It does not require any special talent or intelligence! Hence, it is quite unlikely that a school student would say that his favourite discipline is history, and that he likes to be a historian. Almost everyone wants to be good in science and seeks to become a doctor or an engineer. To be good in literature or humanities means nothing. To be good in Physics or Mathematics means quite a lot. This invariably gives one a heroic status in the classroom. 'Good' students are science students, and those who have failed in science opt for humanities! In fact, the very meaning of schooled consciousness is that it equates intelligence with science, and only science. Here indeed is a blinkered view of intelligence.[13]

Its consequences are disastrous. The cognitive power associated with science often makes it difficult for a science student to realise the meaning of humanities. He looks at all other disciplines with contempt. This makes him poorer. He fails to see the integrity and unity of knowledge. His thinking gets fragmented and divided. Likewise, a student of history/literature/sociology is asked to remain silent before the cognitive power of science. He is trained to see himself as inferior; he fears science."[14] These attitudes (shared by students as well as teachers) affect the style of learning. Science is studied with proud enthusiasm; humanities with passivity and meaninglessness. Science is interesting, and boredom is the meaning of humanities. Not many teachers can challenge this hidden curriculum or create counter-examples.

Another problem lies with the way science is being perceived. It is true that doing well in science, for every school student, is a prestige issue. But then, science by itself is not valued or appreciated. An instrumental meaning is attached to science. Physics/mathematics, it is thought, would enable one to get an entry into the technological world. But not many students are encouraged to pursue their careers in pure/theoretical sciences. In other words, it is applied technology that colonises science. With this instrumentality, no genuine interest can be created in science. Science is about rigorous meditation and contemplation; it is an endless search for truth. It needs patience, imagination, innovation. But then, the meaning attached to science is altogether different. It is seen as a pragmatic means to get an entry into a glamorous, lucrative techno-corporate world.[15] The point we are trying to make is that technology disregards the authentic spirit of science, and the prevalent pedagogy fails to do anything about it.[16]

This narrow approach (because of the colonisation of the

life-world) distorts the meaning of education. Education, it is thought, means a job, prosperity, affluence. 'Good' schooling means 'good' careers. And 'good' careers are lucrative careers in the techno-economic world! In fact, for all practical purposes, this has become the meaning of education, the meaning of 'good' schooling. As a result, the deeper meaning of education is forgotten. It is forgotten that education is not just 'practical' education for market jobs; education is essentially a process of discovery/rediscovery; it is a continual search for truth; it is a creative engagement with the world. Education means inner joy, aesthetics, relatedness. Poetry or mathematics, music or physics, history or economics—nothing is unimportant, if experienced in its correct perspective. But then, as we witness the triumph of instrumental rationality, this deeper meaning of education is not taken seriously. It is said to be 'impractical', or by classifying them as 'extra curricular' activities, schools trivialise the entire process. It is thought that only in some 'super elite' schools can education be experienced in this manner!

In other words, the dominant trend in schools is to generate the consent to technology and to techno-economic careers. Technology is not questioned; the child is not encouraged to see the absurdity/meaninglessness of many corporate jobs. As a result, schooling makes one a conformist —one who accepts the corporate world without any difficulty, thereby failing to see the multiple possibilities in life.

VI
Is There a Way Out?

We are indeed living in troubled times. Because of the socio-economic inequality, there are many who remain deprived of school education. But then, there are those who get school education, but they too are not growing up with emancipatory consciousness. True, there is a lot to be gained from schooling in terms of information and generation of awareness; social mobility and a better quality of life. Yet, schooling, particularly its dominant form of practice, is not conducive to the cultivation of radical/emancipatory consciousness. In a way, it prepares one to accept hierarchy, competition and inequality. It restricts one's horizon, and tends to make one a conformist.

Besides, the present scenario of globalisation, as Krishna Kumar would argue, strengthens the hold of markets everywhere (Kumar 1998). This market-rationality tends to deprive one of the memory of the anti-colonial struggle. Instead, we see 'the claims of neo-fascist elements that they alone represented the cultural and political autonomy' (Ibid: 2914). The result is the shrinking of 'liberal spaces where occasional resistance and critical enquiry might flourish' (Ibid: 2914). Its consequences in the domain of education are devastating. For example, all these new information technologies (globalisation is inseparable from these technologies) do severe damage to the concept of creative/critical education, because the very rationale of these technologies leads to the diminution of space or milieu as a factor in learning. Kumar apprehends this danger with great sensitivity when he says:

> Engagement with the immediate milieu, both natural and social, which Dewey had proposed as one of the foundations of progressive education has run into deep trouble with the advent of online lifestyle as a symbol of status and power. (Ibid: 2915).

This would mean trivialisation of knowledge and the intellectual capacity. It would also mean indifference towards people, their sufferings and struggles; indifference to the costs of capitalist opulence. Can this crisis be overcome through what is being projected as 'value education?' The danger lies in the fact that the idea of 'value education', particularly in contemporary times, has been hijacked by the proponents of *Hindutva*. One begins to sense the assertion of an oppressive/revivalist tradition. It is often forgotten that no authentic value education is possible unless the culture of schooling is changed. Without resisting the hidden agenda of the prevalent from of schooling—hierarchy, fragmentation, duality and indifference—it is difficult to come out of the present crisis.

The visionaries could sense this hidden meaning of schooling. No wonder, they raised the voice of dissent and spoke of alternatives. From Tolstoy to Paulo Freire, from Gandhi to Tagore, from Sri Aurobindo to Jiddu Krishnamurthy—we could see a pattern of alternative education emerging. What characterises this ideal of alternative schooling is the importance it attaches to reciprocity, dialogicity and critical reflexivity. Instead of the examination-centred/competitive pedagogy and fragmented orientation to knowledge, it speaks of integral education, and the child's free/natural/spontaneous growth. Perhaps it would not be wrong to say that this alternative education is closely related to a radical project of remaking our society or creating an intensely harmonic and egalitarian society with sufficient spiritual sensitivity—a society without life-negating individualism and competitiveness.

The question is: why is it that the dominant/mainstream pattern of education continues, and the alternative pedagogic practices remain marginalised?

Notes

1. For instance, literature texts for children are often loaded with *Panchatantra* stories having sound moral messages. Likewise, social science texts assert the ideals like plurality, religious harmony and togetherness. An illuminating illustration is a chapter like 'Thoughts that make us better human beings' in Khan, Singh and Verma 1988: 112-18.
2. This does by no means negate the effect of textual knowledge. No one can deny the importance of school texts or written words in the thinking of children. This is the reason why an entire chapter (Chapter 2) has been written on the sociology of these texts. But then, what we ought to remember is that there are not just *manifest* functions of schooling (say, the noble ideals

that the texts portray), there are also latent or *hidden* functions. It is, therefore, important to see the fate of these texts in the overall culture of learning that characterises contemporary school education.

3. This is not to encourage an 'anti-English' attitude. It is absurd to negate the relevance of English. Moreover, English, for many of us, seems to have become a 'natural' language of communication. At a time when Salman Rushdie, Vikram Seth and many other literary minds have elevated the status of Indian English, how can we deny its historic 'necessity'? Yet, the sociological truth is that the meaning attached to English is closely related to the hierarchy of languages: English at the cost of other Indian languages! Not solely that. English is not and cannot be the 'natural' language of the majority of Indians. English is the 'cultural capital' of the privileged classes. To allow English to dominate in the domain of education is to perpetuate inequality and deprive many of the fruits of knowledge. This was a warning given by visionaries like Gandhi and Tagore.
4. It is important to recall that one of our educational objectives was to fight this dual system of education. For example, the Kothari Commission recommendations in the sixties pleaded strongly for a *common school system* promoting equality. Yet, equality in the sphere of education has merely remained a constitutional aspiration. For further details, see Kaul 1998: 159-74.
5. Krishna Kumar has argued brilliantly. 'The socializing force of English applies not only to the children who study in English-medium schools, but also to those who do not. To English-medium school children, English 'teaches' self-confident articulation and personal advancement, to the children who attend state schools, English is a reminder of their disability and risk of stagnation' (Kumar 1996: 72).
6. It is in this context that Disha Nawani's observations make sense. She demonstrates how the excessive dependence on 'textbooks' deprives school children of experiencing the pedagogic significance of storybooks. As a result, the entire process of learning becomes one-dimensional; it leads to a distorted orientation to knowledge (see Nawani 1999).
7. In fact, enough has already been said and written about the politics of knowledge—how school texts tend to give more

importance to the societal experience and heritage of the dominant class. We have already written about the sociology of school knowledge in Chapter 2. Krishna Kumar is a leading sociologist of education in India who has been writing on the politics of knowledge. He has argued how the dominant form of school knowledge perpetuates symbolic violence to the children of the marginalised castes and tribes. (See Kumar 1989: 59-77).

8. Perhaps this explains the low status of school teachers in the hierarchy of professions. School teaching is seen as a job anyone can do: a job that, as it is thought, doesn't require much talent or inner urge. In fact, this low self-esteem of the teaching professions further demoralises the culture of learning.
9. In fact, herein lies the moot question: Who would educate the educators? To imagine and implement the possibility of dialogic education, the teacher needs to reorient herself. Given the state of school education prevalent today, is it possible?
10. A major reason behind this, it seems, is the preoccupation with order. The teacher tends to think that the restoration of order in the classroom is important. It is also assumed that school children are not yet prepared—emotionally or intellectually—to doubt or question what the teacher narrates or the text prescribes.
11. It is no wonder that this chronic anxiety leads to nervous breakdown; it is not uncommon to hear that the fear of failure leads some to commit suicide. This terrible exam-centred anxiety is a social fact. On the eve of the Class XII CBSE examinations, a leading newspaper in the capital captured this moment of anxiety in the following fashion: 'Rows of anxious parents stood outside the entrance gates of the examination centres, their eyes fixed on their wards trudging into the examination hall. Every time a nervous ward looked back, eyes searching, a thumbs up sign greeted him/her. Giving the parents company were the teachers who made it a point to wish luck to every student who entered the centre' (*Indian Express*, New Delhi, 3 March 2000).
12. For a brilliant understanding of the pathology of the examination-centred pedagogy, see Singha 1984.
13. In fact, there is a deeper meaning of this hierarchy of knowledge. Literature and humanities as 'soft' disciplines are

often regarded as 'feminine'—good for girls, but not for boys who must study 'masculine'/'hard' science and build up their careers. The attitude to knowledge cannot be said to be gender-neutral.

14. It would not be wrong to say that the majority of the students who have not been able to pursue their studies in science subjects suffer from terrible inferiority complex. As a university teacher teaching sociology, I have seen how difficult it is for many of my students to overcome their wounded consciousness and to acquire self-esteem and confidence in what they are studying.
15. This explains the terrible obsession with medical/engineering careers. This also explains the growth of innumerable teaching shops and coaching centres preparing school children for entrance tests for medical/engineering colleges. In fact, it is becoming increasingly difficult for a science student, because of the parental and societal pressure, not to write these tests. It is not very common that a science student voluntarily opts for a course in, say, theoretical physics or mathematics.
16. In fact, herein lies the victory of what can be called positivistic science or instrumental science. Despite environmental studies, science, as it is taught, is closely related to an aggressive brand of modernity that devalues nature, and reduces it into a 'resource' for man's material well-being. Children are given a 'value-neutral' character to the study of natural phenomena, including the non-human living members of nature. Not surprisingly, children are asked to overcome any hesitation or inhibition that they might feel in dissecting for examination a living animal like a frog or a rat. No science text, Krishna Kumar argues, discusses the manner in which animals respond to the violence inflicted on them in the course of study by humans. The meaning of this kind of instrumental knowledge is that it begins to distance the child from his/her own nature. (See Kumar 1996: 42-58).

4

Mirambika: An Alternative School

Possibilities and Contradictions

It is obvious that education, as it exists, has its drawbacks. It deprives the child of the joy of learning and kills the spirit of innovation. It burdens the child with a heavy load of information; the excessive exam pressure on the tender mind leads to chronic anxiety regarding 'success' and 'failure'. This *mainstream* education does not seem to have any higher objective. Its sole aim, it appears, is to prepare the child for a lucrative career. No wonder, it has not been appreciated by many sensitive minds. They want something different; an alternative—a new system of education. Alternative schools, therefore, do exist.

However, it is not easy for these alternative experiments to survive. The overwhelming presence of the dominant/mainstream education would always try to marginalise these creative ventures. Furthermore, as education is inseparable from the wider social system, the new educational practices would find it difficult to take root unless the existing social practices undergo a change. An alternative system of education, therefore, requires a new orientation to life. To accept this orientation is not easy. It means fear of being sidelined—the anxiety that one may not be able to adjust to or cope with the 'system'. This is indeed a paradoxical situation: there is an urgent need for alternatives. Yet, alternatives arouse fear, suspicion and anxiety, making it difficult for alternative schools to survive. It is, therefore, important to comprehend this phenomenon.

Here, we have tried to understand the experience of *Mirambika*—an alternative school located in and run by the Sri Aurobindo Ashram, New Delhi. We want to understand the pedagogic/philosophic significance of Mirambika—the reason for its existence; its innovations and experiments; the dynamic experience of the parents, teachers, and the children; its crises and contradictions and the challenges it faces. However, before we go into the origin and evolution of Mirambika, its aspirations and anxieties, we ought know the basic educational philosophy on which this school is founded.

I
Philosophic Foundations of Mirambika

The name 'Mirambika' comes from *Mira* (Mira Alfasa who was known as the *Mother*—the disciple of saint-philosopher Sri Aurobindo) and *Ambika* (its original Sanskrit meaning is *mother).* As the name signifies, the school derives its inspiration from the charisma of the Mother—her educational philosophy and the way she sought to accomplish the spiritual agenda of Sri Aurobindo. Perhaps it would be more appropriate to say that Mirambika, as a school, is an experimental site which has made an attempt to concretise the educational visions of Sri Aurobindo and the Mother. In fact, Mirambika is conscious of its identity. It does not seem to have any ambiguity regarding its objective. The prospectus of Mirambika states clearly:

> Sri Aurobindo and the Mother are the inspiration from which Mirambika and its philosophy flows... a sacred inspiration, silently nourishing, nurturing, sustaining Mirambika and all those who came in living contact with it... (Sri Aurobindo Ashram).

The prospectus of Mirambika—a text which is worth studying in its own right—asserts its educational principles, quotes extensively from the writings of Sri Aurobindo and the Mother, and argues why it celebrates the concept of 'free progress education'.

> Mirambika's free progress concept was born of a profound spiritual vision and understanding: that education is the process of awakening and evoking the true being, the psychic presence within, and through that process, bringing about a progressive unfolding of the whole person.
>
> This unfoldment would be a natural and joyful process of growth and learning which would flow from within to without. Learning would then be free of structures that bind and stifle and would become more and more a dynamic process of self-discovery and self-actualisation. (Ibid).

The concept of 'free progress education' that distinguishes Mirambika, it is obvious, is profound. It seeks to establish itself as an alternative to the prevalent educational practice which, as we have already said, oppresses the child; and in the process of learning, deprives him/her of the experience of creative joy and inner growth. As an alternative, the main focus of Mirambika is on the child; the child's innate potential and his/her ability to unfold it. This faith in the child frees him/her from the fear of punishment and the life-negating pressure of examinations. No wonder, according to popular opinion, Mirambika is a school that reminds one of 'happy childhood'—a school without homework, exams, grades and ranking. It is seen as a 'child-centred' school where everything is possible!

We would, however, like to point out that the meaning of 'free progress education' is far deeper. It is not just the absence of fear and punishment, or of conventional and routinised form of learning. Nor is it merely a negation of the mainstream. It is something more profound. It has a distinctive agenda—a spiritual agenda to transform the character of the human species. Perhaps the meaning of this agenda would be comprehended better if we first understand the educational philosophies of Sri Aurobindo and the Mother.

Sri Aurobindo, we know, wrote extensively on Indian culture and civilisation. Like Gandhi and Tagore, he too was disturbed by colonialism, its hegemonic urge, its principle of domination and the way it sought to undermine the cultural richness of Indian civilisation. No wonder, at a time when the nationalists began to critique colonial education, Sri Aurobindo came forward and contributed to the development of the idea of national education. In fact, a look at his *A Preface on National Education,* published in 1920-21 shows the kind of education he had in mind for India. What is striking about his critique of colonial education is that it was by no means regressive in nature. Nor was it conservative or chauvinistic. It was not his intention to reject modern systems of knowledge and glorify everything that was associated with ancient India.

> Should we reject modern truth and modern method of science because they came to us from Europe and go back to the imperfect scientific knowledge of classical India, exile Galileo and Newton and all that came after and teach only what was known to Bhaskara, Aryabhatta and Varahamihira? (Sri Aurobindo Ashram 1956: 8).

For Sri Aurobindo, national education was by no means a return to the past. 'Truth and knowledge are one and have no country; education too must be a thing universal and without nationality or borders,' (Ibid: 8) he stressed time and again. In fact, according to him, it was not so important whether one learned English or Sanskrit, modern science or classical Hindu philosophy. The main purpose of education was not the accumulation of information, but how to relate to it, and use this knowledge for 'building the power of the human mind and the spirit'.

It was in this context that he spoke of the essence of India; of what this civilisation demands from man; its supreme *dharma.* As Sri Aurobindo said, man could not be reduced to just an ego, a mind and a reason. Man has a soul. And the aim of existence is not to remain contented with the pleasures of the body, but to elevate the spirit and realise the divine. While speaking of 'national education', it was this lesson that Sri Aurobindo recalled on India.

> India has seen always in man the individual—a soul, a portion of the Divinity enwrapped in mind and body, a conscious manifestation in Nature of the Universal self and spirit. Always, she has distinguished and cultivated in him a mental, an intellectual, an ethical, dynamic and practical, an aesthetic and hedonist, a vital and physical being, but all these have been seen as powers of a soul that manifests through them and grows with their strength, and yet they are not all the soul, because at the summit of its ascent it arises to something greater than them all, into a spiritual being, and it is in this that she has found the supreme manifestation of the soul of man and his ultimate divine manhood, his *paranartha* and highest *purusartha.* (Ibid: 15).

It was this higher spiritual pursuit which, Sri Aurobindo thought, should give a distinctive meaning to our education. It should be our contribution to the world. In other words, an authentic critique of colonial education or a true striving for national education would mean neither a mindless rejection of modernity nor a foolish return to antiquity. It would mean a new education guided by the living spirit of the Indian civilisation.

What is important to note is that Sri Aurobindo did suggest concrete pedagogical proposals to implement this higher ideal of education. In this context, it would not be inappropriate to speak of the three basic pedagogical principles that he suggested. First, according to him, 'nothing can be taught' (Sri Aurobindo Ashram 1956: 20). This principle is indeed radical, because it challenges the idea of the conventional form of teaching: the teacher as a supreme authority imposing his knowledge on the empty mind of the passive learner! Instead, it assumes that the teacher is just a helper, a guide. He shows the child how to acquire knowledge. This means tremendous faith in the child's innate ability to learn and grow from within. Herein lies the second principle. As Sri Aurobindo said, 'the mind has to be consulted on its own growth' (Ibid: 20). This means that the child's specificity and *swadharma* ought to be respected. No adult should be allowed to shape the child according to his will, because

> Everyone has in him something divine, something his own, a chance of perfection and strength, in however small a sphere, which God offers him to take or refuse. The task is to find it, develop it and use it. (Ibid: 20).

The third principle is 'to work from the near to the far' (Ibid: 20). What it signifies is that it is better to learn from all that the child can relate to: the language he speaks, the culture he grows up with, the natural surroundings he comes across every day. These three principles, in fact, reveal a method of learning which is natural and spontaneous, democratic and humane—free from all sorts of artificiality and authoritarianism.

The method of learning Sri Aurobindo talked about, it is obvious, begins with the assumption that every child has a potential, and education should allow this potential to unfold itself. Sri Aurobindo, needless to add, warned us of a wrong method of learning—say, 'stupid and dry spelling and reading books', because that would destroy the child's potential and reduce the process of learning into a dry/mechanical process of rote memorisation. Every child, Sri Aurobindo believed, is a lover of interesting narratives, a hero worshipper and a patriot. It is possible to appeal to these inborn interests, and to let the child, without knowing it, master the living and human parts of his nation's history. Likewise, every child is an enquirer, an investigator, an analyser. And if education can appeal to these inherent qualities, the child can acquire—without knowing it—the right temper and the necessary fundamental knowledge of the scientist.

The main objective of education is to enable the child to realise his/her potential and to develop the *faculties* of learning. Sri Aurobindo gave concrete suggestions on the development of mental faculties, like the power of observation, the ability to differentiate and to judge. For example, he gave the example of a flower, how the child should be encouraged to observe the flower carefully—'the exact shade, the peculiar glow, the precise intensity of the scent, the beauty of the curve and design in the form'. Let the child be given a similar but different flower, and encouraged to observe it with the same care, but with the avowed object of noting the similarities and differences'. An exercise of this kind, if repeated frequently, would sharpen the child's memory; it would also help him/her develop the capacity to compare and contrast!

This natural way of developing the faculties, Sri Aurobindo thought, would enable the child to learn with care, love and creativity; it would be refreshingly free from the oppressive experience of cramming to acquire knowledge. He was hopeful that the child's natural curiosity and his/her observation and comparison of flowers, leaves, plants and trees would lay the foundation of botanical knowledge. Likewise, the observation of the stars would evoke the child's interest in astronomy; with the observation of earth and stones would begin a lesson in geology; the observation of insects and animals would mean a trip to the world of entomology and zoology.

The point Sri Aurobindo was trying to make was that the development of the faculties of learning was important. The goal of education, according to him, was to help the child develop these *faculties*, not to bombard him/her with mechanical book-learning and a storehouse of facts, information and second-hand ideas, because once these faculties are developed, the child would be able to learn everything—and this time with more intensity and creativity.

> There is no scientific subject the perfect and natural mastery of which cannot be prepared in early childhood by this training of the faculties to observe, compare, remember and judge various classes of objects. It can be done easily and attended

> with a supreme and absorbing interest in the mind of the student. Once the taste is created, the boy can be trusted to follow it up with all the enthusiasm of youth in his leisure hours. This will prevent the necessity at a later age of teaching him everything in class. (Sri Aurobindo Ashram 1956: 46).

It was obvious that for a saint-philosopher like Sri Aurobindo, mental/intellectual education alone was not sufficient, because 'the education of the intellect divorced from the perfection of the moral and emotional nature is injurious to human progress' (Sri Aurobindo Ashram 1956: 27). But never did he appreciate the idea of making children moral and religious by the forceful teaching of moral/religious textbooks. He felt that morality or religion should be lived and practised, and, therefore, nothing could be more important than the personal life of the teacher. 'The first principle of moral teaching,' wrote Sri Aurobindo, 'is to suggest and invite; not command or impose. The best method of suggestion is by personal example...' (Ibid: 29). True, he spoke of the necessity of books—books containing the lofty examples of the past or the great thoughts of great souls. However, these ideals, he felt, should not be presented before the child as 'moral lessons', but 'as things of supreme human interest which set fire to the highest emotions' (Ibid: 29). Essentially, the real challenge is not to memorise 'moral lessons' as codified in printed words, but to evoke the noblest emotions from within and live a truly moral and religious life.

The educational ideals of Sri Aurobindo were further elaborated by his disciple—the Mother. For proper education she spoke of the 'science of living'—the necessity of understanding and disciplining the four important components of one's being: psychic, mental, vital and physical. To begin with, let us look at the meaning of physical education. The kind of spiritual pursuits Sri Aurobindo talked about, it has to be kept in mind, should not mean the neglect of the body. Instead, the body ought to be seen as the instrument of the divine. As the Mother said, 'the body should be strong and supple so that it may become in the material world a fit instrument for the truth force which wills to manifest through us' (Ibid: 94). This explains the necessity of appropriate physical education. Its objectives are many: control and discipline of its functions; a total, methodical and harmonious development of all the parts and movements of the body; rectification of defects and deformities, if there are any. For a rational and enlightened physical education, the Mother felt, the child should be encouraged to acquire the basic minimum knowledge of the body, its different organs, their functions and activities. This knowledge would eventually enable the child, as he/she grows up, to control and discipline the body so that its functions become normal and harmonious. Hence, the Mother emphasised the necessity of regular exercises, sports, and games. Besides, it was important for the child to develop a taste for food that is simple and healthy. It was not at all desirable, as she repeatedly emphasised, to make eating an occasion to satisfy the child's greed and gluttony. 'From one's very childhood one should know that one eats in order to give to the body the strength and health, and not to enjoy the pleasures of the palate' (Ibid: 102). Essentially, the deeper meaning of physical education is to train the body so that it can become a perfect instrument of the divine; the goal is to unite the physical with the spiritual. This is important to remember, because, according to the Mother, the body is often used by the mind and the vital for wrong reasons. 'The mind with its dogmas, its rigid and arbitrary principles; the vital with its passions, its excesses and dissipations, soon do everything to destroy the natural balance of the body and create in it fatigue, exhaustion and disease' (Ibid: 94). An appropriate physical education, the Mother hoped, would enable the body to free itself from this 'tyranny'. It would lead to a 'constant union with the psychic centre of the being' (Ibid: 94).

It is not difficult to realise the necessity of 'the education of the vital', because

> The vital being in us is the seat of impulses and desires, of enthusiasm and violence, of dynamic energy and desperate

> depression, of passions and revolt. It can set in motion everything, build up and realise, it can also destroy and mar everything. It seems to be, in the human being, the most difficult part to train. (Ibid: 93).

To educate the vital was, therefore, to become conscious and gradually the master of one's character. Only then would it be possible to channelise the tremendous energy of the vital for humane/divine purposes. For this, the child must be encouraged to observe himself: his reactions and impulses, his desires, his movements of violence and passion. This careful observation would eventually enable the child to achieve 'perfect mastery and transformation of all the elements that have to be transformed.' The Mother also spoke of the necessity of developing the aesthetic sense of the child. 'He must be shown, made to appreciate, taught to love beautiful, lofty, healthy and noble things; whether in nature or in human creation... It will save him from degrading influences' (Sri Aurobindo Ashram 1956: 110).

For mental education, the Mother spoke of the necessity of developing the faculties—the ability to concentrate, observe, record and memorise. Another important thing for mental education, she felt, is to develop the child's interest in learning. 'To love to learn,' said the Mother, 'is the most precious gift that one can make to a child: to love to learn always and everywhere. Let all circumstances, all happenings in life be occasions, constantly renewed, for learning more and ever more' (Ibid: 115-16). However, she said, it should not be forgotten that the mind too needs rest. And that is why, *silence* would play an important role in mental education, because the greatest possible rest, the Mother emphasised, lies in silence.

No education would, however, remain complete without psychic/spiritual education. Because the ultimate goal, as Sri Aurobindo and the Mother emphasised, is to realise the power of the divine within, to transform oneself, and to become a new being. It is, therefore, important to become aware of and discover this spiritual essence—the 'psychic' centre of one's being. The psychic, the Mother said, is 'the seat within of the highest truth of our existence, that which can know/manifest this truth' (Ibid: 91).

The psychic/spiritual education, the Mother felt, would enable one to realise what transcends the body and the immediate circumstances of life. This realisation of 'the sense of universality, limitless expansion, timeless continuity' would lead one 'to live in everything and in all beings' (Ibid: 124). The meaning of this education is that all barriers are overcome; man transcends his preoccupation with himself: his egotistic desires and impulses. And this would mean, as the Mother hoped, 'the creation of a new species that will be in relation to man what man is in relation to the animal and that will manifest upon earth a new force, a new consciousness and a new power.' (Ibid: 130).

This grand agenda of 'integral education', the Mother argued, requires a rigorous practice of austerity—the ability to overcome the temptation of all sorts of 'excesses' and to lead 'a life of light and balance, beauty and joy'. Austerity, it has to be realised, is not contempt for the body. Instead, it is a kind of *tapasya* to build a body that is 'beautiful in form, harmonious in posture, supple and agile in movements, powerful in its activities and resistant in its health and organic function' (Ibid: 135). Hence, the Mother emphasised, it requires 'austere' habits like regularity in food, sleep and physical exercises. This austerity is needed in all spheres—in developing the vital, in the manner of speech, and in the realm of work. But then, the most difficult is the austerity of emotions and feeling—the 'tapasya of love'. The essence of love, the Mother reminded us, is the joy of identity or the bliss of union with the divine reality. What we call love seldom takes us to this higher level, because it is not free from attachment, from feelings of superiority or inferiority. Generally, because of this egotistic desire, it is difficult to avoid misunderstandings, friction and misgivings. That is why, the Mother felt the necessity of the tapasya, so that this love can become truly divine, and as a result, one's personal interests begin to disappear.

> ...The austerity of feeling consists of rejecting all emotional attachment, of whatever kind it may be, whether for a person, for the family, for the country or any other object, and concentrating exclusively on the attachment to the Divine Reality. (Sri Aurobindo Ashram 1956: 159).

This brief and meaningful discussion would help us identify a set of salient features of the educational agenda of Sri Aurobindo and the Mother.

1. Education is not utilitarian—an instrumental means to acquire a technical skill for getting a job or earning money. Instead, education is a kind of *tapasya*—a dedicated quest to realise the divine, alter oneself and become a new being free form egotistic pride and desire.
2. Education is not just intellectual/mental education—a process of acquiring information through learning from books. It is integral education that takes care of all the important components of one's being—physical, vital, mental and psychic. Not only that, education is a process of inner discipline that seeks to unite all these components, and create a new holistic being.
3. Education is egalitarian, because it is against any kind of force or imposition. It assumes that every child is gifted with an innate potential and it is the task of the teacher to arouse the child's interest in learning so that he can unfold this potential. The teacher is a friend, a guide, a catalyst!
4. Education is not just academic. It does not fill the mind of the child with loads of information relating to different disciplines and subjects. Instead, its goal is to develop the faculties of learning, for example, observation, comparison, analysis and evaluation. The assumption is that if these faculties are developed, the child can learn whatever he/she likes.

In other words, instead of the conventional form of 'course-oriented, textbook-dominated' learning, it seeks to engage the child in divergent activities and projects so that the faculties of learning are developed.

5. Education is not formal, mechanical or external. It is essentially a spiritual quest. It requires austere practices so that the learner can overcome all egotistic pleasures and realise the ultimate unity with the divine.

II
Mirambika: Beginning of an Alternative Project

An educational agenda of this kind, as is obvious, would be difficult to implement, particularly because the society we live in has altogether different expectations from schools. Our society—or, to put it more specifically, the career-conscious, ambitious, anxiety-ridden middle class—wants schools to deliver the goods, that is, it wants children to acquire knowledge (information and skill), improve their career prospects and achieve 'success' (or a privileged position in the material world) in life. 'Good' schools, therefore, are required to be careful with their 'products'—the products with a 'market-value'. They have no use for integral education, development of faculties, austerity of life-practices or spiritual awareness. What matters to them is a mode of training that fragments knowledge into different academic disciplines, or sees it as just an instrument for career building.

In this scenario, the existence of Mirambika—a school that seeks to implement the educational agenda of Sri Aurobindo and the Mother—is indeed surprising, mainly because it aims to accomplish what, according to the mainstream way of thinking, would be regarded as an 'impossible' project. No doubt, a school like Mirambika would never be free from difficulties and challenges, as it dares to do what seems to have no meaning in an intensely competitive, fragmented and divided world. Yet, the fact that

Mirambika has been around for more than twenty years shows its innate zeal, its ability to meet challenges and difficulties, and grow, despite the many unresolved contradictions and the resultant anxiety regarding its survival.

A cursory look at Mirambika is enough to convince one that the school is of an altogether different kind. Its *splendid architecture*—its geometrical symmetry, openness, its harmony with nature—is overwhelming. Indeed the architecture reveals the philosophy of the school. Here is a school that does not confine children to an 'enclosed space' for forceful learning. It is a school that does not look like a cage. Instead, its openness invites freedom. No wonder, Mirambika attracts people because of its absolute transparency. They can visit the school at any time, move around, talk to people and experience its beauty and calm. There is nobody—not even a security guard in uniform—who asks questions or expresses doubt about the 'intention' of the visitor. This freedom—freedom from fear and constraints—expresses itself in the body language of the children. Anyone who has visited Mirambika, even if only once, would have noticed the rhythm of these children—happiness in their facial expressions, flexibility in their body movements, and a certain camaraderie with their teachers.

What one notices here is the absence of structured/routinised practices. Instead, the free movement of the children is all pervasive. When some children are engaged in the art room, others may be learning mathematics. Likewise, when someone is playing, his/her friend may be busy in the library for 'project work'. The school, it seems, tries to respect the autonomy of each child. That is why, Mirambika, as one feels when one visits the school, does not look like a learning machine or a factory that breeds anonymity. What characterises it is its intimacy; every child is a 'person' who finds his/ her own space.

The beauty of Mirambika lies in its small/humane size. It is a school with barely 150 children. There is no possibility of anyone getting 'lost' in a crowd. This small size gives the children a sense of belonging, which is indeed a distinguishing feature of Mirambika. A visitor would immediately notice this difference when he sees the two other schools located in the same campus of the Sri Aurobindo Ashram: Mira Nursery and the Mother's International School. The Mother's International School looks quite big—formal and structured. It is a known school that can feel proud of its 'success' rate and its tremendous appeal for the 'educated' class of Delhi. No wonder, from the auto rickshaw driver to the middle class professional—people tend to confuse Mirambika with the Mother's International School, because the general feeling is that a school located in the Sri Aurobindo Ashram ought to be the Mother's International School. This perhaps indicates that Mirambika is not yet a 'known' school. And this is revealing. It just goes to show that in an age when 'good' schools do everything possible to promote and sell their images, Mirambika has refrained from indulging in this practice of advertising itself. This perhaps is yet another sign of an alternative ethos that the school seeks to create.

Indeed, to understand this alternative better, we ought to take a look at how this school was established: Mirambika was born because there was a conscious decision to create an alternative form of education—a school that would try, honestly and sincerely, to implement the educational agenda of Sri Aurobindo and the Mother. It was in October 1980 that the Delhi branch of the Sri Aurobindo Ashram organised a teachers' annual camp. The participants felt that it was necessary to bring about a radical change in the field of education. This led to the establishment of a teachers' training programme at the Ashram. To begin with, Mirambika was conceived as a pilot school for the teachers' training programme. It started functioning in July 1981 with fifty-seven children and ten teachers.

It should be noted that two devotees of Sri Aurobindo and the Mother—Matthijs Corne Lissen and Mrs. Neelijie Huppes—played a key role in the development of

Mirambika. It would not be wrong to regard them as the founders of Mirambika. Both of them were born and brought up in Netherlands. They came to India on a spiritual quest, and eventually engaged themselves in a radical educational agenda. Perhaps a brief look at their spiritual journey would help us understand the meaning of Mirambika. Matthijs was a doctor by profession; deeply interested in psychotherapy. He had been exposed to Indian philosophy even while he was in Netherlands. He had read the writings of Sri Aurobindo and the Mother. Moreover, his engagement with psychotherapy led him to take special interest in Sri Aurobindo. It was in 1970 that Matthijs came to India for the first time. From Caluctta to Boddh Gaya to Varanasi—he moved around and tried to learn Indian philosophy in depth. At Boddh Gaya he learned meditation, and from a professor of philosophy at the Benaras Hindu University, he got to know more about the dynamics of Indian philosophy. It was difficult for him to stay away from India. He came back in 1976 and devoted himself to the spiritual quest.

Neelijie Huppes did her higher education in education and psychology. She too had read the philosophy of Sri Aurobindo and the Mother in Netherlands. She came to India in 1976. For both Matthijs and Neelijie, schooling, as they had experienced it, was not a happy memory.

> There was no respect for the inner being. There was no possibility of learning from within. Things were always forced. Schooling crushed the soul. It negated creativity. It was based on fear and punishment.

Mirambika, they feel, has brought about a much needed change in the field of educational philosophy and practice. It looks at education as a means to realise the beauty within. That is the reason why, they say, Mirambika has never encouraged the idea of a fixed syllabus on different fragmented academic subjects. The goal is to develop the faculties of learning, and academic disciplines are not ends in themselves, but just tools for developing these faculties. Let the children, as Matthijs and Neelijie assert, assume the primary role in the process of learning; develop their own aims and evaluate themselves. The teacher is simply a guide; he should not impose his ideas and knowledge on the child.

The ethos of Mirambika should not, however, be confused with the Western notion of 'child centred' education. Matthijs and Neelijie make this point clear.

> Many schools in the West have become child centred. But their freedom does not have any inner harmony. It often degenerates into egoism. Here in Mirambika, the core element is spirituality. It integrates freedom and harmony. The spiritual dimension lacks in the West.

The spirituality that Matthijs and Neelijie are talking about has to be understood. It is spiritual in the new sense. It is like giving a new meaning to the world and, thereby transforming it. 'The children of Mirambika,' they believe, 'grow up as creative, honest, self-reliant individuals, who are respectful to others. With this orientation they give a new meaning to the world. They transform it.'

In other words, for Matthijs and Neelijie, the goal of Mirambika is indeed radical: creating new values and transforming the world. They admit that it is a school that has addressed the needs of the urban/middle class. But then, they assert, it was a conscious decision. 'It was thought that the middle class, given its ambition and materialism, would not come to a school of this kind. We however, wanted to alter the situation and change the character of this class.'

The goal is radical. The difficulties are many. After all, 'except for the child, all of us (parents and teachers) are the products of the conventional system.' We, therefore, need to orient ourselves time and again. Moreover, there is 'gross materialism' all around. Yet, there is a ray of hope. Matthijs and Neelijie see 'a new sensitivity, a spiritual awakening'. That is why, Mirambika—their creation—has an important role to play. 'Its prospect in the coming age is tremendous,' so they hope. They established Mirambika, saw it evolving and growing, and then in 1992, they left the school and went to Pondicherry for 'deeper spiritual pursuits'.[1]

III
Call of the School: Deep-rooted Parental Engagement

Mirambika, it is obvious, is not a very easy choice to make, because it involves 'risk': the anxiety that the children—with this kind of alternative education—may not be able to compete, 'adjust' to the system or do well in life. The school too knows it. It therefore expects certain similarities between the ethos of the family and that of the school, because alternative education can succeed only if the parents understand its meaning, accept it whole-heartedly and do not create obstacles in its experimental pursuits. In a way, Mirambika has to be chosen, because it cannot be equated with any other 'trusted' school where one normally tries for the child's admission. As a result, not many people choose Mirambika. The school offers admission to 20 children for the Red Group—the junior-most group which is equivalent to the nursery class. And the number of applicants are generally not more than 100. The school is particularly careful about the process of selection, because, as we have already said, it expects the parents to whole-heartedly accept the meaning and objective of Mirambika. As Partho—the present principal of the school—says, 'We want to see primarily two characteristics: intellectual awareness and psychic openness. Psychic openness is really important. We expect the parents—who choose Mirambika—to be open to new ideas.'

The selection process has two important stages. First, the parents are asked to fill up a lengthy questionnaire. Each parent is required to do it separately. The questionnaire contains questions relating to pedagogy, educational philosophy, culture and child-rearing practices. At the second stage, the short-listed parents are called for interviews. The basic objective of these interviews is to see whether the parents are really in tune with the ethos of Mirambika. This indeed is a difficult task. Partho says, 'There is a great amount of intuition in the process of selection.' What is interesting is that in this entire process of selection, children are not interviewed. This speaks of Mirambika's concern for the child. Little children, the school believes, should not be subjected to the oppressive process of examination, interviews, evaluation or ranking. It is only at the end that the parents are asked to bring their children for observation. The children come, they play with one another, and talk to diyas (at Mirambika teachers are called diyas, didis and bhaiyas). There is no surveillance, no authoritarian gaze on the movement of the children. This is just to see whether they are mentally and physically fit and comfortable for the new school life. The process of selection is aimed at choosing only those parents who are willing to appreciate the alternative educational agenda that Mirambika seeks to pursue.

Who are these parents? And how do they relate to Mirambika? One thing is certain. The parents who send their children to Mirambika are well established, and fairly well educated; they have a strong opinion about alternative education. Many of them are what can be called the '*cultural elite*' of our society. They are artists, journalists, designers, NUO activists, media/theatre personalities and filmmakers. Many are in other prestigious professions: doctors, engineers, architects, lawyers, scientists and educationists. In terms of their economic status, they are reasonably well off. For example, the average monthly income of the family, as our findings suggest, is about Rs. 30,000—an amount that, despite the inflated economy, can be said to be good, if compared with the average standard of living in the Indian society. In other words, the social profile of these parents suggests that the character of the school is 'elitist'. In fact, this 'class-confidence' of the parents is obvious from the way they speak, move and conduct themselves. It has to be explored why 'affluent' parents choose Mirambika. According to Partho, Mirambika is, after all, situated in an 'affluent area of Delhi'. Furthermore, as he feels, it is generally the 'English-educated people' who have opted for the kind of education that Mirambika has to offer. Perhaps, as the general argument goes, these are parents who, because of the social/material 'security' they enjoy, can afford to take the 'risk'. Or, it can be argued that unlike government schools, Mirambika is a 'costly' proposition (monthly expenses which include tuition fee, transportation charge and food expenses exceed Rs 1,000), and as a result, it is bound to exclude the lower middle class.[2] Nevertheless, the deeper implications of the 'social background' of Mirambika have to be examined.

But before that, it is important to know how these parents look at, and relate to Mirambika. The reason why they have chosen Mirambika is that it is a school in which they see a possibility—a possibility that is promising in an age in which 'conventional schools' crush the child's free growth and creativity. It is important to note that the parents tend to appreciate Mirambika for its 'child-centred' approach. Here is a school, they feel, that gives 'autonomy to children', seeks to implement the ideal of 'free progress' education and enables them to participate in the process of 'learning without stress'. As a parent comments:

> I have chosen Mirambika because of its open/natural environment. It is non-hierarchical. There is no difference between teachers and students. And Mirambika believes in the development of the natural sense of enquiry.

Mirambika is also appreciated for the emphasis it lays on 'balanced and integral development of the child'. Moreover, Mirambika, as some parents feel, offers 'value-based' education. It has to be realised that the parents who choose Mirambika are not necessarily the devotees of Sri Aurobindo and the Mother. Nor do they necessarily follow or understand the philosophy of Sri Aurobindo and the Mother. In fact, what they really appreciate is the possibilities that Mirambika throws open to its children—something that is refreshingly different form the 'rigid systems' of conventional education.

Many parents feel that 'Mirambika is unique; it cannot be compared with any other school'. The difference between Mirambika and any other conventional school, as a parent puts it, is like the 'difference between a cage and a sanctuary'. But essentially, the beauty of Mirambika lies in its 'holistic' approach to the development of the child, which is quite unlike the 'academic' approach of conventional education.

All this perhaps suggests that parents choose Mirambika for its *uniqueness*—its alternative mode of education. It also implies that the school has succeeded in 'involving' the parents something that it can feel proud of. In a way, Mirambika is also engaged in re-educating the parents. No wonder, a large section of them think that the school has changed their perception of education and the meaning of adult-child relationship. 'Mirambika has changed my whole perception of education and doubled my joy of bringing up kids,' says a mother. Likewise, another parent feels, 'Mirambika has helped create a strong bond between me and my child'. It is heartening to note that Mirambika, for many, has changed their perception of life, their way of relating to the world.

> Mirambika has helped us look into ourselves, to find solutions for problems that we face on a day-to-day basis.

Mirambika, it appears, is not just a school for children. It has become a zone of learning for the parents as well.

> The way we look at knowledge, education, priorities in life, relationship between parents and children, has changed and developed over the ten years we have been with Mirambika. We have learned a lot from Mirambika.

The story of this *relatedness*—or their association with Mirambika—has been repeatedly told by many parents. Take, for instance, Balakrishnan—a professor and computer scientist at the Indian Institute of Technology, Delhi. He recalls his own student days and says that he used to hate history and geography. The way these subjects were taught, according to him, was frightening. It was mechanical cramming meant only for exams, getting marks and ranks. He also speaks of his IIT experience. True, the IIT students are bright. But then, Balakrishnan strongly feels that they do not experience the fire—the creative urge to contribute something meaningful to the fundamentals of knowledge.

Moreover, he is not particularly happy with the value system of the IIT students. They are obsessed with their career and with making money. In fact, Balakrishnan argues that even the brightest products of the mainstream education are not original. It is this dissatisfaction that leads him to look at Mirambika. In Mirambika, he sees a possibility. It arouses the child's interest in learning. The children of Mirambika, he says, may not yet have learned how to answer a set of questions in an exam in a given time, or how to think of marks and grades. But then, they are happy; they are involved in the process of learning. Balakrishnan speaks of his daughter with pride and enthusiasm.

> I am happy with the way my daughter handles the project work. She does it on her own, and does it with lot of interest and creativity. Recently, she did a project on *Kargil*. She used the internet, got relevant information including the UN resolution on Kashmir, and wrote about 8/10 pages on Kargil.

Anil Jain—a senior officer in Punjab National Bank—expresses a similar opinion.

> Mirambika children like whatever they do. They may not know everything. But whatever they know is thorough. For instance, while working on topics like *Birds* and *Time*, my daughter's group was taken to Sultanpur Bird Sanctuary and National Physical Laboratory. They know how to collect resources, get information, and understand things.

Here is the story of yet another parent—a professor and medical surgeon at the All India Institute of Medical Sciences, New Delhi. 'I am a product of the most successful mainstream school—DPS,' he says. His son too used to go to Delhi Public School (DPS). But then, 'the DPS looked like a terribly structured place without any creativity or space left for the child.' It was at this juncture that he came to know of Mirambika.

> We came to Mirambika, saw the school, felt its environment. We felt that it was the right school for our child.

His wife—who is also a doctor at the Safdarjung Hospital feels:

> Academically speaking, Mirambika children are somewhat weak. But then, they develop many other faculties: how to take a decision, or how to grow responsible for one's own work. And, in the ultimate analysis, these are the faculties that matter. In most educational institutions, these faculties are crushed. That is why, even at the college/university level, students cannot take a decision on their own.

They repeatedly refer to their experience with mainstream schools. For example,

> We have seen and experienced what the mainstream education is all about. We don't have any illusion about it.

Babu—a newspaper journalist—says:

> Right from the beginning, I have been looking for a system of education for my daughter that would create good values—not the crude money-making mentality. Moreover, throughout my life, I had 'good' education: one of the 'best' schools in Kerala as well as a university like the JNU. But I have felt that these institutions do not give much importance to values. We wanted alternative education. We came to Mirambika, read the prospectus, and realised that it was the school we were looking for.

Likewise, A. John—an NGO activist—asserts:

> We are against the money-making, competitive rat race. And Mirambika is free from this logic of the market. I also don't have any complaint about my child's development. When I was at school I could not think of doing a project on my own. But my child is doing it. He can think, find and read books, handle resources on his own. This means something is happening.

The parents are, no doubt, deeply involved with Mirambika. It intensifies their hope in further possibilities in alternative education. However, as is to be expected in the case of a unique school like Mirambika, there are moments of tension and anxiety, and there is an atmosphere of uncertainty which has a lot to do with whether or not Mirambika can deliver what it promises. In fact, as we would argue, the school has its 'weaknesses' too, and the parents are no less critical of it. Yet, what cannot be denied is that the school has its own magic, and one cannot remain indifferent to it. In fact, with a school like Mirambika, it would be difficult for anyone to remain content with merely a contractual relationship (i.e. pay the school fee and demand 'results'). Mirambika evokes the feelings of all that is noble and great in us. No wonder, Rekha Kamat—a JNU professor whose child studies at Mirambika—manages time for the children of the school and teaches them English literature. Mirambika, she feels, has influenced her own mode of teaching at the JNU. She asserts with enthusiasm: 'Now I can give more space to my students.' Jain—a bank officer—takes leave from her office, finds tremendous joy in the science lab of Mirambika and implements an alternative method of teaching science. And Manoj Arora—a Supreme Court advocate—comes to Mirambika every Monday and Thursday; spends an hour with the children, trains them in physical activities and games like football. These are just random examples. They demonstrate the parents' deep-rooted interest in the school, and their hope centred on its ability to provide alternative education, generate creativity and reflexivity, and inculcate profound human values in children.

IV
Teaching: Discovery of the Sacred Zone of Meaning

A school like Mirambika, it is obvious, needs teachers who are qualitatively different. For them, being a 'professional' or looking at teaching as yet another 'career', or holding a recognised diploma or degree is not a sufficient qualification. These are the prerequisites for teaching 'academic disciplines'. Given the radical educational agenda that Mirambika has chosen for itself, its teachers ought to be gifted with a set of special qualities. First, it is desirable that they understand, appreciate and imbibe the educational philosophy of Sri Aurobindo and the Mother. In other words, they need to see themselves not as 'specialists' with information and knowledge, but as creative agents organically related to children for cultivating the faculties of learning, and realising the ultimate purpose of existence. They need to be motivated from within. Teaching, for them, ought to be a mission—a radical/spiritual engagement with the world. Second, they ought to be extraordinarily sensitive and open to radical pedagogic experiments, because they are required to question the sanctity of codified texts, fixed curricula and disciplinary devices like examinations and ranking. Mirambika expects them to bring out the child's creativity, curiosity and interest in learning. This means that the teachers here ought to be quite knowledgeable and research-oriented. Third, it is important for them to challenge the hierarchical power relations and practise the egalitarian ideal. They are expected to respect the autonomy of the child. The beauty of the teacher-taught relationship, it is hoped, would not be corrupted by the 'fear of punishment'. To put it briefly, the teachers of Mirambika are expected to fulfil three qualities: commitment and devotion to the philosophy of Sri Aurobindo and the Mother, openness to and familiarity with the new frontiers of knowledge, and a spirit of egalitarianism. As Partho says, 'Mirambika teachers have to be renaissance men.'

No doubt, it is not easy to find such teachers. It is, therefore, important to see how the teachers of Mirambika perceive themselves, how they relate to the process of learning, and define their pursuits in life. Perhaps this would help us understand the dynamics of this important component of school life.

Mirambika teachers can be classified into three types. First, we can speak of the core group, that is, the teachers who have been associated with the school almost from the time of its inception. Second, there are trainee teachers—

young boys and girls—who join the Mirambika teachers' training programme. Third, there are volunteers-professionals, retired officers, parents, housewives—who, because of their interest, offer their services to teach at Mirambika.

Before we learn more about these teachers and their involvement with the school, we need to make a few observations. A teacher at Mirambika, it should be noted, is called *diya*. The word *diya* signifies both *didi* as well as *bhaia*. The fact that children call their teachers *diyas* (not Sir or Madam) speaks quite a lot about the relationship between the teacher and the taught. Here is a relationship that is deeply intimate and personal (we should also not forget that the teacher-student ratio in this school is remarkably satisfactory; for a group of 15 children there are at least 3 to 4 diyas). Theirs is a relationship that seems to have done away with hierarchy and power. The power that prevails is the power of love: mutual trust, reciprocity between the diya and the child. To visit Mirambika is to experience the beauty of this relationship. Children are seen playing with their diyas—they talk, argue, demand, yet respect their diyas. There is no trace of fear, no inhibition, no anxiety. For example, Partho does not look like the 'head' of the institution monopolising power, maintaining an unbridgeable distance and excluding children from his 'sacred' zone. Instead, any child can come to Partho's room at any time and initiate a dialogue. Partho's deep involvement with the children is also obvious from the way he teaches, talks and argues with them. Or take, for instance, Jasvirbhaiya who is approaching seventy. Even a little child of seven years would not feel hesitant to share a joke with him. The story goes on. Mirambika has made it possible: the intense/intimate bond between the diyas and the children.

Teachers as Pillars of Inspiration

The diyas who constitute the core group are Partho, Vijayadi, Sulochanadi and Sriladi. In fact, Mirambika, as it exists, cannot be imagined without these four diyas. Amidst the continual flow/flux of trainee teachers and volunteers, these four persons give some kind of stability to the school. Their deep involvement with Mirambika—the way it evolved, grew and is facing new challenges—generates hope and optimism. They guide the trainee teachers, associate themselves with the parents, and participate in almost every other activity of the school. What makes them stand apart is their *missionary* zeal: their eagerness to implement an alternative educational ideal.

To begin with, let us look at the biographical profile of Partho—the Principal who, for many parents, is a source of hope—the main pillar of the institution. Partho was a brilliant student who did remarkably well in school/college examinations. He did his graduation in English literature from one of the best known colleges in the country: St. Stephen's College, Delhi. He was a topper. The college Principal wanted him to go abroad for higher studies. He, however, decided not to go abroad. In fact, the process of disillusionment with the existing system of education had already begun.

> Since I was a good student, it was not difficult for me to realise that one could fool the prevalent educational system so easily.

Partho left the college: his association with higher education. He tried to help his father in his business, but soon realised that it was not his cup of tea. He began to read a lot: psychology, physics, philosophy and about the evolutionary process. It was at this time (sometime in 1985) that he began to see Ramakrishna and Vivekananda in his dream. The dream surprised him, because he had not read much on Vivekananda. Moreover, he used to think that Ramakrishna was a 'victim of a psychological disorder'. The dream, in a way, was a turning point. He began to make himself familiar with the writings on Indian mysticism and philosophy. He studied Sri Aurobindo, and it had a deep impact on him. Partho decided to become a monk in the Ramakrishna

Mission. But then, he felt that he should first go to the mountains. On his way—from Almora to Mukteshwar—he met many sadhus and lived with them. It was in 1987 that he came to the Delhi branch of the Sri Aurobindo Ashram, and started teaching at Mirambika. Since then—except for a period of five years when he went to Jaipur to start a new school based on similar principles—he has been deeply involved with Mirambika.

'I call myself a hard core Aurobindoite,' says Partho. His mission, he says, is to lead a life based on 'Sri Aurobindo's principle of evolution'. And he has chosen education as his field. In fact, Partho's missionary zeal, his enthusiasm and faith, his passion for an alternative form of education and his spiritual quest are all very obvious when one sees him talking in group meetings (the meetings in which the parents and diyas come together) or in workshops that the school conducts from time to time to 'orient' the parents and diyas and make them familiar with the philosophies of Sri Aurobindo and the Mother.

'I love children,' says Partho. Indeed, the way the children relate to him proves his point.

> They work hard, read a lot, and have their own ideas. They are original.

Sulochanadi—another important personality at Mirambika radiates strength, determination, and the power of dedication. She too is a devotee of Sri Aurobindo and the Mother. Her commitment to Mirambika, it seems, is total. In fact, Sulochanadi was one of the leading persons who started the movement for *integral education*—a project based on the ideas of Sri Aurobindo—in Orissa. Her father—an Aurobindoite—influenced her thinking, and her philosophy of life. Sulochanadi joined Mirmabika in 1982. She has witnessed and experienced the different phases of Mirambika—its moments of optimism as well as of crises. But then, for the 'new generation', she asserts, Mirambika must grow and evolve, because it has a lot to offer through its 'integral education'.

> Our children are unique. They have a mission.

Barring a few exceptions, she says, nobody has ever regretted being a student of Mirambika. Today, Sulochanadi feels, her existence is 'inseparable from Mirambika'. Indeed, her presence can be felt as she works in silence. She is with the children; she is with the diyas; and she is with the parents. Mirambika too, it would not be wrong to say, gets its identity from Sulochanadi: her simplicity, her *karmayoga*, her devotion.

Sriladi joined Mirambika in 1981. Earlier she was with the Pondicherry branch of the Sri Aurobindo Ashram.

> I too was a product of the conventional system. But I disliked it. I disliked its overemphasis on memory. This disillusionment with the conventional system, I am sure, must have been felt by many others who have come to Mirambika to teach.

Her emphasis is on the uniqueness of Mirambika—the way it generates the 'qualities of leadership'. The children of Mirambika, she adds, learn to take the initiative, and value freedom. They become 'good citizens'. To become a good teacher, Sriladi thinks, one needs the right 'attitude, philosophy and skill'. That is the reason why, as she says, the teachers who join Mirambika have to be perpetually reoriented. Anyone who knows this school would concede that Sriladi and Mirambika are inseparable. 'Mirambika has shaped my philosophy. Now I can practise it,' is how Sriladi articulates her intense/selfless association with the school.

For Vijayadi—another member of the core group—'Mirambika is the only answer to education in the 21st century'. It helps develop a child's faculties of learning and makes him/her 'sensitive and humane'. The possibility of Mirambika, Vijayadi believes, is tremendous. The teachers, she feels, should be open, sensitive and always eager to learn. Besides, she feels, the teachers who have worked with Mirambika are capable of making a difference wherever they go. For Vijayadi, Mirambika is a part of her being. 'The more I understand Mirambika, the easier it is for me to overcome all outside influences'. This is not at all surprising, considering that she chose Mirambika to fulfil her mission.

> Right from my school days I was not very happy with the prevalent system of education. I began my search. When I was at the university, a professor who was influenced by Sri Aurobindo's philosophy—told me about Mirambika. When I came to Mirambika I felt that it was meant for me.

These four core persons convey a message: Mirambika is for those who want to fulfil a great mission in life. It needs simplicity, dedication and commitment. It needs sensitivity, openness and eagerness to learn. Essentially, it requires faith—the faith born of conviction and clarity of thought, the faith that gives one the strength to pursue a project that, as far as the mainstream logic goes, appears to be an impossible dream!

Do we see this faith in the other diyas as well—particularly, the trainee teachers who assume the primary responsibility of teaching the children every day?

Enthusiastic Trainee Teachers

Generally, the trainee teachers stay at Mirambika for three years. They are not paid, although they get free accommodation and food at the Ashram. What distinguishes them is the intensity of the work they do—something that is seldom noticed in a conventional B.Ed. college. It can be said without the slightest hesitation that they are a real exception in an environment that has trivialised the teachers' training programmes in the country. They are given the concrete practical responsibility: relating to the children and teaching them, interacting with the parents, evolving plans for the children's cognitive skills, physical activities, art music and craft, evaluating them and writing reports. This sincere/intense engagement makes a difference. It makes them grow confident and responsible.

The fact that they have chosen Mirambika shows their willingness to involve themselves in an alternative project and to make a difference in the field of education. Moushami, for example, was teaching at a kindergarten in Calcutta. This kindergarten was like any other: not inseparable from the psychology of 'fear and punishment'. Moushami began her search for an 'ideal' school—a school without the fear of punishment; a school based on the principles of freedom—a school she thought perhaps did not exist. It was at this time that she came to know of Mirambika. She joined the school in 1997.

Shanu is an electrical engineer, not because she liked engineering, but because it is taken for granted that a good student ought do science and eventually get into either medicine or engineering.

> I was a rebel. I did not like the way things were happening around me. After engineering I thought I would do something relating to human relations. I thought of doing Master of Social Work or M. Sc. in psychology. But because of my engineering degree I was not allowed to do what I wanted.

Meanwhile, she took up a job in Ahmedabad, earned some money and thought of doing something on her own. Her parents did not appreciate the idea. She, however, chose her own way. She began to teach at a kindergarten school in Ahmedabad and realised that she could make a difference in the field of teaching. It was at this time that she came into contact with a person who wanted to start an experimental school in Ahmedabad. She was required to go to the Pondicherry Ashram for this project and that is where she came to know of Mirambika. It was in 1995 that she came to Mirambika for two months. Eventually, in 1996, she joined Mirambika. 'At Mirambika,' she says, 'I found what I was searching for!'

Before joining Mirambika, Satyabrata, a sincere young man from Orissa, was already familiar with Sri Aurobindo's writings—particularly his essays on the *Bhagvadgita*. Moreover, as he says, he was 'desperately looking for an alternative system of education'. Likewise, Vijay, before joining Mirambika, was involved with the 'integral education' system in Orissa. He too was familiar with the educational philosophy of Sri Aurobindo. Anumpama, whose brother taught at Mirambika, was teaching at Sri Aurobindo International School in Hyderabad. She was familiar with the writings of Sri Aurobindo and the Mother. Perhaps, it can be said that, for these teachers, Mirambika was their logical destination. They were striving for an opportunity to work with an alternative system of education. It was this search that led to their discovery of Mirambika.

Many teachers compare Mirambika with their own schools. Both Anumpama and Sudhir say that they had no freedom; everything was based on force, fear and coercion. But Mirambika, they assert with pride, is entirely different. Anumpama adds:

> In conventional schools, everything is ready-made. There are fixed books, and fixed answers. But here, children are encouraged to discover things on their own.

Sushant recalls his own school days and says that there was no communication between the teacher and the child. He says, there were only five or six children in a class who used to do well and they were the ones who got the teacher's attention. But at Mirambika, he feels, 'there is space for everyone'. The school takes care of everyone's specific needs and interests.

Baren sees no comparison between Mirarnbika and his own school—an over-crowded school 'without the required infrastructure', in which communication between the teacher and the child was impossible. Baren feels that unlike the children of conventional schools, the children of Mirambika may not be able to present a thing in a precise manner. But what distinguishes them is that their understanding of things is thorough; they enjoy whatever they do; they can express their ideas through songs, drama, etc.

An awareness of this clear contrast between Mirambika and conventional schools suggests that the teachers attach great importance and meaning to their practices. Their teaching at Mirambika, they assert with pride, is no ordinary/routine affair. They feel that one ought to develop great qualities—not merely academic skills—to become a good teacher at Mirambika. For Shanu, it is important to understand the 'significance of inner change'. For Moushami, a good teacher needs to be perpetually creative and joyful. Satya speaks of the importance of 'sincerity to oneself'. Vijay believes that a teacher must overcome laziness and remain alert and attentive to the child's needs. For Sushant, three qualities are important: punctuality, sincerity and flexibility. And Anumpama feels that it is one's 'obsession with learning' —learning from all kinds of circumstances—that distinguishes a teacher of Mirambika. In other words, the qualities they talk about transcend what is otherwise appreciated in conventional schools: academic skills! These qualities cannot to be quantified in terms of academic achievements, degrees and diplomas. These are primarily to do with one's inner strength. Perhaps Baren summarises it well:

> After joining Mirambika, I realised that a good teacher ought to be a *yogic person.* This means the development of the psychic being, sincerity to oneself. It is not important to be good in the English language. Nor is it important to be good in some academic subject. After joining Mirambika, I did a lot of reading on Sri Aurobindo's and the Mother's philosophy, and eventually practised meditation. All this helped me to orient myself, and become a good teacher.

It is obvious that the teachers at Mirambika are deeply involved with the school. Here is a school that has shown its faith in them, made them believe that they can make a difference. Everyone agrees that they get complete freedom while they evolve their plans for the children. Perhaps, freedom and responsibility are inter-related. Mirambika, as a result, does have a deep-rooted impact on the teacher's orientation in life. It is not merely a 'workplace' to which one is instrumentally related; it becomes a philosophy of life. No wonder, most of the teachers feel that the school has changed them, given them confidence, and made them aware of their innate potential. Baren, for example, wants to go back to Orissa and start a school like Mirambika for poor people.

Sudhir, Vijay and Satya too speak of a similar project—their desire to take the 'Mirambika experience' to the ordinary people of Orissa. For Anumpama, Mirambika is a source of confidence. Every moment at Mirambika, she asserts, is a moment of learning. She would go back to her old school in Hyderabad, and she is confident that the rich experience of Mirambika would enable her to make a difference. Sushant feels that the school has taught him the art of 'self-understanding'. Moushami feels that she is no longer submissive; Mirambika has made her confident. Shanu is absolutely certain that she would be able to apply her Mirambika experience even in a hostile environment. In a way, Mirambika becomes an integral component of one's being. This perhaps explains Nishi's 'coming back' to the school. As a child, Nishi was a student of Mirambika. When she grew up, she completed her M.Sc. from Pantnagar. But then, Mirambika could not be forgotten. She came back, and this time as a trainee teacher. 'At Mirambika,' says Nishi, 'I don't feel burdened. Whatever I do, is done with a sense of freedom.' Teaching at Mirambika, she feels, is really a challenge. It means 'the ability to unlearn all that one has learned in a formal school'; it means 'adaptability', faith in oneself, intense imagination and creativity. Mirambika, it seems, is inseparable from her own identity. 'Wherever I go, I can make a difference'—that is her confident assertion. And she believes that there is no escape from this 'premier institution', because in the coming years 'Mirambika would be a role model'.

These young trainee teachers—with their faith, enthusiasm and dynamism—give a distinctive identity to Mirambika. What strikes one is their simplicity—something that stands out in posh south Delhi. The way they speak, behave, and dress does not give the impression that they are teaching the children of the 'elite/affluent' class. As a matter of fact, they do not look like the typical 'English-speaking teachers' of select public schools. Perhaps this simplicity further softens the environment of the school. Yet, a question continues to confront many: granted that these teachers are simple, honest and morally sensitive, but are they sufficiently 'qualified' and 'capable' of practising an alternative pedagogy with sufficient rigour and detail? More about it later.

Dedicated Volunteers

Another distinguishing feature of Mirambika is its team of voluntary teachers. What attracts them to Mirambika is its open structure—the way it allows innovations and experimentation. These teachers get no remuneration. It is their authentic will to make a difference in the field of education that drives them to work. This reveals the character of the school. Mirambika has the magic that inspires people—even in this age when everything tends to be measured in terms of its monetary value—to work for higher and nobler purposes. Indeed, to feel this school is to feel it as a sacred zone of meaning!

Look at Jasvirbhaiya who is 67 years old, but whose enthusiasm and passion for an alternative form of mathematics teaching is boundless. He teaches what he calls *initial mathematics.* The children of the four groups—Yellow, Orange, Progress and Harmony—are his young disciples. It is his firm conviction that mathematics should and can be taught in an altogether different way. For example, one should begin from the concrete, and then go to the abstract. Children, Jasvirbhaiya asserts, have an intuition about numbers. For example, they experience and know what it means to have a full or half glass of milk. But then, they do not know abstract mathematical symbols. It would be wrong to negate the children's experiential knowledge and burden their tender minds with mathematical symbols, which is the 'accepted' form of teaching mathematics and which causes widespread 'mathematics phobia'. Jasvirbhaiya believes that the teacher should begin mathematics with the children's personal experiences; their own understanding of numbers. The teacher should not try to solve the problem for them. He insists: let the children struggle, suffer and solve the problem.

He feels that what really matters in teaching is: respecting the children's own understanding of things around them, making them active participants in the process of learning, arousing their interest through concrete examples from everyday life, and eventually enabling them to see that mathematics is essentially a language to represent a segment of the reality. It is this radical form of teaching that brings Jasvirbhaiya to Mirambika.

He admits that he is not a devotee of Sri Aurobindo or the Mother. He has not read their educational philosophy and does not have any connection with the Aurobindo Ashram. But he likes the school and its children.

> I am grateful to Mirambika. It has given me the opportunity. It has complete trust in me.

Jasvirbhaiya is clear and convinced about his agenda: the need for a radical change in teaching mathematics. It is this intense passion that perhaps explains why he, who at one time was the GM (Finance) of the ITC, Calcutta, attaches so much meaning to his association with the little children of Mirambika. He took voluntary retirement sometime in the late 80s, and came back to Delhi. One day, he happened to see an advertisement for the recruitment of teachers at Mirambika. He applied, got selected and began to teach.

There were, however, moments of crises. At times, he used to feel that Mirambika would not survive and that he would leave the school.

> But the fact is that I have been teaching here for the last ten years. I do believe that there is a force in Mirambika. It would survive.

How does a man, who at one time was successful in the corporate world, relate to Mirambika? Jasvirbhaiya admits that Mirambika has given him 'a sense of fulfilment'. He has got an enduring relationship with some of the children he has taught. Indeed, for him, Mirambika is a sacred zone of meaning.

The same can be said about Tarunda—another senior

teacher who is teaching the children of Perseverance and Aspiration groups. Tarunda was a nuclear scientist, worked in Hyderabad, did extensive work on military science—particularly on missile technologies. He worked hard, wrote research papers, travelled abroad. But for some reason, after his retirement, a disturbing thought used to haunt him.

> Throughout my life I have been involved with destructive science. It is useless.

He was perhaps searching for the meaning of existence. He went to the Pondicherry Ashram. From there he came to Delhi, taught at the Mother's International School for sometime, and finally started teaching at Mirambika. Initially, he was not very sure whether he would be able to teach children. But then, as he says with a lot of enthusiasm and satisfaction, 'things began to change and he became really successful with them'. He feels that there is fire within the children and there is excitement among them. His primary agenda is to arouse the children's curiosity. He wants to give them a 'solid academic foundation' in Mathematics, but not in a conventional way.

Mirambika, according to Tarunda, shows a lot of promise—the possibility of a new generation with moral values. And, for him, this is very important. Tarunda repeatedly asserts:

> At Mirambika, the children are getting a good education. They are becoming good human beings. The only thing I am trying to do is to develop their academic foundation without disturbing the basic objective of Mirambika.

Jasvirbhaiya and Tarunda's association with Mirambika reveals how passion for creative pursuits with children and the search for a new meaning to existence inspire voluntary teachers to join the school. This, as we have already indicated, conveys a message. Unlike a conventional school where paid teachers teach, hold exams and rank children, Mirambika appears to be a *sacred zone of meaning*. It opens up new possibilities, and with its enriching experiences, rescues one from despair and meaninglessness.

Take, for instance, Gandhibhaiya, who has been managing the library at Mirambika since 1989. He used to work at the Central Telegraph Office, Delhi. He is single. His mother's death in 1981 was a turning point. He began to feel terribly lonely, as his brothers too had deserted him. He went through a period of depression and even thought of committing suicide. In 1981 he took voluntary retirement and came to the Ashram. Taradi told him to work at the Mirambika library. He liked the new place, and has been working here for the last ten years. Here, he feels that he matters; that he is wanted. Mirambika, he confesses, has given meaning to his existence.

These enlightening stories give us an insight into the ethos of Mirambika. They suggest the limits to utilitarianism, and tell us that a school can have so much strength that it can give meaning to one's existence. Yet, there are questions—questions born of concern and anxiety: can a school exist without its paid employees, without a permanent staff? Can it survive solely on the basis of 'good will'? Would it be able to attract and retain 'bright'/'talented' teachers, if they are not paid? More about these anxieties later.

V

Involved Children: Creative Engagement with the School

The quality of a school reflects the way its students think, feel and act; the way they grow up, and develop the faculties of learning. And for a school like Mirambika—a school that intends to pursue a higher objective—it is important that the children imbibe the ethos of the school, and grow up with radical, life-sustaining ideals. It has yet to be seen whether Mirambika is able to make a difference to the concrete actions of its children. Before we explore this aspect in depth, it would not be wrong to give our views based on some broad observations.

Here is a school in which, as we have already said, one can breathe and sense freedom everywhere. There is freedom in the way the children study and relate to their diyas, the way they play and participate in cultural activities, the way they move around and radiate their experiences of joy. Perhaps this freedom has a lot to do with the way the school seeks to treat each child: as a *person* with an identity of his/her own. A Mirambika child, it has to be accepted, does not look like a 'standardised' product—an assembly-line product of the factory system of learning. This explains why there is no school uniform, no 'fixed' work for children of the same age. This striving for a distinctive identity explains the meaning of the different groups—Red, Blue, Green, Yellow, Orange, Progress, Peace, Perseverance, Receptivity, Courage, Equality and Aspiration. These are not typical 'classes', say, from Nursery to Class X. Beneath the idea of these groups lies a philosophy: treating children not as objects of control in a hierarchical system of division and grading, but enabling them to realise a meaning in what they do, and to experience the beauty of these noble virtues—courage or harmony, perseverance or equality!

Here is a school that values freedom—the absence of fear, constraints and inhibitions. But seldom does this freedom degenerate into chaos. Instead, a noble order emerges out of freedom. The children get to know of their responsibilities; the importance of their participation. For example, it is not difficult for these children to respect time, to live with it and maintain a schedule, in spite of the fact that there is no 'disciplinary' school bell to tell them when they should do what! Children do not feel oppressed by this sense of responsibility in following a schedule or carrying out any other activity. Indeed, one witnesses a beautiful rhythm in the daily activities of the school with which the children appear to be well acquainted. The school begins at 8:15 am, when the children come to the field and participate in sports and physical activities. This process of 'warming up' continues till 9 am–9:30 am—and it is time for music. With music begins silence. The entire school becomes silent; even the little children of the Red Group begin to appreciate the worth of silence. The activity begins from 9:35 am. For example, the children of the Receptivity Group learn Mathematics from 9:35 am to 10:35 am After that, the project work continues till 12.00 noon. From 1.00 pm onwards, they get engaged in learning language and literature, be it Hindi or English or French. There is also an activity centred on craft and art. And before the school ends at 3:40 pm, they sit together, concentrate and reflect on all that they have done during the day.

Throughout the day, there is intense activity amidst freedom. The school does succeed in creating an alternative work culture: working without being burdened, and working without experiencing alienation. This is indeed a remarkable achievement in an environment in which, right from early childhood, one is asked to separate work from play, spontaneity from 'hard/serious study', inner joy from the 'real business of life'.

Creative Merger with the Rhythm of the School

The children of Mirambika, as my dialogue with them reveals, seem to be proud of the identity that the school gives to them. They are convinced that they are studying at a school that is unique, that gives them the freedom they value, and makes learning an enormously creative process of inner growth and development. They are also aware—at least theoretically—that education is not just about learning from books; that it is a quest for a noble objective. While talking to the children of the Aspiration group, I asked them to tell me the significance of the name of their group. A boy stood up, went to the group and immediately brought a piece of paper, on which was written:

> The desire for attainment of eternal/fraternal knowledge. The essence of seeking goals. Aspiration is attaining final nirvana. Becoming one with your true self.

And then, they explained why they gave the name 'Aspiration' to their group. Because 'this is the time to aspire and accomplish'. Indeed, time and again the children assert the special/distinctive purpose of Mirambika. The fact that they have internalised the ethos of the school becomes fairly obvious when they say—almost unanimously—that for outsiders, it is not easy to understand the depth of this school, because many of them tend to equate Mirambika with a place where there is no serious study, no exam, no homework; where there is only fun for children! This, they say, amounts to trivialising what the school strives for. The real meaning of Mirambika, they point out, is freedom—freedom to learn and explore, and this freedom is not an antithesis of self-discipline. They work not out of 'fear of punishment'. They work because they enjoy it. And this freedom to pursue creative work, as they tell me repeatedly, is something that is absent in the conventional schools.

Mimansha, an eleven-year-old child from the Perseverance group says:

> Unlike conventional schools, children here have a different experience of learning. Once they are given a problem, they are asked to solve it on their own. Moreover, they can express their doubts, and ask their teachers questions without any fear or anxiety.

And Karan of the same group agrees with Mimansha when he says:

> I can tell my teacher what I want to study. This is something impossible in a conventional school.

In fact, they refuse to accept what others think of Mirambika ('Oh, you are lucky; you don't have exams!'). Instead, they assert with pride and confidence that they work hard and work in a different way precisely because the school has given them freedom and creativity. For example, they speak with tremendous enthusiasm about their 'project work'—the way they conduct research, collect information, enjoy their activities, and make a difference to the process of learning.

Shiv (Perseverance) recalls his project on 'War and Weapons'; Karan (also Perseverance) talks about his work on 'Inventions'. Anna of the same group speaks of the creativity involved in working on 'Light and Lens', and 'Shakespeare'.

Sharanth (Prudence/12) says:

> We understand whatever we do. While working on our projects we use labs, consult libraries. We don't have any problem consulting even the British Council Library. We enjoy our work. But at other schools children forget everything after writing the exam.

This pride in what they do has its significance. It is the reason why they do not attach much importance to the necessity of exams in evaluating one's talent and creativity. Besides, they dislike the competitive spirit of children studying in conventional schools, and seem to be convinced that their alternative form of learning is what really matters. I recall that I tried to provoke Aditi and Amalia (12+, Receptivity) by telling them that there is no life in Mirambika kind of sports, because there is no competition, no winner, no loser. Their instant reaction was:

> There should not be any competition. One is trying to improve one's own performance; the aim is not to defeat others.

Talking to these children is an experience in learning. It is refreshing to know that they think so differently from the way the children of 'mainstream' schools do, who have absolutely no understanding of the alternate form of living and learning. Mirambika has definitely made a commendable difference to the lives of the children who study there. The children's pride in their school is linked with the unfolding of their creativity, their freedom of expression, and most importantly, a sense of equality. No wonder, even the little children can understand and appreciate the meaning of the architecture of Mirambika.

Swati (11 +, Perseverance) expresses it beautifully:

> It is in tune with our school. It goes with our school. It is not like a cage. It is free and open.

Learning to Enquire: Meaning of Project Work

A question that is often asked is related to Mirambika's 'academic output'. Granted, the children of Mirambika like the school and enjoy the freedom, but do they get sufficient 'academic training' to 'do well' in life? Here, it would not be wrong to say that both insiders as well as the outsiders do feel a certain anxiety in this respect: perhaps the children do not get rigorous academic training.

Before we respond to this anxiety and reflect on the academic life of Mirambika, we need to remind ourselves of its core philosophy. The school seeks to develop the faculties of learning with the hope that these faculties, once developed, would invariably enable the child to emerge as an independent learner who would explore the world. Moreover, instead of attaching importance singularly to 'academic achievement', the school sees it as just a component organically related to the higher pursuit of life: integral development and realisation of the spiritual truth.

This core philosophy does have an impact on the daily activities of the school. For example, what strikes one is that the children are not 'academically burdened'. The relative absence of 'homework', 'weekly tests', and 'textbooks' on multiple academic disciplines characterises the school. But then, this freedom from 'academic pressure' does not mean that there is no serious learning. In fact, the method of learning and the meaning attached to it are radically different. The children learn everything—from science to literature, from geography to history—without being excessively conscious of the fact they are learning these subjects and without reducing them to 'course material' to be memorised for exams and grading. Moreover, the entire activity is seen as a means to achieve the higher pursuit of life. This can be understood better if we look at, say, the yearly plan of the Orange Group (equivalent to Class III).[3] What is significant is that the plan document has not given any special importance to different academic subjects like mathematics, science, social science and environmental science. There is no mention of textbooks or syllabus. Instead, the document speaks of primarily three objectives—physical growth and development, channelisation and utilisation of life-energy, and mental development. For physical development, as the document states, it is important to develop certain physical skills like 'skipping, catching, passing, throwing, dribbling, jumping, climbing, cycling and swimming'. And the activities to be pursued for the development of these skills are 'touch ball, football, German games, trampoline, relay race, skipping, cycling and fun games'. For channelisation and utilisation of life-energy, the possible activities the document has suggested are 'drawing and painting, carpentry, knitting, music, embroidery, drama and dance, clay modelling... and story telling'. For mental development—or for logic and reasoning, practical thinking, problem solving, observation, memory, creativity and imagination—the activities to be pursued are 'project work, maths, puzzles, riddles, poem and story writing'. The document has also spoken of the necessity of language development (both English and Hindi), and for that, activities like 'reading books', 'creative writing', or 'ability to look up a dictionary' have been suggested.

This document, we would say, is quite revealing. First, it does not fragment knowledge into disciplinary boundaries. Second, it does not reify academic subjects and associated texts. Third, it attaches refreshingly positive meanings to the pursuit of knowledge: it is for physical growth, mental development and creative use of life-energy.

And this entire approach, as we have already said, makes a difference in the way the children learn. They work without being burdened and become active participants in the process of learning. This explains the significance of what everyone at Mirambika—from a little child of the Yellow Group to a senior student of the Aspiration Group—is fond of saying: the 'project work.' Doing a project is like doing a piece of research. This is to formulate a problem, evolve different ways of coping with it, read necessary literature, meet resource persons, collect information, process the data, arrive at a conclusion, articulate it in the written form, and present it in the group. Its pedagogic significance is tremendous. It involves the learner, makes him/her independent and confident. It is intense and rigorous. It is refreshingly different from learning a chapter from the text or memorising it for the examination. Essentially, the learner enjoys the work; it reduces the possibility of alienation. The children are encouraged to take up different themes for project work. In fact, it is through such project work that they study different subjects. As a result, in the daily schedule, time is not allotted for different subjects (except mathematics and language) as such. The assumption is that the project work would take care of all possible disciplines. In a way, this transcends the disciplinary boundaries, and frees the child from the burden of learning different disciplines and knowledge-systems. An example of the daily schedule is as follows:

The daily routine of the Aspiration Group:	*The daily routine of the Prudence Group:*
8.15-9.15: Games	8.15-9.15: Sports
9.30-10.15: Mathematics	9.30: Music
10.20-12.00: Project work	9.35-12.00: Project work
12.00-1.00: Lunch	12.00-1.00: Lunch
1.00-1.45: Science	1.00-1.45: Hindi
1.45-2.35: Hindi/English	1.45-2.30: Mathematics
2.35-3.15: Project work	2.30-3.15: Science

But what kind of project work do the children do? What kind of material do they study? And what is the standard of their work? To begin with, let us take an example from the Perseverance Group. During my observation of their project work, I have felt that they have acquired the capacity to cope with a problem, as well as to take care of the details. It is interesting to watch an eleven-year-old child write on 'evolution on earth'—reflecting on Charles Darwin's theory of natural selection or Mendel's theory of genes. Another student of the same group has worked on 'water'. What surprises me is the level of alertness of the mind—the ability of the child to understand an issue from all possible angles. Hence, in her project on water, the child has written about drinking water, sea water, water cycle, properties of water, hard and solid water, distribution of water, water in the beginning, liquid water, solid water, substance of water, water in the atmosphere and water in the human body.

This confidence—or the capacity to acquire a comprehensive understanding of the problem—once revealed itself in a project on *newspapers* that the children undertook. They worked, understood the meaning and purpose of a newspaper, wrote, edited and eventually printed a newspaper called *The Perseverance Times* (May 1999) . Let us look at its contents: Manisha interviewed Partho bhaiya, asked him about Mirambika and his experiences as the Principal of the school. Subhadeep wrote on 'global warming'; Mimansa wrote an essay on 'Three Hundred Years of the Khalsa'. Moreover, there were book reviews, poetry, news on sports, and an interview with an important theatre personality. This work reveals the creativity of the children—their ability to go beyond formal/textual knowledge, and to articulate their ideas, thereby making a difference to the process of learning.

This creativity—or the intensely participatory form of learning—can be seen in all the groups. For example, when I see the project work completed by a child of the Aspiration Group, I get delighted at the depth of his work. While working on the 'origin of life', he has incorporated the Cosmozoan theory, the bio-chemical evolution, Mitosis, Mieosis, DNA and even Sri Aurobindo's theory of evolution. From the *World Book of Encyclopedia* to the *Dictionary of Biology* to Carl Sagan's *Cosmos*—the books he has consulted for this work are diverse and many. A significant amount of work has also been done on science—states of matter, elements, molecules, compounds, periodic tables, composition of light, properties of light, splitting light, etc. A work on the 'history of civilisations' or a reflection on 'capitalism-trade-money' or an understanding of major world religions reveals the variety and level of project themes that the children are encouraged to pursue. One can get a glimpse of this child's research temper in the way he has reviewed the works of authors like H.G. Wells, *The War of the Worlds;* Jules Verne, *Around the World in 80 Days*, H.G. Wells, *First Man on the Moon*, and Shakespeare, *Macbeth.* As a matter of fact, this kind of training increases the children's interest in learning. They feel encouraged to take up any theme (not just bookish/syllabus oriented) and reflect on it. Devika showed me the work she did during her summer holidays. She wrote an essay on 'birds'; she reviewed Humphrey Carpenter, *More Shakespeare without the Boring Bits.* Apurva of the same group worked on 'cell theory' and 'structure of the cell'. Khusi worked on 'light', and tried to solve problems like: (a) Why does the sky appear to be blue during the daytime and red and orange during the early mornings and late evenings? (b) Can you imagine how space above you would appear if you are standing on the surface of the moon or Mars? (c) Why do diamonds sparkle? Amal wrote comments on diverse historical themes like the French Revolution, the Industrial Revolution, the Russian Revolution, Rise and Fall of Communism, Nazism and Hitler, the Fall of the Berlin Wall, the American Cold War, the Rise of the Sikhs in India, The Sepoy Mutiny, Satyagraha and Quit India Movement, the Partition of India. And Sharanth wrote creative essays on 'the pros and cons of a circus', 'the joys of cricket', 'everything is possible', 'non-violence is more powerful than violence', 'never again' and 'the joys of freedom'.

What is striking is the children's inner joy—their intimate association with ideas, their confidence in articulating their own point of view, the courage to remain an autonomous learner without being crushed by 'textbooks' and 'old question papers'. No wonder, even the little children of the Orange Group (8+) can be seen expressing their ideas in their own idioms—something that can never be gained through the conventional process of reading the 'prescribed' chapter, cramming it, and completing the 'syllabus'. For example, while working on a simple/elementary project on 'village and city', the children commented on the problem of pollution in the city—why one should not cut trees, or why one should not use leaded petrol. What is interesting is that these children get the training to develop the power of concentration and observation, to choose a problem, think of it, and evolve an answer to it. For example, while working on Mirambika itself, they were inspired to interview the Principal to learn more about the founding members and why the photographs of Sri Aurobindo and the Mother could be seen everywhere in the school. Not only that, they even counted the number of trees in the school, and enquired about the people who planted them.

Learning Takes Place Everywhere

The kind of work that the children do—the work that is challenging and imaginative—requires the support of the library. Indeed, the school library is an important centre for learning, and the children use it for their project work. The library is always vibrant, full of children talking, discussing, reading and writing. A close look at the library suggests that the emphasis is on an alternative pedagogy and research-oriented works. It is a small library with 12,000 books. But its collections are meaningful—the collections that stir the child's imagination, help him/her learn and explore. For example, what strikes one is the collection of different series of encyclopaedia—The American People's Encyclopaedia, The Children's Encyclopaedia, Illustrated Science and Invention Encyclopaedia, Popular Mechanics: Do It Yourself Encyclopaedia. There are good resource books on Mathematics, Physics and Chemistry. There are books with imaginative/bright illustrations—on plants, animals, birds and insects. Then there are books on 'life world library series', which are about different countries and civilisations. Moreover, there are the children's atlases, NBT Indian biographies, NCERT and Eklavya textbooks, the works of Sri Aurobindo and the Mother, and books on pedagogy, education, psychology, psychotherapy and philosophy. Besides, there is a reasonably good collection on English literature.

A library of this kind, it is obvious, attracts the children as well as the diyas. In fact, this small library, as we have already said, symbolises the state of learning at Mirambika —the way little children learn how to find the appropriate books from the racks, collect the necessary information, discuss it with friends, initiate a dialogue with the diyas, prepare their project proposals and write the final drafts. That the library occupies a special place in the order of things is clear from the piece of writing pasted on the main door of the library:

> The library is a place for concentration and study—it cannot and must not be used for playing, chatting or sleeping. Every place has its own quality which must be respected.
>
> A silence of eternal rest and peace supports an eternal action and movement.

This is not to bombard the child's mind with the moral dictum, but to sensitise him/her and create an environment that is sacred and noble. In fact, the Mirambika notice board displays such writings, rather than carrying the official circulars written in bureaucratic language. For example, one fine morning I happened to look at the school notice board, and saw the following:

(a) A beautiful poster against nuclear testing;
(b) A paragraph from Sri Aurobindo's writings on *sadhana;*
(c) An article on TV violence.

As I see it, the entire school is a zone of learning. Wherever one looks be it the library or the art room, the notice board or the dining hall, the resource centre or the meditation room —there is something to learn; something that sensitises us, and tells us about a new way of living, relating, experiencing and understanding.

Problem-posing Pedagogy: Dialogic and Participatory Form of Learning

Mirambika, we have said, is different because of a very enriching relationship between the teacher and the taught. This relationship can be felt in the way the diyas interact with the children in the classroom and in the concrete practice of teaching. The diyas as individuals differ. Their personalities are different; their way of working is different. Yet, there is something that unites them, and gives a distinctive identity to their method of teaching. The Mirambika way of teaching, to begin with, is *participatory*. The agency of each child is realised; he/she is encouraged to recognise his/her innate potential and to participate actively in the process of learning. There are no external constraints like the fear of punishment, or of 'failure' in the exam. Instead, the focus is on cultivating the child's interest in learning so that the motivation or inspiration can come from within. It is, therefore, quite possible that a Mirambika child, unlike his/her counterpart in a conventional school, may not be mechanically efficient in 'learning', that is, memorising the bundle of information, spelling out difficult words, recalling the tables and remembering divergent theories and formulae. The 'progress' in the child's cognitive development may be slow. But then, the beauty of the Mirambika way lies in the fact that learning, for the child, is an experience of inner discovery and joy. It may be slow, but it is deep, life sustaining, and has a permanent impact on the child's development.

Let us take a look at what really happens during the process of teaching and learning. I wish to give some random examples. Meenakshi and Dushmant—the diyas of the Yellow Group (equivalent to Class II]—are working with 17 children. They are working on a project on the Indian states. They do some concrete work on the project from 9.45 am to 10.30 am. To begin with, Meenakshi and Dushmant explain to the children what the work is all about. The method is absolutely dialogic. Initially, the children make a lot of 'noise', but when the teachers begin to listen to them, there is order amidst chaos. The children are asked to form four groups. Now Meenakshi and Dushmant give a sheet (containing pictures representing the clothes worn in different states) to each group. The children are asked to look at these pictures, then draw them on their own and paste them on a chart. The idea behind this exercise is to know what kind of dresses are worn in each state. There is tremendous enthusiasm among these little children. They can be seen deeply involved in their work.

This is significant. There is no textbook, no importance is given to 'book learning'. Instead, through their own activities and creations—drawing, cutting, pasting, talking to the diyas—the children get a reasonably good idea about the different Indian states, and the variations in food and costumes used in these states.

Now we are at Neerjadi's language class in the same group. Neerjadi—an old lady with a lot of enthusiasm—is comfortable with the children. She enters the class, and begins her dialogue. She asks the children what they did in the previous class. She listens to them carefully. She then gives them pencils and notebooks and utters a word, which she asks them to write down in their notebooks. Other words follow and the children write them down: fish, rice, vegetable, egg, meat, chicken, roti, curry and chapati. Now, Neerjadi persuades the children to check the words and correct them, if necessary. Neerjadi, in a truly dialogic spirit, gives her own example: how she herself makes mistakes, and often corrects her mistakes while revising. She now goes to each child, and looks at what he/she has written. There is no fear or anxiety of any kind. It seems that the children have already got the message: the mistakes do not matter; what matters is the willingness to learn and participate. Neerjadi has a lot of affection for these children, and she appreciates them without any reservation. For example, while admiring a child's handwriting, she says, 'It is so good, I wish I had the same handwriting'.

Here is yet another example. The children of the Orange

Group are working on a project on plants and animals. Barenbhaiya is working with them. What is significant is his ability to involve the children in the process of learning, and making them feel that they are the creators and active participants in the project. In the classroom, colourful pictures of animals have been pasted. In addition, there are charts that indicate and demonstrate different parts of a flower, a tree and a fish. Baren comes to the classroom, sees the kind of work the children have done at home: crosssword puzzles on animals and plants, and quiz questions. Now he requests three children who have prepared the quiz to put these questions to the rest of the class. The questions are of the following kind:

(a) What is this animal called?
(b) Which is the world's tallest living animal?
(c) Where does the flower grow from?
(d) Which part of the plant manufactures flowers?
(e) Name our national animal.

What one notices here is the total involvement of the children. They are answering the questions posed by their own friends. The distinction between the teacher and the taught is disappearing. The hierarchy is collapsing. Barenbhaiya is acting like a catalyst. Now it is time for Baren to give them a set of questions to answer.

(a) What are the different parts of a flower and a plant?
(b) What is the difference between downstroke and upstroke?
(c) Why does a plant breathe in carbon dioxide at night and breathe out oxygen during daytime?
(d) What do the birds use to make their nests with?
(e) What is photosynthesis?

After the question-answer session, the children are asked to draw pictures of animals and plants and identify their different parts. The children do this with great enthusiasm. They learn through a number of ways. They draw pictures, construct clay models, prepare crossword puzzles, set questions for the quiz and visit the zoo. Work becomes play, and learning tends to become an aesthetic endeavour.

Tarunda's deep affection for the children, and his enthusiasm to give a 'solid mathematical foundation' to them can be seen in the way he conducts himself in the classroom. He invites me to his class. The children of the Receptivity Group are learning mathematics from him. To begin with, he shows me an old question paper that he prepared for the children. He tells me that he is reasonably happy with their performance. I look at the question paper, and find a couple of interesting questions like:

(a) In a school of 1000 students, 600 play hockey, and 450 play cricket. How many play both hockey and cricket?
(b) Today Rekha is five times as old as her son. Six years hence, she will be 60, three times as old as her son. How old is Rekha at present ?

Tarunda has now asked the children to solve all the questions of Chapter 8 (Profit and Loss) from O.P. Sinhal's *A Textbook of Mathematics for Class VII.* True, Tarunda's method, at times, looks somewhat conventional: giving importance to a specific textbook, and asking the children to concentrate on it. But what cannot be denied is his soothing presence—the way he teaches the children without letting them feel even the slightest fear or anxiety. Although it is a mathematics class, it is full of humour and joy. Tarunda takes care of each child. He cracks jokes, encourages them to give correct answers. This 'tension free' environment in a mathematics class reveals the absence of any jealousy or envy among the children. I have not seen anyone trying to establish his/her dominance or superiority in the class. On the contrary, they communicate, and help one another to understand and solve the questions. The credit goes to Tarunda and his ability to make them believe that mathematics is something to be loved and excited about, not feared and hated.

Perhaps it would be difficult to talk about the existing

system of education at Mirambika without referring to the charisma of Jasvirbhaiya: his intense involvement with the children, his passion for mathematics, and his radical form of teaching. For me, attending Jasvirbhaiya's classes is a great experience. Let me give some examples. He is teaching what he calls Initial Maths to the children of the Yellow Group. He comes to the class, draws a circle on the blackboard and poses a problem: 'Imagine it is a circular path, and two gentlemen —Atal and Nawaz are walking along this path in the same direction. Atal walks two times faster than Nawaz. Where would they meet?' The moment the children hear these two names they begin to laugh. Some of them say: These two gentlemen are Atal Behari Vajpayee and Nawaz Sharif. Jasvirbhaiya remains silent.

Now he demonstrates what he means: he begins to walk at different speeds, to show the children what it means to walk faster, and what it means to walk two times faster. The children enjoy this concrete demonstration. It makes sense to them. They understand what Jasvirbhaiya is talking about. He comes near the blackboard, moves his finger along the circumference, and asks the children where Nawaz would reach when Atal completes the circle. They understand, and ask him to stop at the right place. Again (he demonstrates on the blackboard), when Atal completes two rounds, Nawaz completes one round. And that is the point where they meet.

Now it is time to tell a story.

> I went to Hauz Khas Market, bought 4 sweets, and ate 1. Then I went to Green Park Market, bought 5 sweets, and ate 2. Finally, I came to Yusuf Sarai Market, bought 6 sweets, and ate 3. Now he asks: how many sweets did I eat? And how many did I have with me when I came back?

The children begin to give all sorts of answers. He comes to the blackboard, and begins to explain. This time a child asks: 'Did you really eat sweets today?' He replies: 'Yes I did. This morning I was hungry'.

Let us take another example from the Orange Group. Each child is provided with an Abacus. Jasvirbhaiya asks them to demonstrate different numbers—46, 460, 101, 1010, 8808 and 880800—on the Abacus. The children love to work on the Abacus.

He than gives them a mathematical puzzle to solve: 'There is a room whose length and breadth are the same. A gentleman has got many carpets which are all the same size. And 16 carpets can cover the the entire floor of the room. There is another room of the same length, but its breadth is half. How many carpets are needed to cover the floor of the second room?'

This time the children begin to ask naughty questions like: what about the bathroom? Is it also covered with carpets? Jasvirbaiya remains firm, asks them to concentrate. The children give all sorts of answers: 2, 4, 6, 13, etc. He comes near the blackboard, draws two rooms, and explains. Now they understand and give the correct answer: eight carpets.

What distinguishes Jasvirbhaiya's method of teaching is that he gives concrete examples. He seeks to sensitise the child, makes him/ her see that mathematics is essentially a language that helps one describe, explain and understand the reality. In other words, he seeks to mediate between the concrete and the abstract. Irrespective of whether he is teaching counting, tables, fractions, divisions or multiplications, he gives concrete examples. The journey is from the concrete to the abstract, not vice-versa. His method of teaching makes his class immensely interesting. He has demonstrated how the mathematics class can be full of activities, drama, humour and jokes. For example, one day he asks a child of the Yellow Group. 'There are 18 legs. So how many children are there?' She fails to answer. He waits, giving her sufficient time. She tries again, but fails to give the correct answer. He now asks the children of the group to come forward, and stand before her. The girl is asked to see with her own eyes the number of children, and the number of legs. Finally, the girl answers that there are nine children, and 18 legs. It takes not less than ten minutes, but Jasvirbhaiya does it. This is because his method of teaching respects the intuitive or the experiential knowledge of the child. He does not begin with a textbook of mathematics; nor does he bombard the child's mind with any mathematical formula. He wants the child to discover the solutions to problems through first hand experience, instead of being taught or provided with a readymade formula. Jasvirbhaiya is affectionate; his method of teaching is participatory. He, however, does not fail to convey his message: he wants discipline; he wants the children's attention. At times, it is not easy to distinguish his firmness from harshness. For example, a girl of the Yellow Group, because of her lack of concentration, took a long time to solve an elementary problem of subtraction. He told her: 'Darling, even a Red Group child can answer this; why did you waste so much time of the entire group?'

What impact does the Mirambika way of teaching have on the child? It is obvious that the children enjoy their academic pursuits, and it would not be wrong to say that they evolve a creative/research orientation. But then, a question that often comes up is: does this form of education sufficiently equip them to cope with the 'mainstream' definition of what good academics are, that is, facing the exam, completing the CBSE syllabus, and doing well? True, while doing project work, the children learn the related subject thoroughly. But then, they may not learn everything that is prescribed in the regular syllabus, because they do not follow any fixed curriculum, or text. There is some kind of creative anarchy in the selection of themes for project work. They gain a creative edge; but creativity, it is feared, is not necessarily 'efficiency'—the efficiency to understand the logic of linear academic development, of acquiring a huge stock of information and doing well in the examination. In the next section, we will discuss more about the anxiety related to these concerns. What is, however, interesting is that the children often show their 'confidence' by arguing that they are not afraid; that they can cope with the mainstream syllabus and face the board exam. It is difficult to say whether this confidence is real, or whether it is only a cover-up for their real anxiety.

We should, however, remind ourselves that Mirambika cannot, and should not, be evaluated in terms of what the mainstream calls 'academic excellence'. Instead, we should focus on its real achievements—the way it makes each and every child an active participant, strengthens his/her faith and confidence. Seldom does a child acquire a stigmatised identity, or develop a sense of failure. The message that the school conveys to each child is simple and profound: try, participate, involve yourself; success/failure is unimportant!

No wonder, one can feel that the school spares no effort to encourage the child. Even the little children of the Red Group get the message: they are important; their creations are important. Their paintings and drawings, for example, are properly displayed, and are often pasted on the notice board. The standard of these works is not at all important; what matters is the child's unique creative expression.

This perhaps explains the existence of Mirambika newsletters which are published from time to time. These newsletters, let it be stated, do not look like typical school magazines in which the written works of only select 'talented' students are published. Instead, the newsletters break all such barriers and distinctions. Every child is invited and encouraged to create; the newsletter gives space to each one of them. The 'standard' is not important. What is important is one's effort—the urge to create. That is why, one comes across writings of the following kind in the Mirambika newsletters:

> In my dream my mummy came as Santa Claus and put some gifts under my pillow. When I got up in the morning I found two toffees there. I was very happy!
>
> —*Anushka*/Blue Group/January 1997

> Once there was a circus tent. There were many animals in the tent—an elephant, a horse, a bear, a tiger and a lion. The elephant was riding the cycle, and the bear was riding the

motorcycle. The bear fell down. And the horse brought the ambulance. Everybody laughed. It was good fun.

—*Ananya*/Green Group/December 1997

There was a cat,
who was very fat,
she met a rat,
who sat on a mat,
wearing a hat,
And played ball and bat

Akriti, Yellow Group, October 1999.

One may not find much 'worth' in the writings of this kind. But then, we would argue, these are spontaneous/authentic creations. The fact that these little children are displaying such creativity, is in itself very promising.

In fact, the principle of participation that is so characteristic of Mirambika can be seen in every aspect of its alternative form of learning; be it sports or cultural programmes. For example, at Mirambika, sports remind one of a new possibility in an age in which games and sports have lost their meanings (joy, participation, freedom from the 'instrumental' logic), and become extremely competitive, aggressive and pathological. The children participate—and participate intensely—in all physical activities and games; but there is a no 'winner', and no 'loser'; there is no 'champion'. The absence of competition, or of narcissism in Mirambika sports tends to demonstrate what the school seeks to inculcate in the child: the spirit of participation without the neurotic anxiety of 'success' or 'failure'. Likewise, in the cultural programmes that the school organises from time to time, all children participate. They seem to have realised that they themselves are the creators; seldom do they feel alienated from the rhythm of the school.

Looking Beyond Cognitive Skills: Concern with the Child's Innate Strength

As a matter of fact, the school, as we have said earlier, gives importance to the child's integral development—not just the development of cognitive/academic skills. That is the reason why the school sees and observes how the child is growing and evolving, how he/she acquires autonomy and confidence, and evolves the art of relatedness. No wonder, the reports that the diyas write for the child are strikingly different, because they do not quantify, say, how much the child scores in different 'academic' subjects. Instead, these reports are qualitative in nature, and give special attention to the ethical/spiritual features of the learner. The goal is to initiate a dialogue with the parents, and collectively create a situation conducive to the child's integral development. Let me quote from a few reports:

> Of late, however, we have noticed two worrying tendencies in her communication with the other children. Anna sometimes whispers about somebody to another child, rather than choosing to bring the issue out into the open. She has developed the habit of ordering other people around...
>
> Anna's maturity in dealing with her asthma has impressed us all. She has taken on the responsibility of her daily treatment, recognising her symptoms and responding accordingly; it is good to see her taking such care of herself.
>
> —From the report of Anna, Perseverance Group, 1998-99

> ...Aishvarya very often wants paper from the group to take home to make cards with, and she is usually quite sure of what will do and what won't. Often we don't have the paper cut to the correct size or are pressed for time. In such a situation, we usually tell her why we cannot give her what she wants. She generally persists. Then we have a brief chat about the reasons for taking the paper. We also suggest alternatives, different paper or other material, which is more easily available. Also, if we are inconvenienced, we tell her so. Still, very often, Aishvarya persists, but stops if the message is firm enough. Of course, then she goes to another diya to try her luck.
>
> In this entire transaction, we have to be quite sensitive to Aishvarya's needs. Is it really important to her or is she acting on a whim? And as Aishvarya grows older, this is also what she will have to learn about herself. She will also have to learn

> to explore alternatives. Most important, she must learn the value of other people's feelings. And the beginning has to be made with the adults closest to her—her parents...
>
> —From the report of Aishvarya, Red Group, 1998-99

> ...Ankit feels that he is not trusted by his parents. He feels that he is responsible for himself, but his parents do not understand that.
>
> He feels pressurised in terms of work and feels that his parents do not sufficiently appreciate the quantity and quality of the work he is actually doing. But he understands that his parents are not wholly unjustified. 'After all, I goof up so often'...
>
> He seems to be battling a complex inside himself—something that makes him somewhat unsure of himself; and so his occasionally insensitive behaviour, his tendency quite clear every now and then, to 'boss over', an intolerance of others' defiance. But all these are still nascent. If he becomes more comfortable with himself, as he is, without needing to prove his worth to anyone else (sometimes the anyone else can be one's parents, relatives), his complex will be resolved in no time...
>
> —From the Report of Ankit, Aspiration Group, September 1998.

What is obvious in these reports is that they do not quantify, hierarchise and grade the children. The reports are critical; but every word is written with deep affection and care. The objective is to see the possibility in the child—the possibility that ought to be explored, and for which the diyas as well as the parents have to play a key role. Indeed, a school that can appreciate 'Anna's maturity in dealing with her asthma' (instead of being bothered only with her academic performance in mathematics or history) has evolved a new way of seeing and relating to the child. It is, therefore, not surprising that the school would be concerned with how Aishvarya—the little girl of the Red Group—would also learn to became accommodative, and appreciate the value of other people's feelings. Or, when the report speaks of Ankit's inner world, it does reveal that the school is appreciating the moral/ spiritual development of the child. The conclusion that one feels tempted to draw is that here is a school that goes beyond what is generally equated with education, i.e. academic achievement!

VI
Crises and Contradictions

A statement on Mirambika would remain incomplete unless we take into account its moments of tension and anxiety; its contradictions. True, Mirambika has been trying to make a difference in the field of education. Yet, the school is not without its 'darker' side. In a way, this is inevitable, because an alternative form of schooling would always have difficulty surviving in a system that is hostile to it. Moreover, the terrible pressure from the mainstream on everybody to conform to its ethos has created a situation in which one is confronted with a series of anxiety-ridden questions: is the alternative form of learning at all desirable? Can it enable the children to 'adjust' to the 'real' world? Does an alternative school have the innate strength to cope with the pressure of the mainstream? As we have already indicated, Mirambika, for many, is a conscious choice, an excitement, a possibility, a new beginning. Yet, there are tensions, anxieties and apprehensions. There is deep-rooted fear: can the school survive?

In fact, as we would like to point out, to experience Mirambika is also to sense this all persvasive anxiety. This anxiety can be felt in the way the children, especially those from the higher groups, are leaving Mirambika and joining the 'successful', 'prestigious' mainstream schools. Each time a child leaves the school, it causes terrible anxiety among the parents of other children. Many of them begin to rethink and ask: 'Are we doing the right thing by keeping our children at Mirambika?' One can see this anxiety even among the little children, because they clearly see the dilemma of their parents; they also get affected when they see their own friends leaving the school. It is important to understand the underlying reasons behind this anxiety and fear. It is also important to weigh the crises and contradictions of the school as against its endless possibilities.

Unhappy Parents

To begin with, let us look at the parents—their ambiguities. No doubt, they see a great possibility in Mirambika. But then, for many of them, Mirambika is also causing terrible anxiety; the main reason being its present state of indecision and confusion. Although the school has expanded and the senior-most children of the Aspiration Group are at Class X level, nobody knows where their future lies. The school is not willing to get itself attached to the CBSE, because it fears that to follow the CBSE pattern of syllabus and curriculum, is to lose its specific identity and autonomy. It feels that the children should prepare for the National Open School exam. However, the idea of the National Open School, for most of the parents, is difficult to accept. The result is that there is terrible anxiety, demoralisation and confusion. Even the Aspiration Group that consists of only seven children, is breaking down; the children are either leaving the school or preparing for entrance tests for the other mainstream schools. This confusion regarding the future of the school (whether it would be able to expand itself to include Class X, stabilise itself, and get affiliation from the CBSE or the ICSE) affects almost everyone. No wonder, children from all groups are leaving the school. At times, it appears that the school is no longer certain of its future; that it is losing confidence in itself, and the parents are in a state of acute anxiety. Even a parent who is otherwise convinced about the possibility of Mirambika says:

> If every day students leave the school what would happen? My only hope is that in each group there would be at least 8/9 committed parents.

Another parent expresses his anguish:

> More and more children are leaving the school. This has led to some kind of panic. Every parent is enquiring whether others are shifting their children. There are parents who say one thing in the school (all good things about the school) and do exactly its opposite (shifting the child to a new school). Only yesterday, one parent who used to speak of his commitment to Mirambika, has shifted his child to the DPS.

A parent who has shifted her child to the Mother's International School says:

> I cannot conceive of my child doing National Open School. I feel the management is shirking its responsibility by not pursuing affiliation with the ICSE. They don't want to do the needful.

There are many other valid reasons for this crisis, or the critique of the school that many parents are articulating these days. For example, they do not seem to be happy with the standard of the teachers, particularly those teaching the senior groups. Besides, the continual flux of the teachers worries the parents. As it is often expressed, the need is to 'establish a reasonably permanent set of teachers—well qualified and sympathetic to Mirambika's philosophy'. What cannot be denied, however, is 'the absence of skilled teachers at higher levels'. Furthermore, 'the diyas are not able to understand the child's needs and aptitude for learning'.

A parent feels:

> There is a problem regarding the consistency of teachers. Teachers come and leave. As a result, at times, parents begin to doubt whether the teachers are really gifted, experienced and qualified.

Here is yet another parent who expresses a similar anxiety.

> Mirambika has to think seriously about the quality of teachers. Good teachers can be retained only if they are paid.

In fact, it has been felt by some that the school seeks to hide these problems. Instead of initiating a free/open discussion on these problems, it pretends that everything is in order. This lack of transparency, it is felt, leads to all sorts of gossip and rumours; it causes suspicion and anxiety regarding the trajectory of the school. Some parents have felt that whenever they have articulated their problems, they have been misunderstood and treated as 'problem-posing parents'. A parent who has shifted his three children from Mirambika to the DPS argues:

> For the last two years, there has been lot of confusion regarding the future of the school—the board affiliation, the payment of teachers, etc. The problem is that the school does not open up, doesn't clear things. The management gets irritated if one enquires much. I used to argue quite a lot. They did not like it. I was called a 'problem-parent'. The fact is that the school needs good/stable teachers. For that, the teachers have to be paid. Moreover, the school should become more transparent. It should make everything clear to the parents.

Another parent introduces himself: 'I am a bad critic of the school'. Reasons:

> Till Class VI the school is perhaps one of the best in the world. But for higher classes it does not have the resources and good/experienced teachers. The school fails to arouse and sustain the creative interest of the child. I have expressed my opinion time and again. Now the school dislikes me. I have no illusion about mainstream schooling. But then, Mirambika too fails to do something different. The future of Mirambika is bleak. Only the rich who need not think of their children's careers—would send them to Mirambika.

The questions that the parents are raising are genuine. But then, it is also important to see their own ambiguity, the contradictions in their way of looking at the school. For example, it is not particularly easy to internalise the deeper meaning of Mirambika (not just intellectually, but to experience it in one's own life). Even when one chooses Mirambika, one may not be sure of what to expect. True, Mirambika may be perceived as a zone of freedom, a place that the children enjoy, and where there is no burden of learning. This, one can argue, is good for small children; but, as they grow up and come to higher classes, this 'experiment' becomes irrelevant; what matters is 'serious academic study' for which Mirambika, it is thought, is by no means the right place! In other words, the deeper meaning of Mirambika—something that gives a new meaning to knowledge and life's pursuits, and supersedes the conventional notion of 'academic achievement'—is not easily appreciated. As a result, two things happen. The parents begin to evaluate Mirambika—particularly when their children come to higher classes—in terms of the conventional notion of academics. This evaluation, needless to add, makes them unhappy, and they become eager to shift their children to more stable/successful schools. Second, they put excessive pressure on the children in order to prepare them for the 'mainstream education'. This unhappiness and confusion among the parents demoralises the children, and severely affects the rhythm of the school.

The question is, why does this happen? We have already spoken of the terrible pressure from the mainstream. To live in society is to experience it every day! It is, therefore, not easy to remain permanently attached to an alternative philosophy of life or education. True, the parents have chosen Mirambika. But this faith has to be perpetually renewed. This requires inner strength and one's own realisation of this alternative path. But then, the socio-economic background of the parents and their professional profiles often clash with the beauty of this realisation. The society they live in is filled with the ethos of competition, achievement, success and failure, power and glamour, because this is precisely what the metropolitan/upper class living is all about. The result is incompatibility between their life-practices and the ideals of the school. True, as we have repeatedly said, the parents have chosen Mirambika; they do appreciate its alternative agenda. Yet, these contradictions and dilemmas are no less real. In a way, it can be said that Mirambika, because of its own social location, cannot escape the contradictions of the metropolitan middle class. Perhaps the school can engage in a meaningful dialogue with the parents, and keep their faith alive. Yes, the dialogue does take place. Yet, a question haunts many: is the school sufficiently confident of its own mission?

Absence of Good Teachers

It is in this context that we need to speak of the diyas. What one notices is a widening communication gap between the diyas and the parents. The absence of mutual trust, we would like to stress, is detrimental to the spirit of Mirambika, because a school of this kind can exist only if it retains the spirit of togetherness, and close communication between the diyas and the parents. As we have already mentioned, there are parents who do not seem to be happy with the quality of the diyas. It is argued that the diyas are not necessarily sufficiently qualified, experienced or talented. But then, the diyas too are not always happy with the parents. They often point out that not many parents understand Mirambika. Moreover, the values that they affirm go against what the school seeks to uphold.

> Ninety-nine per cent of them are materialistic. They do not understand the spirit of Mirambika. They put excessive pressure on the school. At times, we ourselves tell them to shift their children from the school if they are so unhappy.
>
> For example, in my group that consists of 19 children there is only one parent who is in absolute harmony with the school. The rest do not understand the spirit of Mirambika, and put excessive pressure on the diyas and the school.
>
> Seldom does one meet a parent who understands Mirambika. Many of them do not have even the slightest respect for what we are doing.

The question is, why this mistrust? After all, the parents have been chosen by the school and vice-versa. We agree that it is not easy to go against the system, and remain absolutely loyal to an alternative philosophy. There are tensions, anxieties and dilemmas. It would be wrong on the part of the school to expect that it can find appropriate/ready-made parents. The parents too have to be educated. And, as we have found, there are parents who, despite their 'upper class' orientation and resultant contradictions, like Mirambika, learn from it, and intend to change their educational philosophies. Perhaps, as one fears, there is lack of proper communication between the diyas and the parents, which, if not checked, could further intensify the already existing differences and prove to be a major setback in the smooth functioning of Mirambika.

Irrespective of this conflict, what cannot however be denied is the actual problem regarding the quality of the diyas. We have said earlier that the diyas are intensely and creatively involved with the children; that theirs is a relationship that intends to overcome all hierarchical barriers —a relationship that affirms mutuality, dialogicity and love. We have also mentioned that a distinguishing feature of Mirambika is its radical pedagogy, and the diyas play a key role in it. Yet, it has to be remembered that to become a good teacher at Mirambika is no easy proposition. A good teacher has to reconcile the moral/spiritual component of 'free-progress education' and mastery in different branches of knowledge. Because to teach in a radical/non-conventional fashion one needs more clarity, rigour and thoroughness. In fact, herein lies the anxiety expressed by many parents. They fear that the diyas, even though morally sound and honest, are not necessarily good in academic skills.

Hence, this is a real problem, and there is no easy solution to it. It is not difficult to find academically skilled persons, but they may not appreciate the deeper meaning of Mirambika, and its free-progress education. And, at the same time, it is not always easy to find a spirited person who is also good in academics. In a way, a school like Mirambika has to learn to live with these contradictions. It is, of course, true that the school does try and bring 'resource persons' from outside, and there are parents who offer their services to the school. It is also true that there are diyas who evolve, grow and learn quite a lot (even academically) in the process of teaching at Mirambika. But then, the fact is that the teachers are not paid, and for basic reasons of survival, they have to leave the school. As a teacher puts it, 'the tragedy of the school is that by the time the diyas begin to understand Mirambika, they have to leave the school.' As a matter of fact, the continual flux of teachers, for many, is a destabilising factor. But then, to retain a permanent set of paid professionals is to restructure the entire school: the teacher-taught ratio, the curriculum, and the philosophy. It would perhaps mean the death of Mirambika. This is indeed a paradoxical situation: the real difficulty that an alternative school faces in order to survive.

There is yet another problem. The diyas too find it difficult to understand Mirambika. It should not be forgotten that they too are the products of the mainstream/conventional system of education. Moreover, they need to develop courage and self-confidence in order to cope with the pressure of the mainstream, or to deal with parents whose dilemmas and contradictions affect the rhythm of the school. The danger lies in the fact that in the absence of proper training and confidence, they may bow down, get demoralised, and begin to doubt the desirability of the Mirambika project. This would shake the foundation of the school; the diyas may become too defensive, or they may start evaluating the achievement of the school against the conventional yardstick, or may even think of some kind of 'compromise' and 'balance'. It is not altogether uncommon to find the diyas talking of the 'limits to freedom', or 'the necessity of board examinations.' We wish to argue that if a school like Mirambika becomes defensive, or if its teachers lack the confidence to pursue an alternative project, it would become self-defeating. Perhaps one way of overcoming the crisis is to orient the teachers, make them see and realise the historic necessity of free progress education. But then, the moot question is: who would educate the educators?

Elitism Shaping the Perceptions of the Children

The children too are affected by these crises and

contradictions. We have already said that the children of Mirambika feel proud of the distinctive identity of the school. The alternative/radical form of pedagogy, and its intense relatedness shape their daily rhythm. In a way, their process of growing up is refreshingly different. Yet, a deeper understanding of their minds suggests that they too experience the anxiety—the anxiety that they notice among their parents regarding the 'future' of the school. As many of their friends leave the school, they begin to redefine their own position. For Karan, for instance,

> Mirambika is not sufficient for future careers. After all, you have to enter the normal life, you have to adjust to it.

Likewise, Nimay says,

> Almost everyone from our group has been preparing for the entrance test for other schools. I want to shift to any school, be it DPS or MIS. It would help me for CBSE.

As the children grow up and come to higher classes, their anxiety becomes more acute. This tension is the beginning of their demoralisation, and it destabilises their minds. The resulting uncertainty and doubts make it difficult for them to remain an integral component of the school.

What is striking is that some children are becoming critical of their diyas. Like their parents, they too have begun to doubt the 'quality' of the diyas. For a school that is known for the intimate/dialogic relationship it promotes between the teacher and the taught, any kind of disruption in this relationship is something to be worried about. When a child says, 'not all the diyas have the capability to communicate with us', he/she questions the very foundation of the school. Or, look at the language of yet another disillusioned child:

> There are many young trainee teachers from Orissa. They are horrible. We know better than them.

Like a 'pragmatic' adult, a child comments:

> Teachers ought to be paid. Without payment how can you find good teachers? Here, anybody can come, and experiment with us.

This cynicism—although limited to only a few children—has a trace of elitism. A distinguishing feature of Mirambika, as we have already pointed out, is the simplicity of its trainee teachers. This simplicity is noticeable, especially in a school located in posh south Delhi. When a child looks at these teachers with contempt, it shows the clash of outlooks, life-patterns and classes. Perhaps this is an indication of the elitist background of the children—the background that gives rise to arrogance and hierarchy. This elitist/arrogant outlook can also be seen in the way many children relate to different languages. It has to be accepted that even in the post-colonial Indian society, the dominance of English continues. English is not just a language. It is one's cultural capital; it symbolises power and privilege. The politics of language has its hierarchy, and the entire vernacular tradition is seen as inferior. Elite schools, we know, privilege English, and reproduce this hierarchy. What is important to note is that the children of Mirambika too tend to develop this elitist outlook to languages. English, for many of them, is superior to, say, Hindi. Learning Hindi, they would argue, is not so important. The following extracts from the interviews I took with the children would make my point clear.

> I hate Hindi. I communicate with my parents in English.
> I am comfortable with English. I hardly issue Hindi books from the library.
> When I become angry, I speak in Hindi. Because in English you can't be rude.
> I speak Hindi only with my maid.
> I speak English because it is the international language.

It is, of course, true that the family plays a key role in the hierarchy of languages that these children have grown up with. But then, the school, it seems, has not been able to do sufficient work to sustain a truly bilingual tradition, as is evident from the collection of great classics in English literature which fill the racks of the school library. On the other hand, the rack that contains Hindi books looks terribly wounded. One gets the impression that English is the main language for all purposes. Not much work has been done in Hindi, or, for that matter, in any other Indian language. This is indeed sad. If even a school like Mirambika cannot challenge this hierarchy, how can it expect its children to relate to the larger society? Not to know the language of the people is to remain perpetually alienated from them.

The elitism that we are talking about reflects itself in many other forms. For example, it is not difficult to come across a group of children who speak the language that characterises the elitist thinking in India. They devalue the country they live in, and attach special importance to the Euro-American world. Yes, there are children who insist that 'India is our motherland', and that one should not leave the country. But then, there are others who find no particular reason to stay in India. Instead, the affluent/prosperous Western world attracts them. 'I wish to settle down in the USA, because it is a place for prosperity, money and technological pleasure'—asserts a child. 'Most of my relatives are in Europe and America. I won't mind settling down there'—says another child. In fact, this attitude is not at all surprising, because for the elite, the West is the secular symbol of salvation, and it is not easy for the children of Mirambika, given their social background, to think or feel differently.

However, it is important to note that the children of Mirambika are quite sensitive to the problem of pollution, as well as to many other social problems like poverty, and over-population. Yet, what is striking is their tendency to keep a 'safe distance' from political ideas/issues. This lack of awareness of socio-political movements is quite obvious. For example, many of them have not even heard of Baba Amte and Medha Patkar. This is surprising and shocking, particularly because the school is otherwise trying to sensitise the children, and make them conscious of the need for environmental protection. Is it possible to speak of the environment without relating it to the movements? Perhaps this is an indication of the inadequacy of the 'environmental lessons' that the school teaches. Or, perhaps, the method of teaching/learning is thoroughly depoliticised, and a lesson on 'pollution control' or 'environment protection' becomes merely cosmetic. Moreover, during the process of interviewing these children, I also found that many of them do not know anything about Karl Marx. Any reference to him is essentially in negative terms. They generally equate Marx with communism, and communism, for them, is not a nice thing. 'Why should a doctor and a nurse be equal?'—asks a child. The negative meaning attached to Marx suggests something far deeper. It suggests a worldview that is hostile to any idea of socio-economic equality. No wonder, a child can say: 'The problem is that the beggars do not want to be rich: Or, as another child puts it, 'there is crime in society because people are idiots.' These viewpoints indicate how the elitist arrogance is reproduced in the thinking of these children. It can also be said that this is an escape from or a dislike for the ideas of collective concern. Although the children have good things to say about Gandhi and Sri Aurobindo, it is, nevertheless, shocking to find a child who can assert with absolute arrogance: 'All that Sri Aurobindo said was rubbish.'

One can, however, argue that children are, after all, children, and it is not fair to expect 'politically correct' statements from them. True. But then, one cannot ignore the fact that the opinions that they express are an assertion of their elitist values, the values that they have learned from the family, the school or the social milieu that they belong to. In fact, this elitism or the culture of consumerism (which often manifests itself in lavish birthday parties held in hotels and restaurants) has got many parents worried about the values that the children are learning from their peer groups. For example, a parent—who, otherwise, appreciates the uniqueness of Mirambika—says,

> The children from the affluent classes are coming to Mirambika. As a result, the school, at times, looks 'western'.

Another parent expresses his concern as his child often reminds him: 'Papa, we don't have a car. Everyone else has.'

The child, he feels, has to be continually reminded of an alternative value system; he needs to be told that not owning a car does not mean that one is insignificant.

> I tell my child that he has got many things which-some of his friends don't have. He has got stability in his home. He gets constant and continual attention from his parents.

Here, one can clearly see a conflict between the actual cultural practices of the children and the philosophic foundations of Mirambika which seek to affirm the values of harmony, cooperation, simplicity, integration and equality. These values, needless to add, are not in tune with what can be called the 'elitist' outlook with its hierarchy, competitiveness, divisiveness and consumerism. Although the children of Mirambika, because of the cultural richness of the school, do develop some remarkably positive and life-sustaining qualities, the conflict that we are talking about is no less real. In fact, the elitist culture (even though its influence is not so pronounced at Mirambika, as compared to the other public/English-medium schools) is one of the chief contradictions of Mirambika. A major reason behind this contradiction is, we assume, the *elitist appropriation* of Mirambika. Because of this appropriation, Mirambika, for a section of the parents—it is felt—becomes merely a 'child-centred' school; not necessarily related to life's fundamental truths. The deeper meaning of the school is forgotten. It is seen as a place where the members of the affluent classes can send their children for stress-free/relaxed schooling. In other words, the school can be appropriated without changing oneself.

Why is it that the school has not been successful in fighting this trend? It is, of course, true that there are limits to what the school can do. After all, a significant part of the child's education takes place in the family, and if the parents do not imbibe the ideal of Mirambika, it is difficult for the school to accomplish its goal. But then, the school too needs to look at its shortcomings; to see how elitism creeps in, and to realise that to fight it, one needs profound socio-political imagination: an awareness of the political economy, and the contradictions that prevail in a fractured society because of its hierarchy and inequality. It is true that the school has a strong spiritual-philosophic foundation. But one feels that the diyas—or all those who matter—lack the appropriate political education, as a result of which, it appears, many of them, cannot make sense of the prevailing contradictions.

One may ask: is there something that is fundamentally wrong with Sri Aurobindo's philosophy? Sri Aurobindo, we have already said, was a great spiritual leader. The spiritual age he strove for meant reciprocity, dialogicity and harmony; it meant transcending all dualities and divisions. In fact, this spirituality negates everything that elitism stands for: hierarchy, inequality, narcissism and egotism. No wonder, Sri Aurobindo was also a revolutionary driven by the urge to resist colonialism and its exploitative nature. Moreover, he wrote extensively on politics: the meaning of state, socialism and democracy. He could see the possibility of a new world order that strengthens its unity from the ethos of decentralisation and pluralism; a new age that would transcend the formal/bureaucratic/technical rationality, and enable humankind to unfold its spiritual potential. It is difficult to see any trace of elitism in his project.

One can, however, argue that Sri Aurobindo's philosophy could not become the philosophy of the masses. A possible reason being that the masses are so deeply preoccupied with their survival that a spiritual journey, for them, becomes a difficult proposition. Or, to put it in another way: in the absence of the necessary 'objective conditions', the spiritual project cannot become a project for the entire humankind. Sri Aurobindo's philosophy, it is felt, is too advanced or 'abstract' to have any relevance in the life of the common people. Here, it is possible to see a difference between the way Sri Aurobindo and Gandhi thought. Eventually, Sri Aurobindo left the political realm, the domain of active struggle, and devoted himself to the spiritual quest. But Gandhi sought to reconcile the two, and found spirituality in politics. In other words, it can be argued, Gandhi's interaction with the masses was more direct, real and intense. Gandhi's idea of basic education, we have seen, emerged from people's productive experiences and knowledge. Gandhi could communicate with the rural peasantry, whereas Sri Aurobindo made sense primarily to the intellectually refined and sophisticated sections of the Indian society. It is, therefore, not surprising if Mirambika gets appropriated by the cultural elite.

Yet, we would argue that Sri Aurobindo's spiritual journey cannot be equated solely with one's preoccupation with one's own salvation. It implied radical transformation in society, polity, economy and culture. In fact, it is important for the devotees of Sri Aurobindo to reconcile the inner and the outer, and realise that a spiritual project needs to manifest itself in concrete social practices—the practices that are conducive to the culture of harmony, reciprocity and equality. The problem arises when spirituality is separated from the socio-political practice. Perhaps the elitism of Mirambika is a part of this crisis. May be the cultural elite, who send their children to Mirambika, tend to see spirituality as a project conducive to their 'personal development', but not as a creative/radical link with the collective. As a result, as we have already indicated, Mirambika may be seen as a school promising 'happy childhood' to the children of the elite, but not as a radical intervention in the people's struggle for a better society. The crisis of Mirambika can be seen in the absence of political imagination. For example, while the school celebrates *Holi, Christmas* and *Janmashtami,* it remains somewhat reluctant to celebrate with equal intensity, say, Gandhi's birthday or the Republic Day. Besides, the school has not yet been able to evolve a policy to attract the children of the relatively poorer and weaker sections of society. This is sad because the pedagogic/educational principles of Mirambika are universal. There is no reason why only the children of the elite should enjoy free-progress education. The challenge before Mirambika is to rescue the school from being hijacked by the elite.

Hard Times: Real Challenges

This critique does by no means suggest that Mirambika has failed. In fact, the crises and contradictions we are talking about indicate the difficulties that an alternative project is bound to experience in a world that is otherwise conservative, and seeks to retain the status quo. In a way, a system that dares to differ, experiment and dreams of a 'utopia' would certainly expect to encounter these crises and contradictions. The critique, therefore, need not be seen as a sign of pessimism; something that declares the death of an alternative project, and celebrates the 'inevitability' of the mainstream/conventional education. As a matter of fact, an awareness of this critique means that the school would undergo a process of self-introspection, and implement appropriate measures to accomplish—more rigorously and confidently—what it has set out to do.

The sociology of education tells us that no school can be seen in isolation; an alternative school in isolation cannot revolutionise our consciousness if the larger social system remains unaltered. But then, this meaningful sociological insight should not be interpreted as a device to devalue the worth of alternative projects, and plead for 'social determinism.' True, in the absence of structural transformation in the spheres of economy and polity, an alternative school has to realise its limitations. Nevertheless, the concept of an alternative project, despite its contradictions and limitations, is always promising, because it is seen as a source of inspiration, a beginning of a radical practice, an affirmation that dissent is possible, and a model to emulate by the future society. With this critical/constructive orientation, we would suggest certain measures that Mirambika should adopt in order to fulfil its mission:

1. All those who belong to the school must renew their faith in the alternative project of education, because without faith, it is impossible to dissent, differ, and create a new agenda. This requires regular meetings of parents and diyas—for studying, sharing, debating,

thinking and involving themselves in concrete educational projects. A communicative interaction, and the realisation of a shared identity would definitely sustain an alternative project. In fact, it is important for a school like Mirambika to organise more, and still more workshops, debates, seminars and discussions so that it can create an environment which is conducive to perpetual learning on the part of the parents and the diyas.

2. The school also needs to reflect on its selection procedure. It ought to see beyond the exclusivist club of elite South Delhi, and spread its message amongst those who may genuinely be striving for new education, but do not have the necessary cultural/ symbolic capital to make their presence felt in a school like Mirambika. This is perhaps one way of reducing elitism in the school.
3. The school needs to be absolutely democratic and transparent, because an experimental project of this kind can succeed only if it shares its difficulties and possibilities with all those who are closely associated with the school—mainly the parents. Regular meetings and workshops should ensure that there is no communication gap between the school and the parents.
4. The school must be absolutely alert in the process of giving proper orientation to its diyas. This is important, because the teachers of Mirambika need to be extraordinarily sensitive, imaginative and creative. Important resource persons—scientists, professors, artists from universities, research centres and the other areas of cultural life should be invited to the school, and the diyas should be encouraged to keep in touch with them. This living contact would enable them to learn and feel confident of new areas of knowledge. It should not be forgotten that a Mirambika teacher must have a solid foundation in

different knowledge systems; only then would it be possible for him/her to teach the children in a radically different way. In other words, the school, through its missionary zeal, must invite, attract and retain creative people from every sphere of life. A school of this kind can exist only with this spirit of cooperation and collective endeavour.

5. It is equally important for the parents to realise that the routinisation or bureaucratisation of Mirambika would mean its downfall, for it cannot retain its *swadharma* with just a group of paid professionals. What is required is a genuine desire to make a difference in the field of education, or the willingness to devote oneself to a great cause. That is why, the parents need to involve themselves with the school; they must give their time, energy and resources. Mirambika is a collective project. The parents should not see themselves as passive clients; they are active creators!

But then, a question that is often asked is: what would the school eventually do? For instance, anyone who has sent his/her child to Mirambika is likely to face the question: 'Are you happy with Mirambika? Would you let your child stay on in the school? Would the school survive?' All these questions, in spite of the fact that the school has been around for more than 20 years. And, one hopes that despite all odds, it would survive, and make its presence felt for a long time to come. There are, however, three possible ways in which the school can deal with the present crises:

- First, amidst the prevalent crises and contradictions, the school may decide not to expand itself, or to go in for higher classes. Instead, it may accept the limitedness of its resources; its inability to meet the needs of the children of higher classes. The school, as a result, may exist as a junior school: a school for little children. This, we would argue, would be self-defeating, because it would reinforce the conventional belief that alternative education (learning without any burden) may be meaningful for little children, but it is of no significance for higher classes when 'serious study' begins! In other words, this option would not communicate the deeper meaning of Mirambika. Unless the school goes in for higher classes with a specific agenda, its alternative project would not be taken seriously.

- Second, the school may begin to re-orient itself to conform to the needs of the 'system'; strive for an affiliation with the CBSE, and go in for higher classes. It may start looking at its 'weaknesses', and in order to compensate for these, it may begin to measure itself in terms of conventional academics, satisfy ambitious parents, get 'good' results for its children, and project itself as another 'successful' school that reconciles 'values' with 'achievement'. This, as is obvious, would be a path of compromise. Because if Mirambika, in order to be 'acceptable' to the system, becomes defensive, and loses its distinctiveness, it would nullify all that it stands for.
- Third, Mirambika may learn the right lessons from its crises and contradictions; make itself more rigorous, determined and confident. It may go in for expansion to include higher classes with its specific identity, and make the CBSE or any other board accept its worth. It may find its rightful place without being defensive. Instead, the power of its alternative philosophy may lead the others to rethink their own educational practices. This third option would be a path of determined, uncompromising struggle.

Perhaps the future alone would be able to reveal the trajectory of this extraordinarily charming school, which, despite its crises and contradictions, is pregnant with enormous possibilities.

Notes

[I studied Mirambika in 1998-99. I am grateful to the diyas, parents and children. Almost everyone I approached cooperated with me. I could take interviews, discuss, observe and participate without the slightest inhibition or constraint. For me, it was a great experience of learning.]

1. I am grateful to Matthijs Corne Lissen and Neelijie Huppes. They were kind enough to give me sufficient time. I interviewed them on 11 November 1998 in New Delhi.
2. It is, however, important to remember that this cost is not higher if we compare it with what is required in the other 'prestigious' schools in Delhi.
3. This document has been distributed among the parents for discussion and suggestions.

5

Conclusion
In Search of Emancipatory Education

Challenges Ahead

Alternative schools, as we have seen, do exist. But then, there are problems and contradictions. In fact, sociologists of education have examined the fate/meaning of these schools in a society that is not yet prepared to alter its educational priorities.[1] Perhaps it can be said that there are limitations to what alternative schools can do, unless of course, the larger society is altered and restructured. It is, therefore, often felt that to think of new education is to think of a new society. A struggle in the domain of education is also a struggle aimed at altering the existing pattern of social institutions and relationships. Before we reflect on this interconnectedness, it is better to identify the outlines of the emancipatory educational agenda that we are proposing.

It is, however, possible to argue that there cannot be any singular educational/pedagogic solution for a country like ours that is so diverse, and lives in many worlds simultaneously. For example, to speak of uniformity, it may be alleged, is to deny diversity. Uniformity leads to centralisation; it negates people's choices, their local histories and indigenous knowledges. Furthermore, it can be said that what is possible in elite/metropolitan schools need not be applied in rural schools. Yet, despite these multiple realities, one can cite the example of what Rudolph C. Heredia would call a 'liberative pedagogy' (Heredia 1995). Regardless of whether one is talking about rural schools or city schools, tribal or middle class children; liberative pedagogy is desirable for all. Because liberative pedagogy is about creativity, social transformation and human emancipation. As Heredia argues:

> ...it must relate the school to society and involve students and teachers in the community so that education is in continuity with life and learning is both relevant and meaningful to it. The emphasis must be on creating a learning environment that is connected to society, not on imposing a teacher's discipline in an ivory tower. Such experience-based learning must be dialogic in all encounters of experience: between one's own and others', the present and the past, the personal and the social, the students and teachers. This will require imaginative and constructive ways of interrogating experiences in all these dimensions, so that the outcome of negotiated meanings is once again both significant and liberating. (Heredia 1995: 895).

The search for a liberative pedagogy, Heredia believes, points to the need to transform people in order to bring about social transformation. It is this search that has led us to identify the following outlines of an alternative educational agenda.

I
For Alternative Educational Practices

Education as Critical Consciousness

One of the primary objectives of alternative education is to arouse one's critical consciousness and humanistic spirit. To begin with, let us understand its meaning. Critical consciousness means that one questions, and one looks at a problem from all possible angles. It means that one does not take things for granted. Nor does it mean that one is faithless. In fact, it is this critical consciousness that leads one to *authentic faith.* Criticality is not cynicism. It fosters a dialogic spirit. It is an experience of learning through examining, sharing and suffering. It is intense. It is passionate. Not surprisingly, criticality leads to profound humanism—commitment to a life-long project that is free from exploitation, domination, injustice and violence. In other words, critical *consciousness requires* an intensely thoughtful, passionate, and a philosophic mind. The irony is that this critical spirit is often suppressed in the prevailing system of education. And particularly in our times when the rationale of the market (or technical rationality) dictates the agenda of education, philosophy suffers. Technology kills philosophy; technical skill becomes more important than the philosophy of life.[2] This is perhaps the reason behind the growing insecurity (or survival anxiety) that all non-technical disciplines experience in our educational institutions.

We, therefore, assert that the alternative vision of education must give due recognition to philosophy. And philosophy, it should be realised, is not just another discipline that can be studied solely for the purpose of the exam. Philosophy is a mode of thinking, a way of seeing, an experience of critical enquiry; it is the spirit of living for love, truth and justice. It is, therefore, important to understand how this sort of philosophy can become an integral part of education. Imagine, for instance, a school student studying literature. In the prevalent system of education, literature is seen as a discrete course material; the emphasis is on mechanical memorisation. However, it is possible to inspire the student to evolve a critical/creative orientation to literature. For example, while studying a piece of poetry by Tagore, the student can come out of the closed space of the classroom, experience the abundance of nature—the landscape, the beauty of the river, the mountain, the infinite sky. It is only through experiencing this inner joy that the learner is able to decipher the deeper meaning of poetry. Or, let us take an example of a student learning the history of Gandhi. Here, it is important to realise how Mohandas became the Mahatma, how he experienced colonialism, and what led him to spiritualise politics. In other words, instead of studying Gandhi as a chapter (arranged in a linear fashion), let the student learn and feel the pulse of Gandhi's time, and experience the meaning of bondage or the therapeutic power of rebellion. Similarly, when the student learns science/ mathematics, let him/her view it in the context of social life and its needs. Indeed, it is important for the learner to see science as a social practice rather than something 'objective' and 'eternally valid,' for scientists too constitute a community of scholars with their own political preferences and social biases. As innumerable studies on the sociology/philosophy of science have demonstrated, science is inseparable from the politico-economic establishment. Not just that, science as a branch of 'pragmatic' knowledge has grown in order to respond to a series of social needs. Hence, the child ought to be encouraged to see science with a critical eye, because to see science as 'sacrosanct' is to encourage yet another kind of superstition—this time in the name of 'objectivity', 'rationality' and 'scientific temper'. This critical orientation to science as an important pedagogic practice ought to be emphasised, because in our times, as Michael Apple puts it, science is often seen as 'high status' knowledge. There is another danger. The criticality of science, as we have already said, is often lost amidst the glamour of technology. That is why, in order to evolve a creative engagement with science, it is important to locate it in the context of the larger society—its needs, priorities and objectives. This means that it is equally important to transcend fragmented disciplinary boundaries, and to look at the domain of knowledge from a holistic perspective. As a matter of fact, with criticality begins the integral/holistic orientation to knowledge and curriculum.

The point we are trying to make is that in the new education agenda, the emphasis is on the cultivation of critical enquiry or the inner/aesthetic realisation of truth. It involves serious rethinking on the curriculum. Instead of attaching importance to the quantity of information one acquires (number of lessons, chapters, books), it privileges the intensity of qualitative knowledge and experience.[3] After all, information is not retained for long. What remains alive is the critical consciousness; the eternal curiosity. New education seeks to develop this asset. Hence, it would drastically reduce the content of the course; it would give more importance to rigour and quality; it would encourage the student to choose a theme and do a project on it (say, a project on Gandhi or Tagore or the behaviour of the atom). Let the student learn it with rigour and intensity, come out of the monotony of the textbook, face the larger world, consult the library, meet people and develop his/her ideas and concepts. Once the mind is developed, the learner himself/herself can arrive at new frontiers of knowledge. The message is that it is not at all important to mechanically remember, say, innumerable pieces of poetry; what is important is to develop the poetic mind and experience poetry in life. It is not important to remember all the discrete pieces of information on the freedom struggle; what is important to realise is what it meant not to be free and the therapeutic effect of the struggle for liberation. The tragedy is that in the prevalent system of education, this simple truth is forgotten, and knowledge becomes a thoroughly de-spiritualised/mechanical bundle of information. New education reverses this trend. It is based on the premise that in the ultimate analysis, there is only one skill matters: *how to think, feel, experience and live.*

Education as Lived Experience

Another significant characteristic of new education is that it attaches great importance to the role that one's life experiences/practices play in the learning process and one's comprehension of the world in general. Here, the learner draws inspiration from life to evolve an *intimate relationship* with knowledge. This is important, because in the prevalent system, knowledge is seen as a 'thing' existing out there: in printed books, libraries, and in laboratories. It is accumulated, consumed and possessed. There is a separation between the knower and the known. For the learner, this is primarily an alienating experience, because one can 'know' without living or experiencing the 'knowledge'. Moreover, what one 'knows' may not have an enduring significance in one's life. Hence to overcome this alienation, a holistic approach to learning is the need of the hour. A series of imaginary situations may enable us to visualise the meaning of new education: To begin with, let us imagine a situation in which an extraordinarily sensitive child refuses to conform to a competitive environment and, instead of being a part of the ruthless exam strategy, spends his 'valuable' time with his friends in an act of mutual learning and growth. As a result, he may not score well in, say, *civics*—a subject that perhaps asserts the ideals of cooperation, brotherhood and solidarity. The irony is that when the child practises what is written in the books, he fails, whereas one who just memorises the 'text' does succeed.

Under the new scheme, things would begin to change, because one's lived experience would be recognised as an integral component of knowledge. It would rescue knowledge from the monopoly of written texts.[4] It would attach importance not just to the writing skills (for evaluation in the exam), but also to the practice of life. Now, in another situation, imagine an urban child whose everyday experience in the school bus makes him feel sick because of air/noise pollution. Let the new education begin with, say, this lived experience and evolve a lesson in environmental studies. These are just examples that tell us how knowledge can be closely related to life-experiences. This approach to learning through real-life situations may also help the learner evolve a critical relationship with the knowledge that is imposed on him/her from above, because when experiences count and are given legitimacy, the learner can challenge/refute all sorts of bookish and, at times, dead knowledge. This is like giving importance to the centrality of the learner, his/her praxis and experience.

Education as Active Engagement with Productive Work

Learning through doing is an important feature of new education, as there is a symbiotic relationship between knowledge and productive work—a fact which is often overlooked in the prevailing system of education. First, the notion of a 'knowledgeable' man, as defined by the elitist perception of education, is a 'thinker' (not a worker). He lives in a world of ideas (not in the sphere of productive activity). He keeps himself away from all sorts of manual labour. Not surprisingly, school knowledge (or legitimate knowledge) does not recognise knowledge born out of human labour or productive activities. It is, therefore, not unusual to find even the subaltern classes developing a negative attitude towards their own heritage (of labour and productive work) after receiving school education. Ironically, this elitist orientation to knowledge manifests itself in the *politics* of reservation, for the implicit assumption is that certain jobs—official jobs detached from productive activities—are necessarily good and preferable![5]

Second, even when this liberal education is challenged by the latest craze for technical/vocational education, the problem remains, the reason being that this kind of technical education is heavily dominated by the logic of techno-capitalism. Moreover, the glamorised technical skills breed new elitism. As we have already said, this market-friendly education is thoroughly anti-philosophical. It is not critical; it does not integrate philosophy with practical work. Instead, it trivialises the meaning of practical work. John Dewey could smell this danger. He did not like the way in which vocational education was becoming trade education—merely a technical programme to suit industries and professions. Instead, he was visualising a kind of education which would also include a

> Study of economies, civics, and politics, to bring the future workers into touch with the problems of the day and the various methods proposed for its improvement. (Dewey 1966: 318).

Hence, we would like to emphasise that the kind of new education that we are talking about is not aimed at boosting the image of a well-fed, well-clothed, but uncritical/non-reflexive techno-personality. The kind of education that we are visualising is qualitatively different. First, it is responsible to the community of peasants, workers, villagers and subaltern people; it does not subscribe to the logic of techno-capitalism. This means that the process of learning is integrally related to the needs/experiences of the community. It is a two way process. First, it includes the productive experiences of people in the curriculum, thereby broadening the scope of education. This further improves and elevates the stock of knowledge and skill of people. Second, this process of learning is inseparable from the deeper philosophical/critical enquiry. To work does not mean that one ceases to be a thinker, or vice-versa. Instead, learning through doing makes one continually reflect on issues like: what is the meaning of work? Whom does it benefit? Does it help one to relate to nature and the larger community? The implications of this kind of education are obvious. It relaxes the mind. It restores the dignity of labour. It privileges the *cultural capital* of the toiling masses. It recognises them as active participants in the process of learning.

To understand this education is to implement something like what Gandhi visualised as *basic education.* How does one implement it? Certainly not by equating it with what is fashionably called 'extra-curricular' activities. The fault lies with the curriculum itself, and that is what needs to be changed. Besides, there is an urgent need to take the entire productive work/experience seriously. This means that schools have to be organically linked with the community.

Education as Creative Teaching-Learning Experience

The above discussion perhaps suggests that we need teachers of an altogether different kind. As things stand, the self-perception of the teaching community is not very good. A school teacher, for instance, does not have a prestigious status in the hierarchy of professions. Moreover, in the prevalent pedagogic culture, he does not have much autonomy. He remains merely a functionary whose task is to follow the prescribed text, cover the syllabus and prepare students for the exam. Not solely that, he remains a dictator in the classroom. Seldom does he allow the culture of critical enquiry to grow.

We do need new teachers. A good teacher is the one for whom teaching is a meaningful vocation, an act of free choice, an experience of immense satisfaction and inner growth. It is this positive self-perception of the teaching community that radiates and elevates the mind of the young learner. A good teacher is the one who is humble, who does not impose his 'knowledge' on the 'empty' mind of the student. Instead, teaching, for him, is perpetual learning. Teaching is a *dialogic* act.[6]

A good teacher does not bombard the mind of the learner with all sorts of information. Instead, his task is to arouse the learner's curiosity and critical consciousness. He does not have a package of fixed/permanent truths. He knows that learning is a lifelong project, and that the teacher and the taught learn from each other through continually exploring the world. A good teacher also knows that there cannot be any better book than one's own life. Teaching, for him, therefore, becomes an act of *self-purification*.[7] Love, honesty, courage, humility, perseverance—these are not empty ideals or 'moral education' chapters. A good teacher seeks to practise these ideals. In a way, teaching is also a kind of spiritual awakening. A good teacher, therefore, is not just a professional. He is also an emancipator.

II
New Education and New Society

The ideals we have outlined suggest the need for a new social agenda—a society that is egalitarian and democratic; a society that is plural, and protects and respects the autonomy of the learner; a society that disregards all hierarchies and dualities (manual labour vs. mental labour, information vs. experience, teacher vs. student); a society that values harmony, reciprocity, dialogicity and equality. It goes without saying that all those who spoke of alternative education pleaded for a new society. Paulo Freire related his dialogic education to an egalitarian society free from exploitation, domination and violence. Gandhi's basic education was integrally related to his worldview; his urge to create a society that fights the evils of ruthless modernity, and evolves a harmonic relationship with nature. Tagore imagined a society that, far from remaining fractured and fragmented, would enable the individual to integrate with the larger universe. And Sri Aurobindo spoke of the spiritual age overcoming the limitations of the age of reason. In fact, as we have already discussed, the idea of new education is inseparable from that of a new society.

What would be the nature of this new society? Here, it is important to note that while constructing the agenda of this new society, the gains of modernity cannot be overlooked, because modernity began with criticality: man's freedom to question the established dogma; his quest for human autonomy and social justice. Yet, we should not forget the discontents of modernity: the way it fractures and fragments the world, and destroys the symbiotic relationship between man and the environment, or the way its 'developmentalism' leads to consumerism and chronic individualism, and negates the beauty of communitarian ideals. Perhaps in the coming age, we ought to spiritualise modernity.[8] The idea of spirituality is often misunderstood. For a modern/rational/secular mind, spirituality is often equated with mysticism; it is seen as an act of contemplation which has nothing to do with one's practical engagement with the world. But then, there are others who see spirituality as an inspiration to alter the hierarchical/exploitative/violent world. Spirituality is an experience of ego-transcendence, humbleness, and fusion of horizons. Not surprisingly, we saw possibilities in the spiritual dimension of ancient education, even though we problematised it. In other words, the vision of the society that we are imagining breaks stereotypes, and succeeds in uniting what appears to be contradictory: a saint and a revolutionary; a mystic and an activist; a Gandhi and a Marx; a Sri Aurobindo and a Paulo Freire; or to put it in more concrete terms, *Eklavya* and *Mirambika*. In a way, what is needed is a paradigm shift: from division and competition to integration, from consumerism to self-purification. Only then would it be possible to implement the kind of alternative educational/pedagogic practice we are talking about.[9]

It is in this context that the challenges confronting our society have to be understood. The Nehruvian brand of modernity that the post-colonial Indian society adopted as the guiding principle, it is often argued, failed to implement what it promised. Because of this disillusionment we have witnessed the emergence of the two other politico-economic projects: the cultural narcissism of *Hindutva* and the economic liberalisation of global capitalism. Enough has been said and written about *Hindutva*—the way it reinforces the communal divide in society, destroys plurality and creates an exclusivist mind-set. Likewise, the principle of economic liberalisation is elitist; it further intensifies the gap between the rich and the poor, delegitimises the role of the state in the promotion of social justice, and invites a culture that, in the name of globalisation, asserts ruthless consumerism.[10] In other words, what we are witnessing is the absence of an agenda that can be regarded as truly egalitarian, participatory, ecological and harmonic. But then, there are also multiple social/political movements initiated by the oppressed, the subaltern castes, the feminists and the ecologists—the movements that derive their inspiration from neo-Gandhism, Ambedkarism and Marxism. Perhaps in all these movements—although not always interconnected—lies the possibility of a new society. An alternative agenda of education, it has to be realised, has to be related to this wider socio-political struggle for liberation. If this relationship is not realised, all ideas of alternative pedagogy and education are likely to remain merely symbolic and ornamental.[11]

Yet, it is important to realise that this relationship between education and the larger politico-economic milieu need not be seen as deterministic, as determinism may lead to defeatism and fatalism. One may be driven to think that since it is difficult to alter the overall system, nothing can be done in the field of education. Instead, we should see this relationship as that of mutual interdependence. In other words, the initiative can come from the field of education itself. What begins in alternative sites of education may have a significant impact on the larger socio-political reality. True, we should not romanticise the alternative educational ideals. But then, nor should we be cynical and devalue their significance in today's world.

In fact, there are three things that we can do. First, as educationists we can broaden our horizons and participate in many other struggles for liberation, because the recovery of education is essentially the recovery of the larger society. Second, as teachers and students; we can work within specific sectors in which we find ourselves. We can initiate some refreshing innovations in our educational practices (making radical interventions in the sociology of knowledge and curriculum, creating democratic space in the classroom, engaging in a continual process of self-purification). Third, we can remain perpetually self-critical. This restlessness would lead to intervention. In other words, no situation is entirely hopeless; it is possible to intervene. Living meaningfully is, after all, an attempt to broaden the scope of the possible.

Notes

1. See, for instance, Shotton 1998. In this context Meenakshi Thapan's ethnographic account of the *Rishi Valley School*—a school based on the educational ideals of J. Krishnamurthy—deserves attention. Thapan has demonstrated how an alternative school of this kind is surviving with multiple

contradictions and ambiguities. As Thapan has shown, it is not easy to remain committed to a radical educational ideal, particularly when, because of the societal/parental pressure, the school is required to prepare the children for the board examination and all that it implies: competition, achievement and success (Thapan 1991).

2. It has to be asserted that technical literacy does not automatically lead to social literacy. For example, a 'bright' product of a management school may learn, say, how to promote and sell a particular brand of cigarettes. But he/she would not be encouraged to ask whether it is at all ethical to induce people to buy cigarettes, when cigarette smoking is injurious to health. In fact, this kind of 'technical' education is merely an armour that an alienated professional needs to legitimise his action. This is the crisis of modern education. It elevates the skill, but kills the spirit.
3. In fact, in the existing pattern of education, the burden of information has become terribly oppressive. These days it is expected that a school student must know (even if briefly) the entire development of science—from Newton to Einstein, or all sorts of theories, experimentations and laws. It is expected that he must know the history of the world, the history of the modern nation, the history of his civilisation—chronicle of events, wars and revolutions. It is also expected that he must know the basic premises of the Constitution. And the story goes on. The Yashpal Committee, for example, reacted sharply to this pathology. A survey conducted in Delhi revealed that the weight of the school bag, on an average, in primary classes in public schools, is more than 4 kgs, while it is around 1 kg in MCD schools. Indeed, as the committee observed, 'a lot is taught but little is learnt or understood.' See, for details, Government of India 1993.
4. In this context it would not be inappropriate to say that this emphasis on experiential knowledge has further been reinforced by recent *postmodern sensibilities,* because in the postmodern times, we are all producers of knowledge. As a result, knowledge generated from a wide number of sources (not just the written text) is recognised. Furthermore, in the postmodern condition there is also a changing role of educational practitioners. Rather than being the source/

producers of knowledge and taste, they become the facilitators of knowledge, helping to engender and interpret the knowledge and tastes produced by others. For an insightful discussion on postmodernity and experiential knowledge, see Usher and Edwards 1994: 172-206.

5. This is not to negate the gains of reservation. It is only to suggest that the rationale of reservation cannot transcend the duality: mental labour vs. manual labour.
6. For an insightful understanding of the role of new teachers engaged in a dialogic act, see Postman and Weingartner 1971.
7. In this context it would not be wrong to derive some positive lessons from the ancient system of education, because, as we have argued in Chapter 1, one of the important ideals of the ancient education was that it attached great importance to the process of self-purification: A learner, it was asserted, ought to grow humble, overcome egotism and realise/experience the noble ideals in his/her life. This culture of learning, we would like to point out, has emancipatory possibilities, particularly at a time when, because of the growing culture of possessive and consumptionist individualism, we get to witness terrible arrogance and snobbery in the acts and deeds of the 'products' of 'good' educational institutions.
8. For an understanding of the discontents of modernity, and the need for spiritualising modernity, see Pathak 1998: 225-29.
9. It is possible to see a close relationship between the fractured/fragmented worldview implicit in modernity and the dominant mode of school education. For example, there is over-specialisation, and knowledge is divided into fragmented disciplinary boundaries. Likewise, the rationale of the assembly-line system of production shapes the practice of school education. Quite often we use the concepts and ideas derived from the factory: 'inputs' or 'outputs' of education, the 'products' of schooling, etc. Hence, it is argued that to alter our educational priorities we need to overcome the dominant paradigm and think of a new paradigm leading to harmony, interconnectedness and holism.
10. For an understanding of the impact of economic liberalisation on education, see Kumar 1998.
11. This is a problem with many 'elite schools'—the schools that speak of many radical measures (like 'project work' or openness

to art, music and sports), but continue to function within the established framework. Seldom do these schools inspire their clients to question the existing order of things—its hierarchy, inequality and exploitation. In this context it would not be inappropriate to mention that the recent NCERT document *(National Curriculum Framework For School Education: A Discussion Document, NCERT, New Delhi, 2000)* has suggested a number of alternative pedagogic practices. It has also emphasised the need for 'value education'. But the question is: is this emphasis on value education merely theoretical? Can we create new values, if nothing is done to alter the larger society? For a critical understanding of the sociology of value-education, see Jayaram 1990: 141-49.

Select Bibliography

Acharya, Poromesh. 1987. 'Education, Politics and Social Structure' in Ratna Ghosh and Mathew Zachariah (eds.), *Education and the Process of Change*. New Delhi: Sage Publications.

—— 1994 . 'Universal Elementary Education Receding Goal', *Economic and Political Weekly*, January 1-8. 29(1): 27-30.

—— 1997. 'Educational Ideals of Tagore and Gandhi: A Comparative Study', *Economic and Political Weekly*, March 22. 32(2).

—— 1998. 'Bengali *Bhadralok* and Educational Development in Nineteenth Century Bengal' in Suresh Chandra Shukla and Rekha Kaul (ed.), *Education, Development and Underdevelopment*. New Delhi: Sage Publications.

Adam, William. 1941. *Reports on the State of Education in Bengal* edited by A.N. Basu, Calcutta.

Advani, Shalini. 1996. "Educating the National Imagination", *Economic and Political Weekly*, 3 August. 31(31): 2077-82.

Altekar, A.S. 1999. 'The Position of Women in Hindu Civilization: Retrospect and Prospect' in Kumkum Roy (ed.), *Women in Early Indian Societies*. New Delhi: Manohar.

Apple, Michael W. 1979. *Ideology and Curriculum*. London: Routledge and Kegan Paul.

Banerjee, Sumanta. 1998. 'Popular Education in Colonial Bengal and Its Legacy: An Examination of a Nineteenth Century Bengali Broadsheet' in Suresh Chandra Shukla and Rekha Kaul (eds.), *Education Development and Underdevelopment*. New Delhi: Sage Publications.

Basu, Aparna. 1978. 'Policy and Conflict in India: The Reality and Perception of Education' in Philip G. Altbach and Gail P. Kelly, *Education and Colonialism*. New York: Dongman.

____ 1982. *Essays in the History of Indian Education*. New Delhi: Concept Publishing Company.

Bhattacharya, Shukla, M.S. Khaparde, M.P. Rastogi and H.L. Sharma. 1988. *Exploring Environment: BOOK TWO: A Textbook for Class IV.* New Delhi: NCERT.

Blackledge, David and Barry Hunt. 1985. *Sociological Interpretations of Education*. London, NewYork: Routledge.

Bourdieu, P. and J.C. Passeron. 1977. *Reproduction in Education, Society and Culture*. London: Sage.

Bowles, S. and H. Gintis. 1976. *Schooling in Capitalist America*. London: Routledge and Kegan Paul.

Carnoy, Martin. 1976. *Education as Cultural Imperialism*. INC, NewYork: David McKay Company.

Chakravarti, Uma. 1996. 'Reconceptualising Gender: Phule, Brahminism and Brahminical Patriarchy' in Kiran Pawar, *Women in Indian History: Social, Economic, Political and Cultural Perspectives*. Patiala, New Delhi: Vision and Venture.

Chandra, Bipan. 1988. *Indian National Movement: The Long Term Dynamics*. New Delhi: Vikas Publishing House.

Chitnis, Suma. 1987. 'Education and Social Stratification: An Illustration from a Metropolitan City' in Ratna Ghosh and Mathew Zachariah (eds.), *Education and the Process of Change*. New Delhi: Sage Publications.

Cohen, Yehudi A. 1971. 'The Shaping of Men's Minds: Adaptations to Imperatives of Culture' in Murray L. Wax, Stanley Diamond and Fred O. Gearing (eds.), *Anthropological Perspectives on Education*. NewYork: Basic Book, Inc.

Collins, Randall. 1979. *The Credential Society*. New York: Academic Press.

Dev, Arjun and Indira Arjun Dev. 1993. *Modern India: A History Textbook for Class VIII*. New Delhi: NCERT (fourth reprint).

Dev, Indira and Shrirama. 1999. *Society and Culture in India: Their Dynamics through the Ages*. Jaipur, New Delhi: Rawat.

Dewey, John. 1966. *Democracy and Education: An Introduction to the Philosophy of Education*. NewYork: The Free Press.

Dharampal. 1983. *The Beautiful Tree: Indigenous Indian Education in the Eighteenth Century*. New Delhi: Biblia Impex Private Limited.

Durkheim, Emile. 1956. *Education and Sociology*. NewYork: The Free Press.

____ 1961. *Moral Education: A Study in the Theory and Application of the Sociology of Education*. New York: The Free Press.

Eklavya. 1999. *Eklavya: A Profile*. Bhopal.

Freire, Paulo. 1972. *Pedagogy of the Oppressed*. Penguin Books.

Gandhi, M.K. 1951. *Basic Education*. Ahmedabad: Navajivan Publishing House.

Ghosh, Arun. 1992. 'Education for All: The Financing Problem', *Economic and Political Weekly*, April 4. 27(14): 679-83.

Ghosh, Ratna and Mathew Zachariah (eds.). 1987. *Education and the Process of Change*. New Delhi: Sage.

Ghosh, Suresh Chandra. 1993. 'English in Taste, in Opinions, in Words and Intellect' in J.A. Mangam (ed.), *The Imperial Curriculum: Racial Images and Education in the British Colonial Experience*. London: Routledge.

—— 1995. *The History of Education in Modern India, 1757-1986*. New Delhi: Orient Longman.

Gore, M.S. 1989. *Non-Brahman Movement in Maharashtra*. New Delhi: Segment Book Distributors.

—— 1994. *Indian Education: Structure and Process*. Jaipur: Rawat.

Government of India. 1966. *Report of the Education Commission, 1964-66*. New Delhi: Ministry of Education, Government of India.

—— 1993. *Learning Without Burden, Yashpal Committee Report*/Report of the National Advisory Committee appointed by Ministry of Human Resource Development to suggest ways and means to reduce the academic burden on school students.

Gramsci, Antonio. 1971. *Selections from the Prison Notebooks*. London: Lawrence and Wishart.

Green, Thomas F. 1971. 'Citizenship or Certification' in Murray L. Wax, Stanley Diamond and Fred O. Gearing (eds.), op. cit.

Guha, Ranjit. 1982. 'On Some Aspects of the Historiography of Colonial India' in Ranjit Guha (ed.), *Subaltern Studies: Writing on South Asian History and Society*. Vol. I. New Delhi: Oxford University Press.

Hargreaves, D. 1980. 'A Sociological Critique of Individualism in Education', *British Journal of Educational Studies*, 28(3): 193.

—— 1982. *The Challenge for the Comprehensive School: Culture, Curriculum and Community*. London: Routledge and Kegan Paul.

Hayward,Tim. 1994. *Ecological Thought: An Introduction*. Cambridge: Polity Press.

Heredia, Rudolf C. 1995. 'Tribal Education for Development: Need for a Liberative Pedagogy for Social Transformation'. *Economic and Political Weekly*, 22 April. 30 (16): 891-97.

Illich, Ivan. 1984. *Deschooling Society*. Penguin Books.

Indian Express, New Delhi, 3 March 2000.

Jayaram, N. 1990. *Sociology of Education in India*. Jaipur: Rawat.

Jhanji, Rekha. 1996. 'Women in the Mahabharata' in Kiran Pawar, *Women in Indian History: Social, Economic, Political and Cultural Perspectives*. Patiala, New Delhi: Vision and Venture.

Joshi, Tarkateertha Laxmanashastri. 1992. *Jotirao Phule*. New Delhi: NBT.

Kamat, A.R. 1985. *Education and Social Change in India.* Bombay: Somaiya.

Kaul, Rekha. 1998. 'Disorders in Education, Private Enterprise and the State' in Suresh Chandra Shukla and Rekha Kaul (eds.), *Education, Development and Underdevelopment.* New Delhi: Sage Publications.

Khan, S.H., Prabhakar Singh and L.N. Verma. 1988. *Our Country India: A Textbook for Class IV.* New Delhi: NCERT.

Kothari, Rajni. 1988. *State Against Democracy: In Search of Humane Governance.* Delhi: Ajanta Publications.

Kumar, Krishna. 1987. 'Reproduction or Change? Education and Elites in India' in Ratna Ghosh and Mathew Zachariah (eds.), *Education and the Process of Change.* New Delhi: Sage Publications.

Kumar, Krishna. 1989. *Social Character of Learning.* New Delhi: Sage Publications.

____ 1991. *Political Agenda of Education: Study of Colonialist and Nationalist Ideas.* New Delhi: Sage.

____ 1996. *Learning from Conflict.* New Delhi: Orient Longman.

____ 1998. 'Agricultural Modernization and Education: Contours of a Point of Departure' in Suresh Chandra Shukla and Rekha Kaul (eds.), *Education, Development and Underdevelopment.* New Delhi: Sage.

____ 1998. 'Education and Society in Post-Independence India: Looking Towards the Future'. *Economic and Political Weekly,* 6 June. 33(23): 1391-96.

____ 1998. 'Freire's Legacy'. *Economic and Political Weekly,* 14 November. 33 (46): 2912-15.

Mani, Lata. 1989. 'Contentious Traditions: The Debate on Sati in Colonial India' in Kumkum Sangari and Sudesh Vaid (eds.), *Recasting Women: Essays in Colonial History.* New Delhi: Kali for Women.

Mannheim, Karl and W.A.C. Stewart. 1962. *An Introduction to the Sociology of Education.* London: Routledge and Kegan Paul.

Mannheim, Karl, 1960. *Ideology and Utopia: An Introduction to the Sociology of Knowledge.* London: Routledge and Kegan Paul.

Manusmriti, V.

Manusmriti, X.

Massey, James. 1995. *Dalits in India: Religion as a Source of Bondage or Liberation with Special Reference to Christians.* Delhi: Manohar.

Miliband, Ralph. 1972. *The State in Capitalist Society.* London: Weidenfeld and Nicolson.

Ministry of Education, Government of India. 1966. *Report of the Education Commission 1964-66.*

Mookerji, Radha Kumud. 1969. *Ancient Indian Education (Brahminical and Buddhist)*. Delhi: Motilal Banarsidass.

Muley, D.S. and A.C. Sharma, 1987, sixth reprint, 1993. *Our Civic Life: A Textbook of Civics for Class VI*. New Delhi: NCERT.

Muley, D.S., A.C. Sharma and Supta Das. 1988, sixth reprint, 1993. *How We Govern Ourselves: A Textbook of Civics for Class VII*. New Delhi: NCERT.

Muley, D.S., Supta Das, Ramesh Chandra and Manju Rani. 1989, sixth reprint, 1993. *Our Country Today: Problems and Challenges: A Textbook of Civics for Class VIII*. New Delhi: NCERT.

Nandy, Ashis. 1983. *The Intimate Enemy: Loss and Recovery of Self Under Colonialism*. New Delhi: Oxford University Press.

Nawani, Disha. 1999. 'Children's Story Books and Their Pedagogic Functions: A Sociological Study of Three Select Schools of New Delhi.' Unpublished PhD Thesis, CSSS/SSS/JNU/New Delhi.

NCERT 2000. *National Curriculum Framework for School Education: A Discussion Document*. New Delhi: NCERT.

Nehru, Jawaharlal. 1983. *The Discovery of India*. New Delhi: Jawaharlal Nehru Memorial Fund.

——— 1984. *An Autobiography* New Delhi: Jawaharlal Nehru Memorial Fund.

Omvedt, Gail. 1995. *Dalit Vision*. New Delhi: Orient Longman.

Panikkar, K.N. 1995. *Culture, Ideology, Hegemony: Intellectuals and Social Consciousness in Colonial India*. New Delhi: Tulika.

Parsons; Talcott. 1968. 'The School Class as a Social System: Some of its Functions in American Society' in Robert R. Bell and Holger R. Stub (eds.), *The Sociology of Education: A Sourcebook*. Homewood: The Dorsey Press.

Pathak, Avijit. 1997. *Living in Modern India: Reflections on Polity, Culture and Society*. New Delhi: Sanchar.

——— 1998. *Indian Modernity: Contradictions, Paradoxes and Possibilities*. New Delhi: Gyan Publishing House.

——— 1999. 'Politics, Morality and Education: Limits to Joshi's Agenda'. *Deccan Herald*, Bangalore. 26 November.

Postman, Neil and Charles Weingartner. 1971. *Teaching as a Subversive Activity*. Penguin Books.

Reynolds, D. and M. Sullivan. 1980. 'Towards a New Socialist Sociology of Education' in L. Barton (ed.), *Schooling, Ideology and the Curriculum*. Lewes: Falmer Press.

Richards, Stewart. 1987. *Philosophy and Sociology of Science: An Introduction*. Oxford: Basic Blackwell.

Sarkar, Sumit. 1997. *Writing Social History*. New Delhi: Oxford University Press.

Sarup, Madan. 1982. *Education, State and Crisis: A Marxist Perspective.* London: Routledge and Kegan Paul.

Schostak, John F. 1986. *Schooling the Violent Imagination.* London: Routledge and Kegan Paul.

Seabrook, Jeremy. 1993. *Victims of Development: Resistance and Alternatives.* London, New York: Verso.

Sen, S.P. (ed). 1973. *Historians and Historiography in Modern India.* Calcutta: Institute of Historical Studies.

Sheridan, Alan. 1980. *Michel Foucault: The Will to Truth.* London, NewYork: Tavistock Publications.

Shotton, John Robert. 1998. *Learning and Freedom: Policy, Pedagogy and Paradigms in Indian Education and Schooling.* New Delhi: Sage Publications.

Shukla, P.D. 1988. *The New Education Policy in India.* New Delhi: Sterling Publishers.

Shukla, Suresh Chandra and Rekha Kaul (eds.). 1998. *Education, Development and Underdevelopment.* New Delhi: Sage.

Singh, Yogendra. 1967. 'The Process of Socialization and Education' in M.S. Gore, I.P. Desai and Suma Chitnis (eds). *Papers in the Sociology of Education in India.* New Delhi: NCERT.

____ 2000. *Culture Change in India: Identity and Globalization.* Jaipur, New Delhi: Rawat.

Singha, H.S. 1984. *Public Examinations: A Critique.* New Delhi: Vikas Publishing House.

Spring, Joel H. 1972. *Education and the Rise of the Corporate State.* Boston: Becan Press.

Sri Aurobindo Ashram. 1956. *Sri Aurobindo and the Mother on Education.* Pondicherry: Sri Aurobindo Ashram, reprint 1997.

____ *Mirambika Prospectus.* New Delhi: Sri Aurobindo Ashram.

Talib, Mohammad. 1998. 'Educating the Oppressed: Observations from a School in a Working Class Settlement in Delhi' in Suresh Chandra Shukla and Rekha Kaul (eds.), op. cit.

Thapan, Meenakshi. 1991. *Life At School: An Ethnographic Study.* New Delhi: Oxford University Press.

Thapar, Romila. 1993a. *Ancient India: A Textbook of History for Class VI.* New Delhi: NCERT (seventh reprint).

____ 1993b. *Medieval India: History Textbook for Class VII.* New Delhi: NCERT (sixth reprint).

Turner, Ralph. 1971. 'Sponsored and Contest Mobility and the Social System' in E. Hopper (ed.), *Readings in the Theory of Educational System.* London: Hutchinson.

Usher, Robin and Richard Edwards. 1994. *Postmodernism and Education.* London/NewYork: Routledge.

Wills, Paul. 1977. *Learning to Labour.* Farnborough: Saxon House.

Index